Y0-EQS-087

TEMPERATURE

Temperature Conversion Table

American Oven Temperature Terms	Degrees Fahrenheit	Degrees Centigrade (Celsius)
	160	71
	170	77
	200	93
	212	100
Very Slow	225	107
	230	110
	250	121
Slow	275	135
	300	149
	302	150
	320	160
Moderately Slow.	325	163
Moderate	350	177
	356	180
	375	190
	390	200
Hot	400	205
	425	218
	428	220
	437	225
	450	232
Very Hot	475	246
	500	260
	525	274
Broil.	550	288

Volume 15

New-Pea

WOMAN'S DAY ENCYCLOPEDIA OF COOKERY

1979 Edition
For WOMAN'S DAY

JEANNE VOLTZ, *Food Editor*

For FUNK & WAGNALLS, INC.

Supervising Editor—**NORMA H. DICKEY**
Production Editor—**KATHIE L. ATTLEE**
Production Executive—**EDWARD HAAS**
Editorial Staff—**DONNA L. AMOS, JUNE V. ROOK**
Art Director—**MURRAY KESHNER**
Layout Artists—**HERBERT ASCHER, MARTIN GORDON, ERLA SIGURDARDOTTIR**

Special Project Staff:

Contributing Editors—**INEZ M. KRECH, JAMES W. TRAGER**

Original Edition

Prepared and edited by the Editors of WOMAN'S DAY

GLENNA MCGINNIS, *Food Editor*

Special Project Staff:

Editor—**NIKA STANDEN HAZELTON**
Associates—**L. GERALDINE MARSTELLER, HELEN FEINGOLD, SUSAN J. KNOX**

First Revised Edition

Special Project Staff:
Editor—**MARIE ROBERSON HAMM**
Associate Editor—**ISABEL CORNELL**

Copyright © 1966, 1973, 1979 by CBS Publications,
the Consumer Publishing Division of CBS, Inc.,
All Rights Reserved.
Distributed by Funk & Wagnalls, Inc.

HIGHLIGHTS

Volume 15

New England-Pea

Arranged alphabetically, the articles in this volume fall between the two words listed above. Among the interesting and informative entries found in this volume, several sections are worthy of special attention. We have listed these below for your convenience.

How to use the Woman's Day Encyclopedia of Cookery

The twenty-two volumes of the Woman's Day Encyclopedia contain a wealth of alphabetically arranged information. If you wish to prepare Apple Pie, look under Apple in volume 1. But to find all of the information in all of the volumes, you should use the twenty-third volume, the Index. Composed of five separate indexes, volume 23 includes: meal and menu planning; information on nutrition and diet; techniques of cookery and equipment use; a listing by author; and an alphabetical listing by ingredients.

This Encyclopedia contains many individual entries that supplement one another. Meal and Menu Planning, for instance, is treated throughout the Encyclopedia in many different entries. The first index in volume 23 collects these entries and lists volume and page numbers for such diverse items as Busy Day Dinners and Low Cost Meals. How to entertain or cook in different national styles will be simplified by consulting such items as Parties or Mexican Cookery. If you want to cook for a crowd or make up a Christmas menu, this index shows you where to find Quantity Cooking and three separate styles of Christmas meals.

If you are learning to cook or beginning to plan diets for a family, two other indexes offer assistance. The Encyclopedia entries that contain information on nutrition and diet are listed in one index, and techniques of cookery and equipment are listed in the other. If you want to know which foods are necessary in your child's diet or how to cut down on cholesterol, see the second index. If you want to find out which pan is appropriate for a layer cake, see Bake in the third index.

The fourth index in volume 23 is a listing by author of all the special articles in the Encyclopedia. Here you will find titles and location of articles by noted cookbook authors and food and health authorities.

A major part of volume 23 is the listing of all the recipes contained in the Encyclopedia, arranged alphabetically by main ingredient and by one or more menu categories. Thus, an Abalone Chowder recipe in volume 1 is listed in this Index under ABALONE and under SOUPS. A Crabmeat Dip recipe appears under CRABS, under DIPS, APPETIZER, and under APPETIZERS.

These volumes offer helpful advice on cooking, meal planning, food budgeting, and entertaining. Brimming with tempting recipes, mouthwatering photos, and interesting tid-bits about the origin and history of some of the ingredients, the Woman's Day Encyclopedia of Cookery is indeed a browsing library for food lovers.

NEW ENGLAND COOKBOOK

Stews and chowders, seafood and fish, baked beans, Yankee pot roast, boiled dinners, muffins, griddle cakes, berries and pies. These are the traditional hearty dishes of New England.

SOUPS

SEAFOOD STEW

4 slices salt pork, diced
¼ cup butter or margarine
½ teaspoon each salt, celery salt, and paprika
2 teaspoons Worcestershire
2 cups bottled clam broth
1 pound cod or haddock, skinned, boned, and cut in pieces
½ pound shelled shrimps, cooked and cleaned
½ pound cooked lobster meat
3 cups milk
1 cup medium cream

Cook salt pork until crisp and browned. Drain off fat and reserve pork. Put butter, seasonings, and clam broth in kettle and bring to boil. Add fish and seafood and simmer, covered, until tender. Add reserved pork and remaining ingredients, and heat. Makes 4 servings.

OLD-FASHIONED NEW ENGLAND FISH CHOWDER

¼ cup (2 ounces) diced salt pork
¾ cup sliced onions
2 cups diced peeled raw potatoes
2 cups hot water
1½ pounds haddock, cod, or ocean-perch fillets
Salt and pepper
2 cups light cream
Butter

Render salt pork in a skillet until it is nicely browned. Add onion and sauté gently. Add potatoes and hot water and cook for a few minutes, or until potatoes are almost done. Then add fish fillets and cook until they are easily flaked with a fork. Season to taste with salt and pepper and add the cream. Heat through and serve in bowls, topping each serving with a generous pat of butter. Makes about 2 quarts.

CLAM CHOWDER

¼ pound salt pork, diced
1 cup finely chopped onions
2 pounds peeled raw potatoes, finely diced
Clam liquor
4 cups shucked clams, chopped
Milk
Salt and pepper

Render salt pork in a skillet; take out crisp pieces. Add onions and cook over low heat until done but not brown. Pour this mixture over potatoes; add clam juice and simmer until potatoes are nearly done. Add clams and bring to a boil. This basic mixture can be stored in the refrigerator or frozen. Before using the chowder, dilute it with an equal quantity of milk. Heat to the boiling point, but do not boil it. Season to taste with salt and pepper. Sprinkle with salt pork. Makes about 2½ quarts.

SEAFOOD

OYSTER OR CLAM SCALLOP

Butter a deep pie plate. Put a layer of cracked crumbs on bottom. Dot with butter. Add a layer of oysters or clams and season with salt, pepper, paprika, and a little sautéed onion. Add another layer of crumbs, then a layer of oysters or clams, and top with crumbs. Dot with butter. Barely cover with light cream. Bake in preheated moderate oven (350°F.) about 30 minutes.

CLAM PIE

Grind enough raw deep-sea clams to fill pastry-lined pan. Sprinkle with cracker crumbs and salt and pepper; add lump of butter and a little clam juice. Cover with pastry and bake in preheated moderate oven (350°F.) for 30 minutes.

OYSTER AND SHRIMP PIE

¼ cup butter or margarine
¼ cup all-purpose flour
½ teaspoon each celery salt and onion salt
¼ teaspoon white pepper
2 cups milk
½ pint (1 cup) raw oysters
1½ cups cooked shrimps
2 tablespoons chopped parsley or chives
Pastry for 2-crust 9-inch pie, unbaked

Melt butter and blend in flour and seasonings. Gradually stir in milk. Cook over medium heat, stirring, until thickened. Add oysters, shrimps, and parsley. Pour into pastry-lined pie dish, top with pastry, and seal edges. Slit top to allow escape of steam. Bake in preheated very hot oven (450°F.) for 10 minutes; reduce heat to moderate (350°F.) and bake for about 20 minutes. Makes 6 to 8 servings.

OYSTERS BAKED IN SHELLS

Select large oysters. Scrub shells well in running cold water. Arrange in baking pan with rounded side down. Bake in preheated very hot oven (450°F.) until shells open. Pry off top shells and serve oysters at once on the half shell. Pass bowl of clarified butter to which fresh lemon juice and grated horseradish have been added. For appetizer allow 6 oysters per serving. For main dish allow 12.

SUNDAY-MORNING FISH BALLS

1 cup raw salt codfish
2 cups sliced peeled raw potatoes
1 teaspoon butter
¼ teaspoon salt
⅛ teaspoon pepper
1 egg, beaten
Fat for deep frying

Cover fish with cold water and let stand for about 1 hour; drain. Place fish on top of potatoes in a kettle; cover with boiling water and cook until potatoes are soft. Drain well; mash fish and potatoes; then beat with fork until mixture is very light. Blend in remaining ingredients except fat. Drop by tablespoonfuls into hot fat (375°F. on a frying thermometer) 2 inches deep and fry until golden-brown, about 1 minute. Drain on unglazed paper. Serve at once. Makes 2 dozen.

CREAMED CODFISH AND BAKED POTATOES

1 pound raw salt codfish
6 medium raw potatoes
⅛ pound fat salt pork
2 cups light cream
2½ tablespoons all-purpose flour
2 tablespoons cold water
1 egg yolk
2 hard-cooked eggs
Pepper to taste

Cover fish with cold water. Bring to boil and drain. Repeat until excessive saltiness has been eliminated. Simmer in fresh water until tender. Drain. Bake well-scrubbed potatoes in preheated hot oven (450°F.) for 45 to 60 minutes, until potatoes are tender. Place thinly sliced salt pork on rack in baking pan and set in oven with potatoes. Watch closely; when pork is crisp and brown, remove from oven. Heat cream in top part of double boiler over boiling water; add flour mixed to smooth paste with water; stir until thickened. Mix in beaten egg yolk just before removing from heat. Add codfish, separated into medium-size pieces, and sliced hard-cooked eggs. Pour into shallow dish or deep platter. Sprinkle with pepper and crumbled salt pork. Serve with hot baked potatoes. Makes 6 servings.

MEAT AND POULTRY

BROILED HONEYCOMB TRIPE WITH MUSTARD SAUCE

Cut tender fresh honeycomb tripe in 6- x 4-inch pieces. Select "pocket" tripe for this. Season with salt and pepper and sprinkle with flour. Dip in olive oil and sprinkle generously with fine, dry bread crumbs. Broil slowly over charcoal or under broiler until well browned and done. Serve with Mustard Sauce.

Mustard Sauce

Melt 1 tablespoon butter in saucepan, and add 1 tablespoon minced onion. Add 2 tablespoons vinegar and simmer for 2 minutes. Blend 2 teaspoons dry mustard with a little water. Mix with 1 can beef gravy. Add to first mixture and cook for 5 minutes. Strain and serve. Makes about 1¼ cups.

MEAT AND VEGETABLE HASH

3 cups coarsely chopped cooked meat
2 large raw baking potatoes, peeled and diced
2 onions, chopped
1 green pepper, chopped
2 celery stalks, minced
1 teaspoon dry mustard
1 teaspoon salt
1 teaspoon garlic salt
¼ teaspoon ground savory
1½ cups meat broth or leftover gravy mixed with water

Meat and vegetables may be forced through food chopper, using coarse blade. Combine all ingredients. Pack into well-greased shallow baking pan. Bake, covered, in preheated moderate oven (375°F.) for 45 minutes. Uncover and brown under broiler. Serve with catsup or chili sauce. Makes 6 servings.

YANKEE POT ROAST

4 pounds bottom round, chuck, or rump of beef
Fat
Water
4 medium onions, minced
2 medium white turnips, diced
4 carrots, diced
2 cups diced celery
Few sprigs of parsley
2 teaspoons salt
¼ teaspoon pepper
½ cup tomato juice
4 medium peeled raw potatoes, quartered
All-purpose flour

Brown meat slowly on all sides in small amount of fat in heavy kettle. Pour off fat. Put meat on small rack in kettle. Add 1 cup water and remaining ingredients except potatoes and flour. Cover and simmer for 4 hours, or until meat is tender, turning occasionally. One hour before meat is done, put potatoes on top of meat. When done, remove meat to a hot platter and surround with potatoes and vegetable mixture. Add enough water to liquid left in kettle to make desired amount of gravy. Thicken with flour blended with a little cold water. Makes 4 servings, with meat left over.

VEGETABLES AND SALADS

BACON-CORN FRITTERS

Mix 1½ cups drained canned whole-kernel corn; 2 eggs, beaten; ¼ cup all-purpose flour; 1 teaspoon baking powder; ½ teaspoon salt; and dash of pepper. Add 2 slices of bacon, cooked and crumbled. Drop by tablespoonfuls into hot bacon fat in skillet. Cook until browned on both sides and done. Serve with butter, and with syrup, if desired. Makes 4 servings.

BOILED WHITE BEANS

1 quart dried pea or yelloweye beans
2 quarts water
1 cup meat broth
½ cup maple syrup
2 onions, chopped
1 tablespoon salt
1 teaspoon white pepper
4 beef marrow bones
¼ pound salt pork, sliced

Soak beans in water overnight. Next morning simmer until tender, adding more water if necessary. Add broth, maple syrup, onions, and seasonings. Put marrow bones in bottom of bean pot. Add beans. Put salt-pork slices on top, cover, and bake in preheated very slow oven (250°F.) for 4 to 6 hours, adding more broth if necessary. Makes 8 to 10 servings.

PARSNIP CAKES

2 cups mashed cooked parsnips
1 tablespoon melted butter or cooking oil
1 tablespoon all-purpose flour
1 teaspoon salt
Dash of pepper
1 egg
Cracker crumbs
Butter for frying

Mix parsnips with next 5 ingredients. Shape into flat cakes. Dip into crumbs, covering completely. Put in refrigerator to chill. Fry until brown in hot butter. Makes 4 to 6 servings.

BAKED PUMPKIN

Scrub 1 small pumpkin (about 3 pounds) and cut into serving pieces. Scrape out seeds and stringy portion. Brush with melted butter and sprinkle with salt and pepper. Arrange, cut side down, in greased baking pan. Add a small amount of water. Bake in preheated hot oven (400°F.) for 30 minutes. Turn, brush again with butter, and sprinkle with salt and pepper. Bake for 30 minutes longer, or until tender, brushing occasionally with butter. With fork, mash in shell; serve. Makes 4 servings.

GLAZED PARSNIPS

2 pounds parsnips
¼ cup butter or margarine
Salt to taste
½ cup maple syrup

Wash parsnips and cook in boiling water until tender. Cool, scrape, halve, and remove cores. Melt butter in skillet; add parsnips and sprinkle lightly with salt. Add maple syrup. Cook until slightly browned and glazed, turning once. Makes 6 to 8 servings.

JELLIED CRANBERRY SALADS

1½ cups fresh cranberries
½ orange
1 cup sugar
1 package (3 ounces) lemon-flavored gelatin
Water
½ cup diced celery
½ cup chopped walnuts

Force cranberries and orange through food chopper. Add sugar and let stand, stirring occasionally, until sugar dissolves. Dissolve gelatin in ½ cup boiling water. Drain fruits and measure juice. Add enough water to juice to make 1½ cups liquid. Add liquid to gelatin and stir in fruits. Add celery and walnuts. Pour mixture into custard cups. Chill until firm. To serve, unmold in lettuce cups and serve with mayonnaise mixed with equal measure of sweetened whipped cream. Makes 4 to 6 servings.

BOILED DINNER, NEW ENGLAND STYLE

3 pounds corned-beef brisket
Water
1 medium onion
1 bay leaf
1 garlic clove
5 peppercorns
4 whole beets
4 peeled raw potatoes
5 or 6 small carrots
5 or 6 small onions
1 tablespoon caraway seeds
1 head cabbage, coarsely shredded

Wash corned beef; put in kettle and cover with boiling water. Add medium onion, bay leaf, garlic, and peppercorns. Cover and simmer for 3½ hours, or until meat is tender. Meanwhile, cook beets separately and slip off skins. Add potatoes, carrots, and small onions to meat during last 35 minutes of cooking. Add caraway seeds and small amount of broth to cabbage. Cook for 10 to 12 minutes, or until tender. Put cabbage on center of platter, cover with sliced meat, and arrange other vegetables around. Leftover meat can be served cold or chopped with vegetables for hash. Makes 4 servings.
NOTE—Dilute broth with water to use in making bean or pea soup.

BREADS

ANADAMA BREAD

2 cups milk
½ cup yellow cornmeal
2 teaspoons salt
⅓ cup molasses
3 tablespoons butter or margarine
2 packages active dry yeast or 2 cakes compressed yeast
⅓ cup lukewarm water*
5 cups sifted all-purpose flour

Combine milk, cornmeal, and salt in top part of double boiler. Cook over boiling water at least 5 minutes, stirring constantly. Add molasses and butter and cool to lukewarm. Pour into mixing bowl. Sprinkle or crumble yeast into water. *Use very warm water (105°F. to 115°F.) for dry yeast; use lukewarm (80°F. to 90°F.) for compressed. Let stand for a few minutes, then stir until dissolved. Add dissolved yeast to cornmeal mixture. Add 2 cups flour. Beat thoroughly. Add remaining 3 cups flour and beat thoroughly. Turn out onto board, adding more flour if necessary, and knead for 10 minutes. Put in greased bowl and let rise until doubled in bulk. Knead and shape into 2 loaves; put loaves in greased loaf pans, 9 x 5 x 3 inches. Let rise until doubled. Bake in preheated moderate oven (375°F.) for 50 minutes. Makes 2 loaves.

INDIAN MEAL RAISED BREAD

1½ cups milk
2 packages active dry yeast or 2 cakes compressed yeast
½ cup lukewarm water*
½ cup dark molasses
1 tablespoon salt
6 to 6½ cups sifted all-purpose flour
¾ cup yellow cornmeal
1 tablespoon melted lard

Scald milk; cool to lukewarm. Sprinkle or crumble yeast into water. *Use very warm water (105°F. to 115°F.) for dry yeast; use lukewarm (80°F. to 90°F.) for compressed. Let stand for a few minutes, then stir until dissolved. Add dissolved yeast to milk with molasses, salt, and 3 cups flour. Beat thoroughly. Cover and let stand in warm place until full of bubbles. Beat thoroughly again; add cornmeal, lard, and enough flour to make a stiff dough. Turn out on a lightly floured board and knead until smooth, about 10 minutes. Form into ball and place in greased bowl Brush with a little melted fat, cover, and let rise until doubled in bulk. Punch down; divide into halves; form into 2 loaves. Place in greased loaf pans, 9 x 5 x 3 inches. Cover and let rise in warm place until doubled in bulk. Bake in preheated hot oven (425°F.) for 15 minutes; then reduce heat to moderate (375°F.) and bake for 30 minutes longer. Makes 2 loaves.

BLUEBERRY BREAKFAST CAKE

⅓ cup shortening
1 cup sugar
1 egg
½ teaspoon salt
¼ teaspoon baking soda
1 teaspoon baking powder
½ teaspoon each ground cinnamon and ground nutmeg
2½ cups sifted all-purpose flour
1 cup buttermilk
1 cup fresh blueberries

Cream shortening and gradually beat in sugar. Beat in egg. Sift dry ingredients together and add alternately with buttermilk to first mixture. Fold in blueberries. Pour batter into greased 9-inch square pan. Bake in preheated moderate oven (375°F.) for 35 to 40 minutes. Serve hot with butter. Makes 4 to 6 servings.

MOLASSES JOHNNYCAKE

1 cup sifted all-purpose flour
3 teaspoons baking powder
1 teaspoon salt
1 cup yellow cornmeal
1 egg, beaten
¼ cup molasses
1 cup milk
¼ cup shortening, melted

Sift flour with baking powder and salt. Mix in cornmeal. Combine egg, molasses, and milk; stir into dry mixture. Blend in melted shortening. Pour into greased 8-inch square pan. Bake in preheated hot oven (400°F.) for 25 minutes. Makes one 8-inch square cake.

DUMFUNNIES

2 tablespoons sugar
1 egg, beaten
½ teaspoon salt
2 tablespoons melted butter
3 cups sifted all-purpose flour (about)
1 teaspoon baking soda
1 cup buttermilk
Fat for deep frying
Maple syrup

Beat sugar into egg; add salt and butter. Sift 2 cups flour with soda and add to first mixture alternately with buttermilk, a small amount at a time. Add enough more flour to make dough stiff enough to knead. Turn out on floured board and knead well. Place in greased bowl; cover with cloth and let stand for 2½ hours. Turn dough out on floured board. Cut off strips about 1½ inches wide and twist into rings. Fry in deep hot fat (350°F. on frying thermometer) until golden-brown on one side; turn and brown on other side. Drain on unglazed paper. Serve warm with warm maple syrup. Makes 3 dozen.

FRIED TOADS

2 cups rye meal
1 cup yellow cornmeal
1 cup sour milk or buttermilk
1 egg, well beaten
1 teaspoon baking soda
⅔ cup dark molasses
½ teaspoon salt
Fat or lard for deep frying

Combine all ingredients except fat and blend well. Add a little extra sour milk if mixture is too thick. Drop by teaspoonfuls into hot deep fat (380°F. on a frying thermometer) and dry for about 30 minutes. Serve at once. Makes about 4½ dozen toads.
NOTE: This is the New England version of Hush Puppies.

HASTY PUDDING

4 cups water
1 teaspoon salt
1 cup yellow cornmeal

Bring water and salt to boil over direct heat in top part of double boiler; sprinkle in cornmeal, stirring constantly. Cook over boiling water for 30 minutes, stirring occasionally. Sweeten to taste with maple syrup, honey, molasses, or sugar; serve in deep bowls with milk or cream. Makes 8 servings.

DESSERTS

INDIAN PUDDING

Originally, Indian pudding was baked in the warm ashes of an old brick oven for many hours longer than the three specified here; but this adapted recipe gives a result as close to the original as a modern stove can do.

4 cups milk
¼ cup yellow cornmeal
⅔ cup dark molasses
⅓ cup sugar
¼ cup butter or margarine
¾ teaspoon ground cinnamon
⅜ teaspoon ground ginger

In top part of double boiler scald 3 cups milk. Mix cornmeal with ¼ cup milk and stir it into the hot milk. Cook the mixture, stirring occasionally, for 15 minutes over simmering water; then add molasses, sugar, and butter. Season this batter with cinnamon and ginger; cook another 5 minutes; then pour it into a well-buttered baking dish. Pour on ¾ cup cold milk (do not stir in!) and bake pudding in preheated slow oven (300°F.) for 3 hours. Let stand to "whey" for 30 minutes. Serve warm, with vanilla ice cream, if desired. Makes 4 to 6 servings.

STEAMED CHOCOLATE PUDDING

½ cup soft butter or margarine
½ cup sugar
1 egg, beaten
1 teaspoon vanilla extract
1 cup sifted all-purpose flour
2 teaspoons baking powder
½ teaspoon salt
⅓ cup milk
2 squares (2 ounces) unsweetened chocolate, melted
Hard sauce

Cream butter and sugar until light and fluffy. Add egg and vanilla. Beat until blended. Add sifted dry ingredients alternately with milk, beating until smooth. Stir in chocolate. Put in greased 1-quart pudding mold, cover tightly, and put on rack in kettle. Add boiling water to come halfway up sides of mold. Cover kettle and steam pudding for about 1 hour. Turn out of mold and serve warm with hard sauce. Makes 4 to 6 servings.

APPLE SLUMP

6 large Rhode Island greening apples
2 cups water
1 cup sugar
1½ cups sifted all-purpose flour
¼ teaspoon salt
2 teaspoons baking powder
¼ cup butter or margarine
½ cup milk

Peel and core apples and slice into large skillet. Add water and sugar, cover, and cook over medium heat until apples are almost tender. Make biscuit dough with remaining ingredients. Pat out into round the size of skillet. Place dough on top of apples, cover, and simmer about 20 minutes, or until dough is cooked. To serve, turn bottom side up on chop plate. Pass cinnamon sugar and heavy cream. Makes 4 to 6 servings.

MRS. PARSON'S RECIPE FOR CREAM

1 cup milk
1 egg yolk, well beaten, or 1 whole egg, well beaten
1 teaspoon vanilla extract
¼ cup sugar
Dash of salt

Combine ingredients in top part of a double boiler and cook over hot water until mixture becomes thick and creamy. Pour into serving dishes and chill. Serve topped with sweetened whipped cream. Makes 2 servings.

OLD-TIME SPICED BREAD PUDDING

6 slices of bread buttered generously with ¼ cup butter
1 cup firmly packed dark brown sugar
½ teaspoon each ground allspice and cinnamon
¼ teaspoon salt
2 eggs
2½ cups milk, scalded
Cherry jam

Dice buttered bread into buttered 1½-quart shallow pudding pan. Sprinkle with sugar mixed with spices. Beat salt and eggs slightly. Gradually beat in milk and pour over bread. Bake in preheated moderate oven (325°F.) until set, about 30 minutes. Top with cherry jam. Makes 6 servings.

PIES

SQUASH PIE

2 cups mashed cooked Hubbard squash
¾ cup firmly packed brown sugar
¾ teaspoon ground cinnamon
½ teaspoon each ground mace and nutmeg
¼ teaspoon ground ginger
½ teaspoon salt
3 tablespoons butter or margarine, melted
1 tablespoon molasses
2 eggs, slightly beaten
2 cups milk, scalded
Pastry for 1 crust 9-inch pie

Combine all ingredients except pastry and mix well. Turn into a 9-inch pie pan lined with pastry rolled ⅛ inch thick. Bake in preheated hot oven (450°F.) for 20 minutes. Reduce heat to moderate (350°F.) and bake for 30 minutes longer or until firm in center. Makes 6 to 8 servings.

APPLE-RAISIN-NUT PIE

Pastry for 9-inch lattice pie
5 cups (8 to 10) cored, peeled, and sliced cooking apples
1 cup seedless raisins
½ cup chopped nuts
1 cup firmly packed dark brown sugar
2 teaspoons ground cinnamon
Dash each ground cloves and nutmeg

Roll out half of pastry and line 9-inch pie pan. Mix remaining ingredients and fill lined pan. Roll out rest of pastry, cut into ½-inch strips, and arrange on top in lattice fashion. Moisten edges with water, and seal. Bake in preheated hot oven (425°F.) for 10 minutes. Reduce heat to moderate (375°F.) and bake for 30 to 35 minutes. Makes 6 to 8 servings.

CHERRY DEEP-DISH PIES

2 cans (1 pound each) water-packed pitted red sour cherries
¼ cup quick-cooking tapioca
⅔ cup sugar
⅛ teaspoon each salt and ground cinnamon
Pastry (1½-cup flour recipe), unbaked

Drain cherries, reserving ⅔ cup juice. Mix juice with tapioca, sugar, salt, and ground cinnamon. Add cherries. Pour mixture into 4 individual baking dishes. Top with strips of pastry, lattice fashion. Bake in preheated hot oven (400°F.) for 35 to 40 minutes. Serve warm, plain or with heavy cream or ice cream. Makes 4 servings.

One-Dish Cherry Pie

Prepare cherry mixture as for Cherry Deep-Dish Pies above, pouring mixture into 8-inch square baking dish. Cover completely with a rectangle of pastry (1-cup flour recipe). Bake in preheated hot oven (425°F.) about 30 minutes, or until crust is browned and juice begins to bubble through slits in crust.

CAKES AND COOKIES

ANTHELIAS' SOUR-MILK GINGERBREAD CUPCAKES

½ cup dark molasses
1 teaspoon baking soda
½ teaspoon salt
1 tablespoon ground ginger
½ cup sugar
1 tablespoon butter, softened
1 cup sour milk or buttermilk
2¼ cups sifted all-purpose flour

Mix molasses with ½ teaspoon baking soda. Add salt, ginger, sugar, butter, and sour milk. Beat well. Gradually beat in flour sifted with remaining ½ teaspoon baking soda. Spoon mixture into greased muffin pans. Bake in preheated hot oven (400°F.) for 20 to 25 minutes. Makes 12 cupcakes.

BOSTON CREAM PIE

½ cup butter or margarine, softened
2½ cups sifted cake flour
3 teaspoons baking powder
½ teaspoon salt
1½ cups granulated sugar
Milk
1 teaspoon vanilla extract
2 eggs
Cream Filling
Confectioners' sugar

Stir butter just to soften. Sift in flour, baking powder, salt, and granulated sugar. Add ¾ cup milk and vanilla. Mix until dry ingredients are dampened. Then beat for 2 minutes at low speed of electric mixer or 300 vigorous strokes by hand. Add eggs and 2 tablespoons milk. Beat for 1 minute longer in mixer or 150 strokes by hand. Pour into two 9-inch layercake pans lined on the bottom with paper. Bake in preheated moderate oven (375°F.) for 20 to 25 minutes. Turn out on cake racks, and peel off paper. Cool, and put together with Cream Filling. Sprinkle top with sifted confectioners' sugar. Makes 8 servings.

Cream Filling

½ cup sugar
2½ tablespoons cornstarch
⅛ teaspoon salt
1½ cups milk
2 egg yolks, beaten
1 teaspoon vanilla extract

In heavy saucepan mix sugar, cornstarch, and salt. Add ½ cup milk, and stir until smooth. Add remaining 2 cups milk, and cook over low heat, stirring constantly, until smooth and thickened. Stir mixture into egg yolks. Return to saucepan, and cook for 2 minutes longer, stirring constantly. Cool, and add vanilla.

OLD-FASHIONED HERMITS

½ cup sugar
⅓ cup shortening
1 egg
3 cups sifted all-purpose flour
½ teaspoon salt
1 teaspoon ground cinnamon
½ teaspoon ground nutmeg
¼ teaspoon ground cloves
½ cup dark molasses
½ cup buttermilk
1 cup seedless raisins

Cream together sugar and shortening. Beat in egg. Sift dry ingredients and add alternately with molasses mixed with buttermilk. Stir in raisins. Drop by teaspoons onto greased cookie sheet. Bake in preheated moderate oven (350°F.) for 8 to 10 minutes, or until lightly browned. Cool on a rack. Makes about 6 dozen cookies.

RIBBON CAKE

1 cup butter or margarine
2 cups sugar
4 eggs, separated
1 cup milk
3½ cups sifted all-purpose flour
3½ teaspoons baking powder
½ teaspoon salt
½ cup raisins, chopped
1 cup dry currants
1 pound citron, diced
2 tablespoons molasses
2 teaspoons brandy
1 teaspoon ground cinnamon
Red jelly
Vanilla Frosting

Cream butter and sugar and add egg yolks. Stir in milk. Sift flour with baking powder and salt and gradually add to first mixture, mixing well after each addition. Fold in stiffly beaten egg whites. Divide batter into thirds. Grease three 9-inch square pans. Pour two-thirds of batter into two pans. Add rest of ingredients except jelly and frosting to remaining batter; mix well and turn into third pan. Bake in preheated moderate oven (375°F.). White layers will take 30 to 35 minutes; fruit layer 45 to 50 minutes. Turn out on cake racks to cool.

Place one white layer on a large plate; spread with red jelly. Set fruit layer over this and spread with red jelly. Top with remaining white layer. Trim sides, if necessary, to make straight edges. Frost top and sides with Vanilla Frosting. Makes one 9-inch square cake.

Vanilla Frosting

1 tablespoon butter
¼ cup hot milk
3 cups sifted confectioners' sugar
1 teaspoon vanilla extract

Melt butter in milk; add sugar and vanilla. Mix well and spread on cake.

Seafood Stew
Old-time Spiced Bread Pudding

BUTTERMILK SNICKERDOODLES

½ cup shortening
1 cup sugar
2 eggs, well beaten
2½ cups sifted all-purpose flour
1 teaspoon baking powder
½ teaspoon each baking soda and salt
1 teaspoon ground cinnamon
½ teaspoon each ground allspice and cloves
¾ cup buttermilk
⅓ cup each seeded raisins and dry currants
½ cup chopped nuts

Cream shortening and sugar. Add eggs. Mix and sift dry ingredients and add alternately with buttermilk. Stir in fruits and nuts. Pour into greased and floured 2½-inch muffin pans, filling two thirds full. Bake in preheated moderate oven (375°F.) about 25 minutes. Makes 24.

A PRESERVE

CHOWCHOW

18 large tomatoes, peeled and chopped fine
1 small head of green cabbage, chopped
2 green peppers, seeded and chopped
1 red pepper, seeded and chopped
1 cup cider vinegar
1 cup sugar
2 teaspoons ground cinnamon
1 teaspoon each ground allspice and ground cloves
6 tablespoons salt
1 large onion, peeled and chopped

Combine all ingredients. Cover tightly and simmer for several hours until vegetables are tender. Spoon into hot sterilized jars; seal. Makes 8 pints.

NOODLE—A food paste, or pasta, made of flour, water, and egg yolks. (It is the addition of the egg solids that makes the difference between noodles and spaghetti or macaroni.) Noodles are a favorite of countries as dissimilar as China and Italy, and they may be prepared in a great variety of ways. Widely available commercially, in many countries they are still made at home, too.

Availability and Purchasing Guide—Commercially made noodles are sold packaged in fine, medium, and wide widths. Some are cut into squares, some are shaped into bows, and some of the fine noodles are shaped into noodle "nests." Also available are noodles enriched with thiamine, riboflavin, iron, and niacin; and spinach, or green, noodles, noodles to which about three per cent of spinach solids have been added.

Noodles are available canned in many combinations, such as goulash with noodles; chicken with noodles; and turkey, beef, and chicken noodle soups. There are dry soup mixes containing noodles and a packaged chicken noodle dinner.

Storage—Store uncooked noodles in a cool dry place.
Kitchen shelf: 3 to 6 months
Refrigerator shelf, cooked and covered: 4 to 5 days
Refrigerator frozen-food compartment, prepared for freezing: 3 to 4 weeks
Freezer, prepared for freezing: 1 year

Nutritive Food Values—Primarily a source of carbohydrates.
Noodles, 1 cup (5.6 ounces) = 200 calories

Basic Preparation—Plan to serve noodles as soon as they are cooked. Cook them in plenty of boiling salted water. Keep water boiling rapidly to prevent noodles from sticking together. To lasagna noodles add 2 tablespoons oil to the cooking water to keep them from sticking. The ideal consistency for noodles is *al dente,* still chewy. All noodles should be drained immediately after cooking, and rinsed in hot water, or separated with a fork to prevent sticking.

BASIC NOODLE DOUGH

1½ cups sifted all-purpose flour (about)
½ teaspoon salt
2 eggs, slightly beaten

Sift flour and salt into bowl. Make a little well in center and drop in eggs. Work with fingers until mixture becomes a very stiff paste; if it is too moist, more flour must be added. Divide dough into halves and roll into two balls. Put floured tablecloth or pastry cloth on wooden board or marble, wooden, or enamel kitchen table. Place dough on cloth and with floured rolling pin roll very thin. You will have to turn dough often, rolling it first on one side, then on the other, flouring cloth and rolling pin occasionally. It takes a strong right arm to get this dough thin enough. Roll up dough tightly into a long roll and, with sharp knife, cut into crosswise slices about ¼ inch thick. Separate slices. Dry for 1 hour, more or less, but do not let all the moisture evaporate or dough will crumble. Store in a jar. Makes about 8 ounces.

To Make Tagliatelli—Roll up dough as above and, with sharp knife, cut into very thin crosswise slices about ⅛ inch thick. Proceed as directed above.

To Make Cannelloni—Roll dough very thin and cut into 6-inch squares; use at once, or store.

To Make Lasagna—Roll dough very thin and cut into 3-inch strips; use at once, or store.

FLORENTINE CANNELLONI

Use Basic Noodle Dough, or buy broad (2½- to 3-inch) noodles. Drop a few at a time into a large kettle of salted water. Cook for 5 to 7 minutes, or until chewy but not raw. Drain. Spread each piece with 1 tablespoon or so of Filling. Roll up like little muffs. Place side by side, one layer deep, in casserole or individual baking dishes. Pour Cheese Sauce over cannelloni. Sprinkle with more grated Parmesan cheese. Set in cold broiler; turn up heat to medium. Broil until mixture is heated through, top is brown, and cheese is melted. Serve at once, very hot. Makes 6 servings.

Filling

½ pound mushrooms
1 small garlic clove
3 tablespoons olive oil
1 cup ground cooked chicken
1 hard-cooked egg, sieved
⅛ teaspoon each dried thyme and rosemary
Cream to hold mixture together (1 to 2 tablespoons)

Grind mushrooms and garlic together in food chopper, and brown lightly in hot oil. Add all other ingredients, and mix. Cool slightly.

Cheese Sauce

2 tablespoons butter or margarine
2 tablespoons all-purpose flour
1 cup chicken bouillon
½ cup light cream
Salt and pepper
½ cup grated Parmesan cheese

Melt butter in skillet. Add flour and stir to form smooth paste. Add bouillon and cream, stirring slowly. Add salt and pepper to taste. Cook until you have a medium-thick sauce. Add cheese.

SHRIMP-NOODLE SKILLET

2 tablespoons butter or margarine
½ cup chopped green pepper
1 garlic clove, crushed
⅛ teaspoon pepper
4 cups clam juice
4 cups (8 ounces) fine noodles
1 can (6 ounces) mushrooms
¼ cup canned pimientos, chopped
2 cans (5 ounces each) shrimps, drained

Melt butter in 10-inch skillet. Add green pepper and garlic and cook over low heat for 5 minutes. Add pepper and clam juice and heat to boiling point. Add noodles slowly so mixture continues to boil. Cook, uncovered, for 5 minutes, stirring occasionally. Add mushrooms and liquid, pimientos, and shrimps. Cook for 5 minutes longer, stirring occasionally, or until thoroughly heated. Makes 4 to 6 servings.

RUMANIAN NOODLES

1 pound fine noodles
1 pound ground fresh pork
1 slice of bread, soaked in milk and squeezed dry
1 leek, minced
2 teaspoons fennel seeds
¼ cup chopped parsley
1 teaspoon salt
½ teaspoon pepper
4 eggs
⅔ cup light cream
½ cup grated cheese
¼ cup butter or margarine

Cook noodles only three-quarters tender. Combine pork, bread, leek, fennel seeds, parsley, and salt and pepper. In greased large shallow baking dish place alternate layers of noodles and meat mixture, ending with noodles. Beat eggs with cream and cheese. Pour over noodles. Dot with butter. Bake in preheated moderate oven (350°F.) for 40 minutes, or until pork is done. Makes 4 to 6 servings.

THE POOR PARSON'S NOODLE DISH

3 tablespoons bacon fat
2 onions, minced
½ cup minced green pepper
2 cans (4 ounces each) sliced mushrooms, drained
4 cups ground cooked meat
3 cups beef bouillon
3 tablespoons all-purpose flour
¼ cup water
Dash of hot pepper sauce
1 teaspoon salt
½ teaspoon pepper
½ teaspoon dried thyme, basil, or other favorite herb
8 ounces medium noodles, cooked

Melt bacon fat and cook onions and green pepper until soft. Push to one side and add mushrooms. Sauté for 5 minutes, covered. Add meat and cook for 5 minutes more. Add bouillon. When boiling, thicken with flour mixed with water into a smooth paste. Stir in seasonings. Simmer for 15 minutes, stirring occasionally. Add noodles, and heat through. Makes 6 servings.

NOODLES POLONAISE

4 cups (8 ounces) wide noodles
¼ cup butter or margarine
½ cup fine dry bread crumbs
1 hard-cooked egg, chopped
1 tablespoon chopped chives or parsley
½ teaspoon salt

Cook noodles; drain. Melt butter in skillet and brown crumbs in it. Add chopped egg, chives, and salt; mix well. Add noodles and toss to coat. Heat through, stirring. Makes 4 to 6 servings.

MEATBALL-NOODLE SKILLET

1 egg
1 pound ground beef
½ cup fine dry bread crumbs
⅓ cup chopped parsley
1 medium onion, chopped
1 tablespoon grated lemon rind
2 teaspoons salt
½ teaspoon pepper
⅛ teaspoon ground nutmeg
¼ cup olive or salad oil
2 tablespoons butter or margarine
1 can (1 pound) tomatoes
Water
1 teaspoon oregano
2 bay leaves
4 cups (8 ounces) medium noodles

Mix together egg, beef, bread crumbs, parsley, onion, lemon rind, 1 teaspoon salt, ¼ teaspoon pepper, and nutmeg. Shape into 1½-inch balls. Heat oil and butter in 10-inch skillet. Add meatballs and cook over medium heat until browned on all sides, stirring occasionally. Cover and cook over low heat for 15 minutes. Drain tomatoes into separate pan; reserve tomatoes. To tomato liquid add enough water to make 4 cups. Add oregano, bay leaves, and remaining teaspoon salt and ¼ teaspoon pepper; pour on meatballs in skillet. Heat mixture to boiling point. Gradually add noodles so that mixture continues to boil. Cook, uncovered, over low heat, stirring frequently, for 12 to 15 minutes, or until noodles are almost tender. Add reserved tomatoes and cook for 5 minutes longer. Makes 4 to 6 servings.

HAM AND NOODLE RABBIT

3 tablespoons all-purpose flour
1 teaspoon salt
2 teaspoons dry mustard
⅛ teaspoon hot pepper sauce
1 pound Cheddar cheese, shredded
3 tablespoons butter or margarine
1½ cups (12-ounce bottle) beer or ale
2 cups diced cooked ham
8 ounces medium noodles, cooked

Mix together flour, salt, mustard, hot pepper sauce, and cheese. Melt butter. Stir in cheese mixture and cook over low heat until smooth, stirring constantly. Add beer and continue stirring over low heat until thoroughly blended. Add ham and noodles and mix well. Heat if necessary. Makes 4 to 6 servings.

Tongue and Noodle Rabbit

For ham in above recipe, substitute 2 cups diced cooked smoked tongue.

PARTY NOODLES SUPREME

½ cup butter or margarine
⅓ cup all-purpose flour
2½ cups hot chicken bouillon
¾ cup light cream
⅓ cup white wine
2 teaspoons salt
½ teaspoon white pepper
6 or 8 large mushrooms
1 cup cooked ham, cut into strips
8 ounces medium noodles
2 cups diced cooked chicken
½ cup grated Parmesan cheese

Heat ¼ cup butter; blend in flour. Gradually add bouillon, stirring constantly. Add cream and cook, stirring, until sauce is smooth and thickened. Add wine and salt and pepper and remove from heat, but keep hot. Slice mushroom stems. Heat remaining ¼ cup butter; in it, sauté sliced mushrooms, whole mushroom caps, and ham. Remove caps and reserve. Cook and drain noodles. Combine noodles and chicken with sauce and sliced mushrooms and ham. Turn into 6 or 8 individual baking dishes. Top each dish with a mushroom cap and some grated cheese. Bake in preheated hot oven (400°F.) for 20 minutes. Makes 6 to 8 servings.

NOODLES WITH EGGS AND BACON

12 bacon strips, diced
1 pound medium noodles, freshly cooked, drained, and rinsed
¾ cup butter or margarine
4 egg yolks
Salt and freshly ground pepper
Grated Parmesan cheese

Fry bacon until crisp, Remove crisp pieces and drain fat from skillet, leaving about 2 tablespoons. Toss drained and rinsed hot noodles with butter until well blended. Pour noodles into skillet with crisp bacon pieces. Add egg yolks and salt and pepper to taste. Cook over medium heat for ½ minute just until eggs are set. Top with freshly grated Parmesan cheese. Makes 4 to 6 servings.

BUTTERED NOODLES WITH CASHEW NUTS

Cook ½ pound wide noodles according to directions on package. Drain. Season. Pour over ½ cup split cashew nuts browned in ½ cup butter. Makes 4 servings.

HUNGARIAN NOODLE AND CHEESE CASSEROLE

3 cups (6 ounces) wide noodles
1 cup cottage cheese
1 cup dairy sour cream
1 garlic clove, minced
3 tablespoons minced onion
1 pimiento, chopped
Dash of hot pepper sauce
¾ teaspoon steak sauce
¼ teaspoon salt
½ cup grated mild Cheddar, Gouda, or Edam cheese

Cook and drain noodles. Combine with all other ingredients except grated cheese. Turn into buttered 1½-quart casserole. Sprinkle with cheese. Bake in preheated moderate oven (350°F.) for 30 minutes. Makes 4 servings.

PORK-CHOP AND NOODLE SKILLET

¼ cup butter or margarine
4 pork loin chops, cut 1 inch thick
2 teaspoons salt
½ teaspoon ground nutmeg
4 cups apple juice
4 cups (8 ounces) wide noodles
4 canned spiced crabapples
Parsley sprigs

Melt butter in 10-inch skillet. Sprinkle pork chops with 1 teaspoon salt. Arrange pork chops in skillet and cook over medium heat until browned on both sides, 15 to 20 minutes. Add nutmeg and ½ cup apple juice. Cover and cook over low heat for 45 minutes, turning pork chops occasionally. Remove pork chops. Add remaining 3½ cups apple juice and remaining 1 teaspoon salt. Heat to boiling point. Add noodles gradually so that mixture continues to boil; cook over medium heat, stirring frequently, about 20 minutes, or until noodles are tender. Add pork chops and heat to serving temperature. Garnish with crabapples and parsley. Makes 4 servings.

GREEN NOODLES WITH BASIL

1 pound green noodles
1 or 2 garlic cloves, minced
1 cup soft butter or margarine
1 teaspoon salt
1 teaspoon pepper
3 tablespoons shredded fresh basil leaves or 2 teaspoons dried basil
1 cup grated Parmesan or Swiss cheese

Cook noodles. Drain; return to kettle. Add remaining ingredients and toss well. Makes 4 to 6 servings.
Note: Use fresh basil if you can; it makes a big difference.

HUNGARIAN ALMOND NOODLES

Cook ½ cup slivered blanched almonds in ¼ cup melted butter until golden. Add 2 tablespoons paprika. Cook for 3 minutes, stirring constantly. Toss with hot cooked noodles (8-ounce package). Makes 4 to 6 servings.

FETTUCINE ALFREDO

1 pound noodles
½ cup unsalted butter, cut into pieces
2 cups freshly grated Parmesan cheese
½ teaspoon pepper

Cook noodles; drain. Place in hot deep serving dish. Add butter, cheese, and pepper and toss thoroughly but quickly. Cheese and butter should melt into a creamy sauce that coats the noodles. Makes 6 servings.

THREE-TONE BUFFET NOODLES

Cook 8 ounces medium plain noodles according to package directions and dress with ¼ cup butter or margarine. Keep hot. Do the same with 8 ounces green noodles of the same size. Cook another 8 ounces medium plain noodles and dress with 1 cup hot plain tomato sauce. Toss thoroughly and drain off excess sauce, if any. Noodles must be dry. Arrange noodles on heated platter in three groups: green noodles first, white ones in the middle, and red ones last. Serve plenty of grated Parmesan cheese separately. Makes 6 to 8 servings.

PRUNE-NOODLE PUDDING

3 cups (6 ounces) wide noodles
Salt
3 eggs, separated
¾ cup sugar
1 cup milk
1¼ cups (8 ounces) dried prunes, pitted, soaked until soft, and chopped
¼ cup chopped nuts
2 teaspoons fresh lemon juice
1 teaspoon vanilla extract

Cook noodles in boiling salted water until tender; drain. In top part of small double boiler beat egg yolks and 1 egg white with ½ cup sugar until blended. Add milk and cook over simmering water, stirring constantly, until mixture is slightly thickened and coats a metal spoon. Add noodles, prunes, nuts, lemon juice, and vanilla. Put in buttered 1½-quart casserole. Beat remaining 2 egg whites with a dash of salt until foamy. Gradually add remaining ¼ cup sugar, beating until stiff. Pile lightly onto mixture in casserole. Bake in preheated slow oven (325°F.) for 15 minutes, or until lightly browned. Serve warm or cold. Makes 6 servings.

NORWEGIAN COOKERY

by Nika Hazelton

The scenery of Norway, from one end to the other, is beautiful beyond belief. The sea surrounds the mountains embracing them with the long arms of the fjords, and the mountains are part of the sea, dotting it with islands that make the heart long to go back to them. But it is the friendliness, the openhearted hospitality of the Norwegian people, that win the visitor at first meeting. Like Americans, Norwegians will take the stranger into their homes, and make him feel welcome immediately.

Norway is a fishing country, and the excellence of the fish and the way it is cooked cannot be praised sufficiently. The cold waters of the northern sea, lakes, and streams give a firmness of texture and sweetness of flavor beyond compare to cod, haddock, herring, plaice, salmon, and trout; fish that constitute the greater part of the Norwegian diet. In the fish markets, which to the stranger's surprise are odorless, fish is bought within hours of its catching, or freshly killed, for all of Norway's towns are close to the fish-rich waters. It is a heartwarming sight to see a Norwegian housewife choosing the daily fish for her family. The fish is cooked with equal care, and since its quality is so superior, the Norwegians cook it plainly. First it is soaked in cold water and then it is briefly boiled or sautéed and served with a butter or herb sauce. The fish is cooked in servings, so that the second helping will come to the table as freshly cooked as the first. The livers, which do not taste like fish oil, and the tongues are eaten sautéed. Herring is a standby in the daily diet, as in all of Scandinavia, and served in a multitude of ways, fresh, pickled, and preserved, the latter as a topping for the open-face sandwiches eaten for lunch or snacks.

A special Norwegian favorite is *fiskepudding,* fish ground extremely fine, mixed with cream, sometimes with butter, and steamed. This mousse is served hot, with butter sauce, or sliced and sautéed, or cold as a sandwich topping. Norwegians also favor shrimps and crayfish.

The meats which Norway produces and eats in quantity are lamb and mutton. Whether it is the sweetness of the mountain pastures, or the tasty grass of the salt-water farms on which they feed, their meat is delicious.

Game birds of every kind, including the Arctic ptarmigan, and venison play a great part in Norway's diet. Much of Norway's terrain is vast forest; only 2.7 percent of the country's 119,240 square miles is farming land, the rest being naked rock or deep forests. The products of the majestic, wonderfully silent Norwegian woods are cooked with great delicacy, often with wine and with sour cream. Reindeer meat is one of the products of the forest cooked this way; the taste resembles that of beef, with just a touch of sweetness. Compotes of lingonberries, prunes, or apples are standard game accompaniments.

As for vegetables, potatoes and cabbage reign supreme, closely followed by carrots, turnips, and green vegetables in season.

Norwegians love fruit. Norwegian apples are excellent, and so are the berries of the north, lingonberries, blueberries, strawberries, and Arctic cloudberries, called *multer,* which look like yellow blackberries and taste both tart and sweet. Cooked and served with cream, they are festive fare, the Christmas dessert.

Like all Scandinavians, the Norwegians make very good pancakes, called *lefse,* and waffles which, surprisingly, they eat cold. The dark and rye Norwegian breads, including the flatbreads, are simply marvelous and the backbone of the diet.

Norwegian food has a certain family resemblance to other Scandinavian food. But it is less rich than the Danish and it relies far more on fish, game, and smoked meats than the Swedish, and the baking is also on a less lavish scale than that of Sweden, although fully as good.

APPETIZERS AND SOUP

KJØTTSALAT
[Meat Salad]

Hearty salads of meat, chicken, game, or fish are popular on the Norwegian appetizer table and for cold suppers.

1 cup julienne strips of cooked beef, veal, or lamb
1 cup julienne strips of baked or boiled ham
1 tablespoon minced onion
6 tablespoons salad oil
2 tablespoons cider vinegar
½ teaspoon pepper
1 teaspoon minced parsley
¼ cup heavy cream or dairy sour cream
1 hard-cooked egg, sliced
1 boiled or pickled beet, sliced

Mix cut meats with onion. Beat together oil, vinegar, pepper, and parsley. Stir cream into dressing. Mix with meats, combining lightly. Garnish with sliced egg and beet. If served on appetizer table, where small servings are spooned onto guests' plates, this amount makes 6 servings, or 2 or 3 servings as a main-dish salad.

HAUGESUNDSK SPEDESILD
[Haugesund Pickled Herring]

2 large pickled herrings
3 tablespoons cider vinegar
3 tablespoons salad oil
1 teaspoon pepper
3 tablespoons sugar
1 small onion, minced
1 cup coarsely chopped pickled beets
Minced parsley

Rinse herrings and soak for 12 hours. Cut into strips, ½ x 1 inch. Arrange pieces to resemble the fish before cutting. Mix vinegar, oil, pepper, and sugar. Pour mixture over herring and let stand for several hours. Serve garnished with onion, beets, and minced parsley. Makes 4 servings.

NOTE: Serve with boiled potatoes and thick dairy sour cream.

ISBJØRNØYE
[Polar Bear's Eye]

12 flat anchovy fillets, chopped
2 medium raw potatoes, cooked, peeled, and chopped
6 onion slices, chopped
1 large beet, cooked, peeled, and chopped
6 raw egg yolks

On each of 6 plates make a circle of anchovies, potatoes, onions, and beets. Carefully place a raw egg yolk in the center of the circle. Chill and serve with flatbread and butter. Makes 6 servings.

KIRSEBAERSUPPE
[Cold Cherry Soup]

2½ pounds ripe cherries
2½ cups sugar
2½ quarts water
1 piece (1 inch) cinnamon stick
Grated rind of ½ lemon
Juice of ½ lemon
2 cups sherry

Wash and stem cherries. Remove pits but do not discard them. Combine cherries, sugar, and water in large enamel or agate kettle and heat to boiling. Simmer for a few minutes. With slotted spoon, put cherries into large bowl. Put cherry pits in a small heavy plastic bag. Wrap bag with a towel and crush pits by hitting them with a hammer. Add crushed cherry pits to hot cherry juice with cinnamon stick and lemon rind and juice. Stir and let boil for 3 or 4 minutes. Remove from heat, strain, and pour over cherries. Chill. Just before serving add sherry. Makes 8 or more soup servings, 12 or more large beverage servings.

NOTE: Should be served very cold, in chilled glasses or bowls. Plain cookies or wafers go with this traditional favorite.

FISH

KOKT ØRRETT
[Boiled Trout]

4 small whole trout
1 cup cider vinegar
Water
1 tablespoon salt
½ cup butter or margarine, softened
½ cup chopped parsley
Lemon wedges

Put trout in a shallow pan and add vinegar and enough water just to cover fish; add salt. When water just starts to boil, remove from heat and let stand covered, for 15 to 20 minutes. Drain and carefully lift fish to a platter. Cream butter until light and fluffy and blend in parsley. Serve parsley butter with fish and garnish platter with lemon wedges. Makes 4 servings.

FISKEPUDDING
[Fish Pudding]

3 pounds fresh fillets of haddock or other mild-flavored white fish
2 tablespoons salt
¼ cup cornstarch or potato flour
⅛ teaspoon ground nutmeg
2 cups light cream
2 cups milk
Shrimp or Lobster Sauce

Rinse fillets; drain. Cut into small pieces and sprinkle with salt. Put fish through food chopper using finest blade. Mix ground fish with cornstarch and nutmeg. Put through chopper 4 more times. (A blender may be used instead of food chopper and milk and cream must be blended with the fish.) Gradually beat in cream and milk. Mixture should be just thick enough to shape into balls which will hold their shape. Spoon two thirds of mixture into buttered 1½-quart baking dish. Cover tightly with foil. Set in shallow pan of hot water. Bake in preheated moderate oven (350°F.) for 40 to 60 minutes. Shape remaining fish mixture into balls about 1½ inches in diameter. Cook in lightly salted simmering water for 20 minutes. Drain; set aside and keep warm. To serve, turn mold out on warmed platter and garnish with cooked fish balls. Serve with hot Shrimp or Lobster Sauce. Makes about 12 servings.

Rekesaus
[Shrimp Sauce]

1 pound raw shrimps
6 tablespoons butter or margarine
¼ cup all-purpose flour
3 cups milk or 1½ cups milk and 1½ cups fish stock
1 tablespoon dairy sour cream
½ teaspoon salt
½ teaspoon sugar
2 tablespoons sherry

Cook shrimps, clean, and cut into pieces. Melt 3 tablespoons butter in a large saucepan. Stir in flour and mix well. Add milk gradually, stirring constantly. Add remaining 3 tablespoons butter, sour cream, salt, and sugar. Mix and cook over low heat, stirring constantly, until smooth and thickened. Add shrimps and cook for 1 minute longer. Add sherry; remove from heat. Serve hot with Fish Pudding. Makes 2 cups.

Hummersaus
[Lobster Sauce]

Substitute 2 cups cut-up cooked lobster meat for shrimps in above recipe.

NOTE: Leftover sauce (either shrimp or lobster) may be reheated in double boiler over hot water. Add 1 teaspoon sherry and use for a fish dish next day.

MEAT

KJØTTKAKER
[Meatballs]

1 onion, grated
⅓ cup butter or margarine (about)
1 pound ground beef round steak
¼ pound ground lean fresh pork
½ cup fresh soft bread crumbs
½ cup milk
1 egg, slightly beaten
1 teaspoon salt
¼ teaspoon ground nutmeg
Dash of ground allspice
3 tablespoons all-purpose flour
1½ cups beef bouillon or water

Cook onion in 2 tablespoons melted butter for 2 or 3 minutes. Combine with meats, bread crumbs, milk, egg, and seasonings. Mix well and shape into firm balls about 1 inch in diameter. Brown a few at a time, shaking pan to prevent sticking. Allow meatballs to brown all over. Remove from pan. Stir in flour and gradually stir in bouillon. Cook over low heat until thickened, stirring constantly. Makes 4 servings.

JULESKINKE
[Christmas Ham]

1 fresh ham (9 to 10 pounds)
Sugar
3 tablespoons fine salt
2 tablespoons saltpeter
4 cups light beer
4 cups dark beer
1½ pounds coarse salt

Rub fresh ham with a mixture of 1 tablespoon sugar, fine salt, and 1 tablespoon saltpeter. Let stand for 24 hours. Combine 1 cup sugar, remaining 1 tablespoon saltpeter, beer, and coarse salt. Bring to boil and pour mixture over ham in a crock or enamelware kettle. Let stand, covered, in a cold place for 3 weeks. Make sure brine covers ham entirely. If necessary, make additional brine. Turn meat in brine every day. Reserve brine. Hang ham to dry in an airy place. Smoke.* To cook ham, simmer for 4 hours in boiling unsalted water. Cool in reserved brine. Remove rind with sharp knife. Serve ham hot or cold with fresh vegetables. Store ham in brine to keep juicy. Makes 12 to 14 servings.

*To smoke ham: Hang scrubbed and well-dried meat in smokehouse. Build a small fire of green hardwood such as hickory, oak, pecan, or apple. Do not use resinous woods. Keep temperature between 80°F. and 90°F. Open ventilators the first day. On second day, close ventilators and smoke until ham has the desired color. A thin haze of smoke will smoke meat best.

PUSS PASS
[Lamb Stew]

2 pounds boneless lamb, cubed
8 large raw potatoes, peeled and diced
8 carrots, sliced
½ head green cabbage, cored and shredded
1 teaspoon peppercorns
2 teaspoons salt
1 tablespoon all-purpose flour
1 cup water

Put meat and vegetables in layers in a large heavy saucepan. Add peppercorns, salt, and flour. Pour water over the top. Cover and simmer for 2 to 3 hours. Makes 8 servings.

LAMMEKJØTT I SURSAUS
[Lamb Shanks with Sour-Cream Sauce]

6 lamb shanks
Salt and pepper
3 tablespoons butter or margarine
1 large onion, chopped
1½ cups dry white wine
½ cup beef bouillon
2 tablespoons all-purpose flour
3 tablespoons water
3 tablespoons chopped fresh dill
1 cup dairy sour cream

Trim excess fat from lamb shanks. Wash and pat dry. Rub meat with salt and pepper. Heat butter in skillet and brown lamb shanks on all sides. Transfer shanks to a deep kettle. Add onion to pan drippings and sauté until tender. Pour onion with drippings over shanks. Add wine and bouillon. Simmer covered, about 1½ hours, or until tender. Remove shanks to a hot platter. Strain stock and return to kettle. Mix flour and water to a smooth paste and stir into stock. Cook over low heat until smooth and thickened, stirring constantly. Stir in dill and sour cream. Return lamb shanks to sauce and reheat but do not boil. Serve with steamed potatoes sprinkled with chopped fresh dill and a cucumber salad. Makes 6 servings.

VEGETABLES AND SALADS

SURKÅL
[Cabbage with Caraway]

1 small head green cabbage, cored and shredded
2 tablespoons all-purpose flour
1 teaspoon salt
1 tablespoon caraway seeds
2 tablespoons butter or margarine
1¼ cups chicken or meat bouillon
2 tablespoons cider vinegar
1 tablespoon sugar

Put shredded cabbage in large saucepan. Sprinkle cabbage with flour, salt, and caraway seeds. Heat butter with bouillon and pour hot mixture over cabbage. Cover and simmer for 1½ hours, or until cabbage is tender. Stir in vinegar and sugar. Serve immediately. Makes 4 to 6 servings, depending on size of cabbage.

Isbjørnøye
Fiskepudding med Hummersaus

BLOMKÅL I REKESAUS
[Hot Cauliflower with Shrimps]

1 large cauliflower
2 cups milk
½ medium onion, minced
2 sprigs of fresh dill
¼ cup butter or margarine
¼ cup all-purpose flour
1 teaspoon salt
¼ teaspoon ground white pepper
2 cups chopped cooked shrimp
¾ cup heavy cream, whipped
12 whole shrimps, cooked and shelled
2 tablespoons minced fresh dill

Trim cauliflower, wash thoroughly, and cook whole in boiling salted water. Meanwhile make sauce. Combine milk, onion, and dill. Bring to a boil. Strain milk and keep hot. Melt butter and stir in flour. Cook mixture over low heat for 3 minutes. Do not brown. Stir hot milk gradually into mixture and cook over low heat, stirring constantly, until smooth and thickened. Cook for 2 minutes longer. Season with salt and pepper. Add chopped shrimps and cook over very low heat until heated through. Fold whipped cream into sauce. Place hot cauliflower on serving dish and pour sauce over it. Decorate with whole shrimps and minced dill. Makes 4 to 6 servings.

SOMMERSALAT
[Summer Salad]

1 head Boston lettuce
2 large raw potatoes, cooked, peeled, and sliced
2 hard-cooked eggs, chopped
1 cup cooked green peas
¼ cup salad oil
2 tablespoons cider vinegar
2 tablespoons prepared mustard
1 teaspoon salt
1 teaspoon sugar
2 large tomatoes, sliced

Trim lettuce and separate leaves. Wash and drain thoroughly. Mix lettuce with potatoes, eggs, and green peas. Chill. Mix oil, vinegar, mustard, salt, and sugar. Toss salad with salad dressing. Pour mixture into a salad bowl. Garnish with sliced tomatoes. Makes 4 servings.

SAUCES

PEPPERROTSAUS
[Horseradish Sauce]

2 cups dairy sour cream
2 to 3 tablespoons grated prepared horseradish
2 teaspoons sugar

Combine all ingredients and blend well. Serve with lamb, veal, chicken, or fish. Makes about 2 cups sauce.

Blomkål I Rekesaus

LØKSAUS
[Onion Sauce]

4 onions, peeled and chopped
2 tablespoons butter or margarine
½ teaspoon salt
¼ teaspoon white pepper
1 teaspoon sugar
2 tablespoons all-purpose flour
1 cup meat bouillon or milk
2 teaspoons horseradish or cider vinegar

Sauté chopped onions in melted butter with salt, pepper, and sugar. Cook over low heat, stirring constantly, until onions are tender but not brown; stir in flour. Gradually stir in bouillon and continue to cook, stirring, until smooth and thickened. Stir in horseradish. Serve with boiled meat. Makes about 2 cups sauce.

BREADS AND PANCAKES

RUGBRØD
[Rye Bread]

2 packages active dry yeast or 2 cakes compressed yeast
1 cup lukewarm water*
1½ cups scalded milk
2 teaspoons salt
1 teaspoon sugar
6 to 7 cups sifted rye flour

Sprinkle or crumble yeast into water. *Use very warm water (105°F. to 115°F.) for dry yeast; use lukewarm (80°F. to 90°F.) for compressed. Let stand for a few minutes, then stir until dissolved. Cool scalded milk to lukewarm. Stir in salt, sugar, and dissolved yeast. Beat in enough flour to make a stiff dough. Pour remaining flour onto a board and knead dough for a few minutes. Put in bowl, brush with shortening, and let rise in warm place until doubled in bulk. Shape dough into 2 round loaves. Put loaves on lightly greased cookie sheets. Let rise until doubled in bulk. Bake in preheated moderate oven (350°F.) for 45 minutes, or until loaves when thumped give a hollow sound. Makes 2 loaves.

KAFFEKAKE
[Coffeecake]

4 eggs
¾ cup sugar
⅔ cup melted butter
1 teaspoon fresh lemon juice
1 teaspoon ground cardamom
3¾ cups sifted all-purpose flour
3¾ teaspoons baking powder

Beat eggs and sugar together until light. Add melted butter, lemon juice, and cardamom. Mix well. Sift flour and baking powder together. Add to egg mixture and mix well. Turn dough out on a lightly floured board. Cut into 4 portions. Shape each into a long roll. Place rolls on greased and lightly floured cookie sheets. Bake in preheated hot oven (425°F.) about 20 minutes; the top should be lightly browned. Remove from oven and let cool slightly. Cut into ½-inch slices while still warm. Spread out slices flat on a cookie sheet and return to hot oven (425°F.) for 5 minutes to brown slightly. It is much like rusk in flavor and texture, not soft but a little dry. Excellent with coffee. Makes 5 to 6 dozen pieces.

LEFSER
[Griddle Cakes]

4 cups riced hot cooked potatoes
2½ tablespoons light cream
2½ tablespoons lard
1½ tablespoons sugar
1 teaspoon salt
2 cups sifted all-purpose flour

Mix riced potatoes with cream and lard. Chill for 1 hour. Add sugar, salt, and flour. Blend thoroughly. Take about ⅓ cup of mixture and form into 2 balls. Continue with remaining dough. Chill balls for 1 hour. On a lightly floured board roll each ball into a paper-thin round about 5 inches in diameter. Cook on heated griddle over low heat until very light tan. Turn and cook on other side. Serve hot or cold. Makes 26.

VAFFLER
[Waffles]

1 cup dairy sour cream, whipped
1½ teaspoons sugar
Pinch of salt
1 egg, well beaten
⅔ cup sifted all-purpose flour

Combine all ingredients in order given. Beat and blend well. Put 1 tablespoon of batter in hot Norwegian waffle iron. Cook until golden-brown. Makes 35 waffles. Makes 4 to 6 servings.

NOTE: Can be prepared in a regular waffle iron. Prepare a double recipe.

DESSERTS, CAKES, AND COOKIES

RABARBRAGRØT
[Rhubarb Pudding]

1½ pounds rhubarb
Water
¾ cup sugar
1½ teaspoons vanilla extract
3 tablespoons cornstarch
1 cup heavy cream

Trim rhubarb and cut into ½-inch slices. Combine with 1½ cups water and ½ cup sugar and simmer until soft. Stir in ½ teaspoon vanilla. Blend cornstarch with a little cold water to make a smooth liquid. Gradually stir cornstarch into rhubarb. Cook over low heat, stirring constantly, until thickened and clear. Pour rhubarb into glass serving dish and chill. At serving time, whip cream. When frothy add remaining ¼ cup sugar and vanilla. Whip until stiff. Pipe whipped cream through a pastry tube in decorative swirls over top of pudding, or cover top of pudding with spoonfuls of whipped cream. Makes 4 servings.

TROLLKREM
[Magic Cream]

3 egg whites
⅓ cup sugar
2 tablespoons fresh lemon juice
1 cup thick well-flavored applesauce or other puréed fruit

Beat egg whites until stiff but not dry. Gradually beat in sugar, 1 tablespoon at a time. Beat in lemon juice and continue beating until mixture is stiff and glossy. Fold in applesauce. Spoon into serving dishes and serve as soon as possible. Makes 4 to 6 servings.

JEG KAN IKKE LA VAERE
[Irresistible Dessert]

4 eggs, separated
½ cup sugar
1 envelope unflavored gelatin
¼ cup cold water
¼ cup fresh lemon juice
Whipped cream
Maraschino cherries
Macaroons

Beat egg yolks until thick and lemon-colored. Gradually beat in sugar. Soften gelatin in cold water and let stand for 5 minutes. Dissolve gelatin by placing over low heat and stirring until gelatin is dissolved. Add gelatin to egg-yolk mixture. Stir in lemon juice. Beat egg whites until stiff but not dry. Fold egg whites into egg-yolk mixture. Pour mixture into serving dish. Chill until firm. Garnish with whipped cream, maraschino cherries, and macaroons. Makes 4 servings.

Krumkaker, Curled Cakes, are baked in a special iron and rolled while still hot.

KRUMKAKER
[Curled Cakes]

½ cup dairy sour cream, whipped
1 egg yolk
2 tablespoons sugar
1 drop of lemon extract
½ cup sifted all-purpose flour

Combine all ingredients in order given. Put 1 teaspoon of batter in the center of a preheated *krumkake* pan. Close the lid and cook for a few minutes, turning the pan once to brown on both sides. Roll the cake while still hot around the handle of a wooden cooking spoon. Makes 12 to 16.
NOTE: These pans can be bought in specialty hardware stores.

SERINAKAKER
[Serina Cakes]

2 cups sifted all-purpose flour
1 teaspoon baking powder
1 cup plus 2 tablespoons sugar
1 cup butter or margarine
1 whole egg, well beaten
1 teaspoon vanilla extract
2 egg whites
½ cup chopped blanched almonds

Sift flour with baking powder and 1 cup sugar. Cut in butter until mixture resembles coarse cornmeal. Add egg, vanilla, and 1 egg white, beaten until stiff and then beaten with 2 tablespoons sugar. Blend well. With floured fingers shape dough into small balls. Beat remaining egg white until foamy. Dip each ball into egg white, then roll in chopped nuts. Put on greased cookie sheets and flatten slightly. Bake in preheated moderate oven (350°F.) for 12 to 14 minutes. Makes about 4 dozen.

FIRE-SPECIEDALER-KAKER
[Four Specie Dollars]

1 cup butter or margarine
1½ cups sifted all-purpose flour
1½ cups sugar
1½ cups coarsely chopped blanched almonds

Cream butter until light and fluffy; beat in flour and sugar. Stir in almonds and mix well. Shape mixture into long roll about 1½ inches in diameter. Wrap in wax paper and chill overnight. Cut into ¼-inch slices and put on greased cookie sheets, about 2 inches apart. Bake in preheated moderate oven (350°F.) for 10 to 12 minutes, or until lightly browned. Makes about 5 dozen.

PLESKENER
[Spongecake Cookies]

4 eggs, separated
1⅓ cups sugar
1 teaspoon vanilla extract or grated rind of 1 lemon
1⅓ cups sifted all-purpose flour

Beat egg yolks until thick and lemon-colored. Beat in sugar and flavoring. Stir in flour. Fold in egg whites which have been beaten until stiff but not dry. Drop dough by teaspoonfuls onto greased cookie sheets, 2 inches apart. Bake in preheated moderate oven (350°F.) for 12 minutes, or until pale golden-brown. Makes about 4 dozen.

KLEJNER
[Fried Twists]

2 whole eggs
2 egg yolks
¾ cup sugar
½ cup melted butter or margarine
½ cup light cream
3 cups all-purpose flour (about)
1 teaspoon baking powder
Fat or cooking oil for deep frying
Confectioners' sugar

Beat whole eggs with egg yolks until thick and lemon-colored. Gradually beat in sugar. Stir in melted butter and cream. Sift 2 cups flour with baking powder and stir into egg mixture. Then stir in enough additional flour so that dough cleans the bowl. Roll on a lightly floured board until ⅛ inch thick. Cut dough into strips or diamonds 3 to 4 inches long and about 1½ inches wide. Cut a slit in center of each strip and pull one end completely through slit. Drop into deep hot fat (375°F. on a frying thermometer) and fry for 2 or 3 minutes, or until golden-brown on both sides. Drain on absorbent paper. Sprinkle with sifted confectioners' sugar. Makes about 4 dozen.

NOUGAT—A confection made with roasted nuts such as almonds or walnuts and sugar or honey. Sometimes egg white is added to bind the mixture. The word comes from the Latin *nux* or "nut."

Nougat of all kinds is a very old confection, possibly of Moorish origin. It has always been popular in Spain, Italy, and France. A variety of nougat much favored in these countries is *touron* in Spanish, or *torrone* in Italian, a chewy candy prevalent especially at Christmastime. There are a great many varieties of nougat: hard or soft, white or colored. Brown nougat, made from caramelized sugar and chopped almonds, is used by candymakers in their confections, or in professional fancy baking.

White nougat usually contains honey and sugar mixed, almonds, and white of egg. It is chewy rather than brittle.

FRENCH NOUGAT

Put 1 cup confectioners' sugar in heavy saucepan. Heat, stirring, until sugar is melted and golden-brown. Stir in 1 cup finely chopped blanched almonds. Put mixture on oiled platter and fold over and over with a spatula. When cool enough to handle, divide in four parts and, with hands, shape to form rolls about ½ inch in diameter. When hard, cut into 1½-inch pieces. Makes about ½ pound.

WALNUT NOUGAT

1 cup sugar
½ cup water
3 tablespoons light corn syrup
2 egg whites
¼ teaspoon salt
½ cup honey
1 cup broken walnut meats
1 teaspoon vanilla extract

Put sugar, water, and 2 tablespoons corn syrup in small, deep heavy saucepan. Bring to boil, stirring until sugar is dissolved. Continue cooking to 290°F. on a candy thermometer. Beat egg whites with salt until stiff. Gradually add syrup, beating constantly with electric beater. Continue beating while cooking honey and remaining 1 tablespoon corn syrup to a temperature of 290°F. Gradually add honey mixture to egg-white mixture, beating constantly. Add nuts and put mixture in top part of double boiler. Cook over simmering water, stirring frequently, about 15 minutes, or until candy begins to dry out. Add vanilla and press into buttered pan, 8 x 8 x 2 inches. Let stand until firm. Then cut into 1½- x ¾-inch pieces. Makes about 1 pound.

NOTE: Use candy thermometer in making this recipe.

NUT—The word is used to describe a large number of dry fruits which generally consist of a single kernel enclosed in a woody shell. Acorns, filberts, and hazelnuts are examples of true nuts. The Brazil nut represents another type of dry fruit popularly classed as a nut: it grows like the segments of an orange, eight to twenty-four of them within a single hard-walled husk. Some nuts are, botanically speaking, legumes. The peanut, for instance, is the pod of a vine of the pea family.

Some fruits whose kernels are not dry are called nuts because of their nutlike shells. The litchi nut, for example, is a fleshy raisin-like fruit enclosed in a shell. But not all the shells of true nuts are hard. The almond and pecan, for instance, come in more than one variety. Some have hard shells, some have soft ones, and some have paper-thin shells.

Nuts are one of man's oldest foods and one of the most useful. They may be eaten raw (usually dried), cooked, or in nut butters and pastes. Some nuts are dried and ground to serve as a coffee substitute or as a flour. Nuts are also used to feed livestock. Sometimes they are strung to make decorative necklaces and very hard nut shells are made into buttons.

Nuts were the traditional playthings of Roman children. They became so closely associated with childhood that it was customary for a bridegroom at his wedding to scatter nuts to the guests signifying that he had put away his childish pursuits.

Early Roman gourmets ate almonds, beechnuts, filberts, chestnuts, hazelnuts, pine kernels, and walnuts, and they were used in cooking. The Middle Ages and the Renaissance had many recipes for the use of nuts. Hugh Platt, an Englishman writing in 1609, tells how to make a sucket, a sort of conserve: "To make sucket of greene Walnuts. Take Walnuts when they are no bigger than the largest hasill nut, pare awaye the vppermost greene, but not too deepe, then seeth them in a pottle [2 quarts of water] till the water bee sodden away, then take so much more of fresh water, and when it is sodden to the halfe, put thereto a quart of vinegar and a pottle of clarified honie."

North America has always had a plentiful supply of nuts, welcomed by the early colonists as a relief from the meager diet on which they were forced to subsist. Many unusual ways of preparing nuts were practiced by the Indians and the colonists learned to copy them. Not only were nuts eaten out-of-hand, but they were roasted and added to various meat and vegetable stews. The Indians ground the dried kernels and used the meal to make breads and puddings much as they used corn. The hickory nut is native to America and an Indian milklike preparation was made from the boiled nuts. Chestnuts were also prepared in this way. The nuts the colonists found included the chestnut, hickory, pecan, black walnut, chinquapin, beechnut, and acorn.

Availability—The nuts available commercially are almonds, Brazil nuts, cashews, chestnuts, filberts, or hazelnuts, Macadamias, peanuts, pecans, pine nuts, pistachios, and walnuts. They are sold in the shell or shelled either by variety or as mixed nuts. Nuts are also sold chopped, ground, blanched or unblanched and in halves. Almonds alone come in the shell, shelled, either unblanched or blanched, chopped, slivered either plain or toasted, and ground either dry or into a paste. Nuts are sold in plastic bags, in boxes, in jars, and vacuum-packed in cans. They are sold dry-roasted (without additional fat), roasted in additional fat, toasted in hot deep fat or vegetable shortening, and either unsalted or salted. Some varieties are spiced, sugared, made into nut clusters, dipped into fondant, candy coating, or chocolate.

Many oils are extracted from nuts; peanut oil is the most popular. Some nuts are made into flour after oil is extracted. Available in health food stores are peanut and chestnut flour and almond meal. Some unripe nuts, such as green almonds and green walnuts, are sold pickled.

Purchasing Guide—If nuts are to be stored for a long period of time they should be purchased in the shell. A very general rule of thumb for the amount to buy is:

1 pound nuts in the shell = ½ pound shelled nuts.

When buying nuts in the shell, look for shells with no scars, cracks, or holes. Kernels should not rattle when nuts are shaken.

In shelled nuts, the nutmeats should be plump, meaty, crisp, and uniform in color and size.

Storage—Exposure to air, light, warmth, and moisture can cause rancidity in nuts. For long storage nuts should be kept unshelled. If shelled, do not chop or grind nuts until ready to use and keep as cool as possible; the colder they are the longer they will keep. Store in an airtight container in the refrigerator to prevent absorption of foreign flavors and odors.

The length of time nuts can be stored varies greatly with the type of nut, but in general unshelled nuts can be kept at room temperature for about 1 year, and shelled nuts, in a moisture-proof wrapping, can be kept refrigerated for at least 4 months, or longer depending too on type of nut.

Nutritive Food Values—Although these vary with the specific nut, nuts are by and large a good source of protein; and a fair source of phosphorus, iron, and thiamine. They have a high fat content and high caloric count.

Basic Preparation

To Salt—In a large skillet heat about 2 tablespoons cooking oil for each cup of nuts. Cook, stirring, over medium heat until nuts are lightly browned, about 3 minutes. Sprinkle with salt and toss lightly to coat all nuts. Allow about ½ teaspoon salt for each cup of nuts. Other seasoning, such as curry powder, Worcestershire, etc., may be added at this point.

To Grate—It is important to grate the nuts so that they will not be too oily when added to tortes or other preparations. Special nut graters are made for this. Nuts can also be ground in a blender or food processor, a small amount at a time.

To Blanch—Cover them with boiling water and let stand for 5 minutes. Drain and cool slightly but rub the skins off with the fingers while they are still warm and moist.

To Roast and Toast—Put nuts in preheated slow oven (300°F.) and bake until lightly browned. Nuts may be blanched or unblanched. Some nuts may be roasted in the shell.

To Deep Fry—Heat the fat or oil to 360°F. on a frying thermometer. Fry nuts for 2 or 3 minutes, or until lightly browned. Sprinkle with salt or other spice or herb seasoning and store until needed in an airtight container.

NUT BUTTER

NUT BUTTER—A spread made from finely ground nuts which may be blanched or unblanched. Particularly good for homemade nut butters are almonds, cashews, filberts, and peanuts. To produce the smooth oily texture needed to make a good nut butter, a food chopper, blender, or food processor is used to crush the nuts.

Nut butters made commercially include the most popular, peanut butter, and the less widely available almond and cashew butters.

Nut butters are used as is; or they may be blended with soft butter; or seasoned with a little salt, Worcestershire, or hot pepper sauce. In addition to their use as spreads, they are used as a flavoring for sauces, frostings, and other cooked dishes.

Nutritive Food Values—Nut butters are rich in fats, with good amounts of high-quality protein and carbohydrates and fair amounts of phosphorus and iron. They are a good source of thiamine.

Storage—Homemade nut butters should be stored in the refrigerator since fats at room temperature tend to become rancid. Commercially made nut butters have additives which prevent rancidity and they may be stored on the kitchen shelf. Read label for proper storing instructions.

NUTMEG—The hard kernel of the apricot-like fruit of the different varieties of the nutmeg tree. This tree, *Myristica fragrans,* is a tropical evergreen, native to the Spice Islands, or Moluccas, of the East Indies, but now also raised in Grenada in the West Indies and in Brazil. It grows to a height of twenty to forty feet. In appearance it resembles the pear tree and it continues to bear fruit for some fifty years.

The fruit, which is intermingled with the flowers, is gathered with long hooked poles. The fruit is carefully split in half to expose the hard seed, which is the nutmeg proper, covered by a false aril which is carefully removed, dried, and used to make mace, sister spice of nutmeg.

The nutmeg itself is also dried in the sun or over charcoal fires. It is oval in shape, gray-brown in color, and contains fat, volatile oil, acid, and starch. It is an aromatic spice, used a great deal in cooking.

Nutmegs were first traded to the Near East by the Arabs. In the 6th century they were used in the food at the court of Justinian in Constantinople. They became a favored and valuable spice in the Middle Ages. Chaucer, the greatest English poet of the Middle Ages, wrote in the 14th century: "Nutmegs, too, to put in ale, No matter whether fresh or stale." The oil taken from the nutmeg was used to flavor butter.

Nutmeg was one of the spices Columbus was looking for when he sailed west across the ocean from Spain in search of the East Indies. On his second trip in 1493 he was so eager to prove that he had indeed found the Spice Islands that he thought many of the native plants were familiar spices. One of the members of the company, Dr. Chanca, a Spanish doctor, wrote home describing some of the territory of Hispaniola, the island which is present-day Haiti and the Dominican Republic: "We found other trees which I think bear nutmegs, because the bark tastes and smells like that spice, but at present there is no fruit on them." The reason there was no fruit was that they were not nutmeg trees.

Later, Magellan sailed off under the auspices of Charles V of Spain to find the Spice Islands and their riches. Although he died before he reached them, one of his crew, Pegafetta, has described some of the spices they found. The nutmeg, he says, "resembles our walnuts as well in the appearance of the fruit as in the leaves. The nutmeg when gathered is like a quince in shape, color, and the down with which it is covered, but it is smaller." The expedition had started out with five ships; it returned with one. Sebastian del Cano, the leader of the remaining ship, was awarded a coat of arms by Charles which included three nutmegs in its bearings.

Imported nutmegs were valued by the early settlers of America. Often, traveling peddlers sold or bartered them. They were usually dipped into slaked lime before they were imported. This prevented them from being regrown by the buyer. It is said that once, when nutmegs without lime covering were sold in Connecticut, the housewives refused to buy because they feared the nutmegs were not real but imitations made of wood. This is the most likely story put forth to explain why Connecticut is called the Nutmeg State.

Nutmegs were used not only for flavoring in colonial America: because of their distinctive shape, they were sold as charms at country fairs.

Nutmeg is sold either whole or ground. Whole nutmegs are ground on a nutmeg grater which can be bought in hardware stores. The warm, sweet flavor of nutmeg improves many foods, particularly creamed dishes and fruit desserts, and is delicious sprinkled on custards and eggnogs.

CREAMY MUSHROOM SAUCE FOR PASTA

6 tablespoons butter or margarine
4 medium onions, thinly sliced
2 pounds fresh mushrooms, sliced
Salt and pepper
¼ teaspoon ground nutmeg
1 to 1½ cups heavy cream
Grated Parmesan cheese

Heat 3 tablespoons butter in heavy skillet; over medium heat, cook onions until golden. Lower heat. Simmer, covered, for 20 minutes, or until onions are very soft. Stir occasionally. Melt remaining 3 tablespoons butter in another skillet; add mushrooms and cook until tender. Season with salt and pepper to taste; stir in nutmeg. Add mushrooms to onions; mix well. Keep sauce hot while pasta is cooking according to directions. Five minutes before serving time, add cream and heat thoroughly. Do not boil. Toss pasta and sauce together. Serve immediately with freshly grated Parmesan cheese. Makes enough sauce for 1 pound of pasta.

NUTMEG LOGS

1 cup soft butter
2 teaspoons vanilla extract
2 teaspoons rum flavoring
¾ cup sugar
1 egg
3 cups sifted all-purpose flour
Ground nutmeg (2 to 3 teaspoons)
¼ teaspoon salt
Rum-Flavored Frosting

Cream butter with flavorings; gradually beat in sugar until light. Blend in egg. Sift flour, 1 teaspoon nutmeg, and salt; add to butter mixture and mix well. Shape pieces of dough on a sugared board into long rolls ½ inch in diameter. Cut into 3-inch lengths and put on greased cookie sheets. Bake in preheated moderate oven (350°F.) for 12 to 15 minutes. Cool. Spread Rum-Flavored Frosting on top and sides of cookies; mark with tines of fork to resemble bark. Sprinkle lightly with remaining nutmeg. Makes 6 dozen.

Rum-Flavored Frosting

Cream ⅓ cup butter with 1 teaspoon vanilla extract and 2 teaspoons rum flavoring. Blend in 2 cups sifted confectioners' sugar and 2 tablespoons light cream; beat until smooth and creamy.

NUTRITION

by FREDRICK J. STARE, M.D.
Professor and Founder, Nutrition Department
Harvard School of Public Health

A scientist would define nutrition as the sum total of all the processes by which our bodies get the materials (nutrients) they need for survival, growth, and repair. He might add that good nutrition comes from eating the right foods in the right amounts, in short, following a balanced diet.

All of which sounds more serious than it needs to be. Good nutrition is perfectly compatible with good eating, good companions, and good fun. Food can make or mar a day, or a holiday. Food can make life pleasant, and the enjoyment of food aids digestion. A person in normal health can eat the foods he likes, and keep in good trim, if he eats in moderation. And a working knowledge of foods and their best use will add to his happiness, health, and long life. Here are some of the essentials.

What is a balanced diet?

A balanced diet is achieved by eating a variety of foods—to furnish all the nutrients required for good health—in the proper amounts and in proper relation to each other. A group, or team, of nutrients functions more effectively than the same nutrients consumed individually. The nutrients are customarily placed in six food groups, depending on their chemical characteristics and the functions they perform in the body. They are: proteins, carbohydrates, fats, minerals, vitamins, and water. The body requires all of them in amounts that have been determined through research. A balanced diet provides better nutrition than an unbalanced one. There is a minimum of waste, the body uses the nutrients effectively, and better health results.

What does a balanced diet accomplish?

Most foods contain several of the nutrients which constitute a balanced diet, and it is important to know which ones, or the main ones. For example, oranges, lemons, and grapefruits are rich in vitamin C or ascorbic acid; and milk in protein, many B vitamins particularly riboflavin, calcium, and vitamin A.

What do the six groups of nutrients do?

Proteins have a main function of building and maintaining body muscles, glandular organs, arteries, skin—all living cells. The amino acids which make up proteins are often called, with reason, the "building blocks" of life. Of the twenty-two or more amino acids, eight are not synthesized or manufactured by the body and must be consumed in food from day to day for good health. Proteins, along with carbohydrates and fats, provide energy, or fuel, for body functions, and this energy is measured in calories which will be explained later. The main sources of proteins are meat, fish, poultry, eggs, milk and its products, and lesser amounts are to be found in the bread and cereal groups, and in legumes.

Carbohydrates (sugars and starches) are the most efficient sources of energy. We consume these in breads, cakes, cereals, rolls, rice, macaroni, noodles, potatoes, etc., which also give us worthwhile amounts of iron, several of the B vitamins, and energy in balanced proportion with that furnished by fats.

Fats provide twice as many calories as do the same amounts of protein or carbohydrate. Carbohydrates and fats are responsible for most of the total calories in the diet, and this permits the amino acids to do their vital building and maintenance work so that they are not burned for energy. Meat, eggs, cream, butter, oils and margarine are a few of many fat sources.

Minerals, some twenty to twenty-two are now known to be essentials, and more may be found to be so in the future. They serve as catalysts to control the utilization of proteins, fats, and carbohydrates, and they function in essential structures on their own. Most persons are aware that they need calcium and iron, but it is now known that our bodies require many other minerals in trace amounts, including copper, chromium, manganese, selenium, zinc, fluoride, cobalt, molybdenum, etc. These are toxic in substantial amounts, but essential to health in minute amounts.

Vitamins are catalysts which enable the other nutrients to do their jobs. All are needed in small or trace amounts. With a balanced diet the normal, healthy person gets all the vitamins and minerals he needs.

Water is essential for the body's functions. Most of us should drink six to eight glasses of water a day, some of which can be in the form of tea, coffee, fruit and vegetable juices, soup, etc., depending on our body size, activity, and the type of climate we live in. Water may provide some of the minerals we need such as calcium, and, in some cases, fluoride which lessens dental decay. A large share of all body fluids are water, such as blood and urine. Water helps the body regulate its temperature and aids in the intestinal process.

While not ordinarily included in the six nutrient groups, *fiber* or *roughage* is another diet ingredient. Animal fiber, as found in meat, and vegetable fiber, such as cellulose, are not digestible, but help the intestinal muscles do their job. Bulk may be found in whole grain bread and cereals, and the skin and fibrous parts of fruits and vegetables.

Variety is essential

Nutrition authorities agree that a few simple rules will help one follow a balanced diet and enjoy many kinds of food.

Be sure to eat some of the "basic four" every day. These provide the "protective" foods, those rich in protein, minerals, and vitamins, and they are:

1. Meats, poultry, fish, eggs—at least two servings every day. Beans, peas, and nuts have good food values and can sometimes be substituted.

2. Milk and dairy products (directly or in cooking)—at least two to four cups of milk or the equivalent ice cream, cheese, or dairy food.

Children ....2 to 3 cups milk
Teenagers ....3 or more cups milk
Adults ....1 or more cups milk

3. Breads and cereals—at least four servings every day—whole grain, enriched, restored. Remember: macaroni, rice, and grits are cereals, not vegetables.

4. Fruits and vegetables—at least four servings a day, including a dark-green or deep-yellow vegetable for vitamin A at least every other day, and a citrus fruit, or other fruit or vegetable for vitamin C every day. Some dark-green vegetables are: collards, kale, spinach, broccoli, cress, etc. Some deep-yellow vegetables are sweet potatoes, pumpkins, yellow squash. Apricots and cantaloupes are deep-yellow fruits.

Pastries, spreads, jellies, relishes, and the like help to add zest to a meal. But be sure you first have your "basic four." Desserts can have a few calories, or many, as you decide.

Eat a variety of foods at each meal. Monotony is the enemy of good nutrition. Changed combinations of foods and new methods of preparation make them more attractive. Adjust portion size to body weight and activity. Some foods taste better hot, others cold. Nutritionally, either way is fine. Avoid noise, rush, and clatter when eating. Pleasant conversation and attractive surroundings aid good digestion. In the family, mealtimes should be fun, occasions for sharing amusing or stimulating experiences and strengthening family ties.

How many calories do you need?

Granted its limitations, the calorie is the unit of energy measurement in nutrition. If too few are eaten, weakness and hunger prevail; if too many, sluggishness and overweight result. The calorie is essentially a heat unit: the energy required to lift the temperature of a quart of water two degrees Fahrenheit. A diet calorie, or kilo calorie, is 1,000 times the calorie used as a unit of measurement by physicists, chemists, and engineers.

The calories expended depend on your body size, age, and physical activity. An adult of 100 pounds burns fewer calories than an adult of 150 pounds, assuming they are living on about the same pattern of physical activity. An average adult of 150 pounds uses up about sixty calories an hour just to live: in heart action, breathing, liver function, and the like. This is called his basal metabolism rate.

If he (or she) does some sedentary work such as writing, sewing, or reading he will burn up to eighty to 100 calories an hour. Cooking, dusting, ironing, handwashing, and rapid typewriting take about 110 to 160 calories per hour. Mopping, gardening, carpentry, or walking moderately fast use 170 to 240 calories an hour. Hanging out clothes, heavy scrubbing, waxing floors burn 250 to 350 calories per hour. Vigorous tennis, swimming, cycling, skiing, or dancing use 400 to 500 calories per hour.

It is just as important in weight control to know how many calories one expends in physical activity, as it is to know how many calories there are in one's foods. Exercise is frequently overlooked as a calorie "burner."

One's daily caloric requirements decrease each year after twenty-five as body processes tend to slow down and one's energy expenditure decreases. Actually the decrease averages about five per cent for each decade past twenty-five years; thus adults of forty-five or fifty years of age need about ten per cent fewer calories than they did when they were twenty-five or thirty and they must eat less to avoid overweight.

Weight control the healthful way

The best way to lose excess weight is to bring one's caloric *intake* below one's *output*, to continue on a balanced diet, and to secure adequate exercise. This permits sensible, healthy weight reduction, and avoids the nervousness, headaches, and short temper which usually go with extreme or crash diets. Establishing a total daily caloric intake at about 500 calories below the caloric output is a good working rule. On this basis the average healthy person will lose a pound a week, or fifty pounds a year. A pound of stored fat represents about 3,500 calories. Records show that the gradual loss of weight also offers a better chance for permanent loss. The subject of weight loss, however, may be more complicated than here described. Medical factors enter, since no two individuals assimilate their food in the same manner. This is one of the reasons why no diet aimed at reducing more than ten to fifteen pounds should be undertaken without a doctor's advice.

The writer, Alexander Woollcott, who was considerably overweight, once remarked that "The most interesting things in life are immoral, illegal, or fattening." Things aren't that bad. If you want to lose weight, don't go at it with a do-or-die attitude and try to cut out everything you like. Keep some of your favorites, but keep your daily caloric total in mind. Reduce the size of servings, and avoid extra helpings. You can substitute lower calorie foods for higher, still secure the nutrients you need, and not feel hungry all the time. For example, a serving of string beans has about twenty-five calories; Lima beans, 100. Half a grapefruit at thirty-five calories is but a fraction of the 350 calories in a substantial slice of pie or frosted cake.

Don't skip meals. The long periods between meals put the body out of balance. Passing up breakfast reduces one's morning output of work by as much as twenty percent, and one may then overeat at lunch and dinner. Avoid "reducing drugs."

For most persons past their teens who wish to lose weight, a 1,400 calorie a day diet is recommended as being safe, within the capacity of most of us, and it will provide the energy needed for a normal day's work.

Individual food requirements

Each member of the family requires the same basic foods, but the quantities vary according to age, physical activity, and other factors.

Children require more food proportionately for energy and body growth than adults. They may need second helpings. They require adequate amounts of the basic four groups of foods, and milk products especially. Children require adequate vitamin C, so citrus fruits, tomatoes, cherries, and other sources can be served to meet this need. Youngsters also need exercise to help avoid overweight; in the United States overweight in children is a serious problem.

Good food habits can help many teenagers attain good complexions, attractive hair, skin, and teeth. Some teenage girls do not get enough vitamins A and C. The boys want to excel in sports, so they usually drink enough milk and citrus fruit juice, and do somewhat better than the girls. High calorie snacks with low nutritive value are to be avoided. Teenagers should be reminded that what they eat determines in large measure how they feel. Excess weight, put on in the teens, tends to stay on into young adulthood.

The modern mother knows the importance of sound diet during pregnancy and lactation, both for herself and her baby. She should increase, as a rule, her intake of the basic four or protective foods in accordance with her doctor's instructions. She will avoid eating too much or too little.

Older persons need a balanced diet and fewer calories. Variety becomes even more important, as taste, smell, and other sensations diminish somewhat with age. One danger for the older person is that it is "too much trouble" to go to the food store, or to prepare an adequate meal. This makes for meals that are really only snacks. With the tapering off of bodily functions such as chewing ability, a balanced diet of protective foods is imperative.

Therapeutic diets are prescribed by a physician to deal with a particular disease or condition, and should be followed carefully. One's health, and possibly one's life, may depend on obeying the doctor's orders.

Changing patterns of eating

Modern living calls for occasional flexibility in the times members of the family eat, because of different school and working hours. While it is advisable to have three balanced meals, some recent scientific evidence suggests that equally good health may come about from eating four, five, or six meals of smaller quantity. There is nothing the matter with snacks, providing they possess nutritional value and do not simply add to one's total daily caloric intake. If one is underweight, snacking may be helpful in increasing food consumption. What is a mistake is watching television by the hour in an easy chair and snacking at the same time.

There is nothing wrong nutritionally in substituting foods for the familiar or traditional ones at certain meals. At breakfast the tendency is toward certain standard items. If a teenager thinks he'd like a hamburger for breakfast, give it to him for a change. It's a perfectly good food. With the great variety of foods at the supermarket or food store the year round there is little excuse for mealtime boredom. Change should be welcomed. Increasingly, Americans and Canadians are trying the unfamiliar foods of other countries or of other sections of our own. For example, do you eat papayas, avocados, Chinese cabbage, black-eyed peas, artichokes, mangoes? Do you enjoy French, Italian, German, Mexican, and other national styles of cooking?

Conserving nutritional values

With the high quality of foods available today it is important that we use them so as to retain their palatability and nutritional values. A few reminders:

1. Many people keep their lettuce, carrots, cabbage, and other vegetables in the refrigerator too long before serving.

2. Despite the educational job that has been done, many people still cook vegetables and other foods in substantial quantities of water and then throw the water away, thus discarding valuable nutrients.

3. Even in a freezer, there is some loss of nutritional value and flavor over a period of weeks or months. Keep the foods moving toward the table.

4. Serving food as fresh as possible helps to keep it appealing to the eye as well as the palate.

5. Don't be timid about using new combinations of foods. You will be surprised at the difference in flavors when you find some new companions for your food favorites.

Food myths and facts

The Food and Drug Administration says that nearly a billion dollars a year is wasted on food fads, myths, and misconceptions. These are fostered by promoters with "wonder" food products to sell at high prices. They are claimed to possess some miraculous nutritional or health building quality in themselves, or as a result of the conditions under which they are grown. Neither of these viewpoints is accepted by responsible nutrition scientists.

Some of the myths are: (1) that all human diseases are due to a faulty diet, (2) that widespread soil depletion causes malnutrition in this country, (3) that prevailing methods of "overprocessing" destroy food values, and (4) that most Americans are in dire need of "food supplements" or vitamin pills. The Food and Drug Administration says that none of these assertions has any foundation, and that the American and Canadian food supply possesses high nutritive value, variety, abundance, and safety. The Food and Drug Administration, other government agencies, and professional organizations combat food myths and fads constructively, but not vigorously.

Standards of food safety and quality are set by professional and governmental bodies, including the U.S. Department of Agriculture, the Food and Drug Administration, the American Medical Association, the American Dietetic Association, the American Home Economics Association, and many other professional organizations. Many standards for the science of nutrition and for the guidance of the food industry are determined by the Food and Nutrition Board of the National Academy of Sciences—National Research Council. These standards are revised from time to time in the light of research done in university and other laboratories.

Nutrition Science

Nutrition is a "new" science in that the major developments in it have occurred in the past generation. Notable progress has been made toward a better understanding of (1) the complicated processes by which the body makes use of foods, (2) the nutritional qualities of food eaten singly and combined with other foods, and, more recently, (3) the role of diet in diseases of a metabolic character, such as coronary heart disease and diabetes. Nutrition science helps to treat and control diabetes and liver injury. It also prepares the body to withstand surgery and to recover properly afterward.

In the United States and Canada the diseases caused by vitamin deficiencies such as rickets (lack of vitamin D) and pellagra (lack of niacin, part of the B-complex) have been overcome. This is not true in the underdeveloped countries where protein and other deficiencies cause disease and high mortality.

In the United States, and Canada also, there has been an enormous scientific and technical improvement in the methods of growing, processing, distributing, and preserving foods. In recent years we have seen the development of the "convenience" foods, in which much of the labor of preparation has been performed before they reach the consumer. Quick freezing and freeze-dry methods have made many foods available in attractive form the year round. "Instant" and dehydrated foods save time and energy in the kitchen. Improvements in food containers and packages have resulted in the retention of higher nutritional qualities for longer periods of time.

However, the familiar phrase, "we have only scratched the surface," applies to nutrition research as well as to other fields of endeavor. Many questions await answers in the laboratories. It could aptly be said that we are in the midst of a nutritional revolution. Advances in scientific knowledge are being translated into nutritious foods for the dinner table and advances in human health. Those responsible for the advances in knowledge and human health are the nutrition scientist, food technologist, physician, public health official, dietician, home economist, teacher, food industry executive, and others.

Today, nutrition scientists are striving to keep people in good health, to lengthen the life span, and to extend one's peak of achievement. The degenerative diseases of later years, or some of them, now appear to have early beginnings. Scientists are endeavoring to find out when and how they start, and what role the diet can and should play at various periods in life. A healthy old age can be given a good start in youth with sound food habits.

Nutrition scientists have devoted a great deal of study of late to the role of fats. Fats may be associated with heart disease and atherosclerosis, along with genetic inheritance, overweight, lack of exercise, smoking, and stress, although no one has quite defined what stress is. Considerable information on the metabolic role of fats has been obtained, some of it conflicting. Agreement does not yet exist on the precise amounts of saturated or animal fats and unsaturated or vegetable fats which should be in the optimum diet. We need both for best health. Definitive information should be available on the subject in the next few years.

Meanwhile, research continues to find many dietary answers to matters of good health, for the individual who wants to feel and be at his best, and for the nation which wants its citizens to be in top physical and mental condition. Sound nutrition is indeed the most important environmental factor in the health of a person or a people.

COMMON TERMS USED IN NUTRITION

ALLERGY Hypersensitivity to a food, pollen, drug, or any other allergen, usually a protein. The skin, gastrointestinal tract, or respiratory tract may be affected.

AMINO ACIDS The "building blocks" of protein, about twenty-two in all, of which eight are essential to man: tryptophan, threonine, methionine, isoleucine, leucine, lysine, valine, and phenylalanine. The body is unable to produce these and must get them from food. The other amino acids may be synthesized in the body.

ANEMIA A condition of the blood characterized by a low hemoglobin content, or reduction in the amount of blood, or a reduction in the number of red blood cells.

ANOREXIA Lack or loss of appetite.

ARTERIOSCLEROSIS A condition of the arteries marked by thickening and hardening of the walls and a loss of elasticity; related to

ATHEROSCLEROSIS A type of arteriosclerosis characterized by the accumulation of cholesterol and other lipids in the artery walls, resulting in a narrowing of the passages.

CALORIE A unit of heat, used as a measure of the energy value of foods.

CARBOHYDRATE Food substances, containing carbon, hydrogen, and oxygen, such as sugars, starches, cellulose, and gums. They furnish heat and energy and carry other nutrients.

CAROTENE A yellow or orange pigment found in green and yellow vegetables and fruits—obvious in carrots and masked by chlorophyll in green leaves. It is a precursor of vitamin A and can be converted to that compound in the body.

CHOLESTEROL A fatlike substance associated with atherosclerosis. It is normally synthesized in the body. Animal tissues are a source of cholesterol in food; however, the cholesterol in food consumed may or may not determine serum cholesterol levels.

DIETETIC FOOD Food processed commercially which may be used to meet diet restrictions. Consult physician before using. Many, if not most, diet modifications can be made using regular foods.

ENRICHED Food that has certain basic nutriments added to it.

ENZYMES Substances protein in nature that are produced by the body which facilitate chemical changes but are not themselves changed in the reaction (e.g., digestive enzymes aid in the breakdown of food).

FATTY ACIDS, ESSENTIAL Collective name for three unsaturated fatty acids, linoleic, linolenic, and arachidonic, found in many food fats, which are considered dietary essentials. They are poorly distributed in animal fats and occur mainly in vegetable oils.

LIPIDS Fats or fatlike substances.

METABOLISM The sum total of all the chemical changes that occur in the body by which food is converted into tissue, reserve nutrients are stored, and waste products are eliminated.

MINERALS Inorganic substances present in the body which have specific functions:

Calcuim A mineral that helps to build sound bones and teeth; helps blood to clot, helps muscles and nerves react normally. Found in milk products and in dark-green vegetables.

Iron A mineral that combines with protein to make hemoglobin (the substance in the blood that carries oxygen to all body cells) and, in each cell, helps develop energy.

Sodium A mineral necessary for maintaining body neutrality and water balance. It is also associated with muscle contraction. The usual source in the diet is sodium chloride, table salt, and it is also obtained in other foods such as baking soda and baking powder.

Other Minerals:

Copper Works with iron in forming hemoglobin in the red blood cells.

Fluorine A constitutent of bones and teeth. Fluoridation of water under controlled conditions is said to be effective in reducing the incidence of dental cavities, but the matter is still under dispute.

Iodine Useful for the cure and prevention of nutritional goiters.

Magnesium Required for the utilization of amino acids in formation of proteins.

Phosphorus Constituent of bones and teeth; necessary for calcium utilization.

Potassium Necessary for muscle and nerve functions, carbohydrate metabolism.

Sulfur An essential mineral found in certain amino acids, vitamins, and in insulin.

Trace Elements Cobalt, zinc, manganese, molybdenum, selenium, etc.

OXIDATION The reaction in the body of oxygen and nutritionally useful compounds which results in the release of energy and the formation of various end products.

PROTEINS Essential constituents of all living cells, distinguished from carbohydrates and fats in that they contain nitrogen. Needed to build, maintain, and repair body tissues; help form antibodies to fight infection; supply energy.

VITAMINS General term for organic substances occurring in many foods, necessary for the normal metabolic functioning of the body.

Vitamin A Necessary for growth, skin health, vision, resistance to infection. Fat soluble, found in butter, Cheddar cheese, liver, kidney. Made in the body from carotene in green and yellow vegetables and fruit.

Vitamin B-Complex Water-soluble compounds which function with the enzymes in the body and are directly related to the production of energy. Included are: *thiamine* (B-1); *riboflavin* (B-2); *niacin; pyridoxine* (B-6); *cobalamin* (B-12); *biotin; folacin* (folic acid); *inositol; pantothenic acid.* Widely distributed in food; in the meat group, many fruits and vegetables, the milk group, and the bread-cereal group.

Vitamin C (Ascorbic Acid) Needed for the formation of intercellular cement, for maintaining the strength of the blood vessels; helps resist infection; helps insure more rapid healing of wounds. It is found in citrus fruits, strawberries, cantaloupes, tomatoes, cabbage, green peppers, broccoli, and other vegetables and fruit.

Vitamin D The sunshine vitamin, so named because ultra violet light from the sun converts a precursor located in the skin into the vitamin. Other forms of vitamin D are available in fish-liver oils, fish, egg yolk, and milk. It is necessary for growth. It aids in the absorption of calcium and phosphorus and helps to build bones and teeth.

Vitamin E (Tocopherol) It acts as an antitoxidant to preserve the fat-soluble vitamins and the unsaturated fatty acids. It may be necessary for reproduction, and it is also effective against certain toxic agents. Seed oils and margarine are the best sources.

Vitamin K There are two natural forms: one may be obtained from food and the other is synthesized in the intestinal tract by bacteria. Food sources include pork liver, cabbage, cauliflower, spinach, soybeans, etc. It is essential for the synthesis of prothrombin and the normal clotting of blood.

Choline A nutritionally important substance necessary for transporting fat in the body. It is widely distributed in food and a deficiency is unlikely. Good sources include meat, egg yolk, bread, cereal, beans, and peanuts.

O

OAT, OATMEAL—Oats are the grains of a cereal-grass plant of the *Avena* genus, or the plant itself. Like the rest of the grains, oats consist of a soft inner part surrounded by a husk which is removed before being eaten by humans. Some varieties of oats, however, are hulless. The grain is used to make rolled oats and as feed for livestock.

Most cultivated varieties of oats have a smooth-surfaced hull, although some wild varieties are hairy. Cultivated oats are thought to be the descendants of two kinds of wild oats, the common and the red which probably originated in western Europe. From there they spread to other parts of the world. They are now largely cultivated in northern Europe and North America since they can be grown more easily and more profitably than any other grain except rye in cold and damp climates. Oats will flourish as far north as the Arctic Circle, and a damp island climate suits oats precisely; that is why they flourish in Scotland and Ireland.

In manufacture, the grain is cleaned, sorted for size, kiln-dried to loosen the hull and develop the nutty flavor of the kernel, cleaned again, and put through machines which remove the hulls, and then sterilized. To produce rolled oats, the husked sterilized grains are flattened by heated rollers, into the flakes familiar to the consumer. To make oatmeal, the groats (edible poriton of the oats with the hull removed) are steel-cut in three sizes and ground in grades from coarse to extra-fine. Even finer grinding produces oat flour or oatmeal flour. Although properly speaking the term "oatmeal" should only be applied to the ground meal of the grain, it is commonly used to describe both rolled and ground oats.

Oats are the most nutritious of cereals, containing a good amount of fat, proteins, and minerals. They are an excellent energy food for people who live an active outdoor life in cold weather. All the people of northern Europe depended on them for their diet until modern times, eating them as a meal in porridges, in baked foods such as bannocks, and as a food stretcher. Oats do not lend themselves to breadmaking since the protein material does not occur in the form of gluten; risen oatmeal bread, to be satisfactory, has to be mixed with other flour.

The highly processed rolled oats that we know today were first made by Alexander Hornby from Craigsville, New York, using a new precooking process developed by two Englishmen. H. O. Hornby Oats, as the new product was called, were baked raw oats steamed under pressure in rotating boilers. This process shortened the cooking considerably and made oatmeal more palatable to people who like a more refined product.

Availability and Purchasing Guide—Rolled oats, both quick-cooking and regular, are widely available. Scotch oatmeal (oat groats cut with stone rather than steel rollers, thus producing a more coarsely ground grain), oat groats, and oat flour are available in specialty or health-food stores.

Many uncooked and dry cereals made with oats are also available. Among the uncooked types are: oat cereal with toasted wheat germ and soy grits; maple-flavored instant-cooking oat flakes; oat granules, maple-flavored, instant-cooking; oat and wheat cereal. Ready-to-eat cereals include: shredded oats with protein and other added nutrients; oats (with or without corn) puffed, with added nutrients; oats (with or without corn or wheat) puffed, with nutrients and sugar-covered; oats (with soy flour and rice) flaked, and with added nutrients.

Storage Kitchen shelf: 2 to 3 months
Refrigerator shelf, cooked: 3 to 4 days

Nutritive Food Values—Good source of thiamine; fair source of riboflavin and vitamin E.

The caloric values for 3½ ounces of the various oat products are:
Oatmeal or rolled oats, cooked = 55 calories
Oat and wheat cereal, cooked = 65 calories
Oat granules, maple-flavored, quick-cooking, cooked = 60 calories
Oat flakes, maple-flavored, instant-cooking, cooked = 69 calories
Oat cereal with toasted wheat germ and soy grits, cooked = 62 calories
Shredded oats with added nutrients = 379 calories
Puffed oats (with or without corn or wheat) with added nutrients = 397 calories
Flaked oats (with soy flour and rice) with added nutrients = 397 calories
The caloric value for 1 cup of oat products are:
Cooked oatmeal = 130 calories
Cooked oatmeal (3 minute) = 175 calories
Puffed oats = 100 calories

Basic Preparation—Sprinkle cereal slowly into boiling salted water and stir while cooking to prevent lumping. Quick-cooking cereals should be prepared as directed on the package as one brand may be more quick cooking than another. A quick-cooking cereal can be cooked over direct heat. Some quick-cooking oatmeal can be "cooked" right in the cereal bowl by adding boiling water and stirring.

With regular oatmeal, long slow cooking gives the best flavor. To prevent sticking and possible scorching, cook the cereal in the top part of a double boiler over boiling water.

OATMEAL BREAD

1 cup sifted all-purpose flour
2 tablespoons sugar
2 teaspoons baking powder
½ teaspoon baking soda
¾ teaspoon salt
¾ cup quick-cooking rolled oats
¼ cup butter or margarine
¾ cup buttermilk

Sift flour with sugar, baking powder, baking soda, and salt. Stir in rolled oats. Cut in butter until butter forms small particles. Add buttermilk all at once and stir until smooth. Pour mixture into well-greased 8-inch square pan. Bake in preheated hot oven (400°F.) for 30 minutes. Cut while warm into squares. Makes 8 servings.

OATMEAL DROP COOKIES

½ cup soft butter or margarine
1 cup sugar
1 egg
1½ cups sifted all-purpose flour
½ teaspoon each salt and baking soda
¾ teaspoon ground cinnamon
½ teaspoon each ground cloves and allspice
1¾ cups quick-cooking rolled oats
⅔ cup raisins, cut into small pieces
½ cup chopped nuts
⅓ cup milk

Cream butter until light and fluffy. Gradually beat in sugar. Add egg and beat until light. Sift flour with salt, baking soda, and spices; add oats, raisins, and nuts. Add to first mixture alternately with milk and mix well. Drop by teaspoonfuls onto greased cookie sheets. Bake in preheated moderate oven (350°F.) about 15 minutes. Makes 3 dozen.

ROLLED-OATS-MIX MAGIC

ROLLED-OATS MIX

4 cups all-purpose flour
4 cups quick-cooking oats (not instant)
1½ cups dry nonfat milk powder
¼ cup baking powder
1 tablespoon salt
1½ cups vegetable shortening (not oil)

Put first 5 ingredients in large bowl and stir until very well mixed. Cut in shortening until well blended. Cover and refrigerate; will keep 1 month. Store in covered glass jars or canisters, if preferred. To measure, spoon into cup, pack lightly and level off. Makes about 10 cups.

OAT-RAISIN COOKIES

2½ cups Rolled-Oats Mix
1 teaspoon ground cinnamon
¾ cup sugar
⅓ cup seedless raisins
1 egg, beaten
1 teaspoon vanilla extract
¼ cup water

Mix all ingredients and drop by rounded teaspoonfuls onto greased baking sheets. Bake in preheated moderate oven (375°F.) 12 to 15 minutes. Makes about 2 dozen.

DATE-NUT OAT BREAD

8 ounces imported pitted dates
1 cup boiling water
1 cup sugar
1 egg
3 cups Rolled-Oats Mix
1 cup broken walnuts or pecans

Cut dates in half and put in bowl. Cover with water and mix well. Stir in sugar and let stand until lukewarm, then add remaining ingredients and mix well. Put in greased 9 x 5 x 3-inch loaf pan and bake in preheated moderate oven (350°F.) 1 hour, or until done. Turn out and cool before slicing. Makes 1 loaf.

OAT CRUMB COFFEE CAKE

2 cups Rolled-Oats Mix
1 cup firmly packed light-brown sugar
¼ teaspoon each ground cinnamon and nutmeg
1 egg, well beaten
½ cup water

Mix first 2 ingredients, measure ¼ cup and set aside. Add spices, egg and water to remaining mixture and beat well. Spread in greased 8-inch square pan and sprinkle with reserved crumbs. Bake in preheated moderate oven (375°F.) about 30 minutes. Cut in squares and serve warm, plain or with butter. Makes 6 to 8 servings.

OIL—In cookery, this is an edible fatty or greasy substance occurring in the seeds of certain plants. Although there are some edible fats procured from mammals and fish, whale and cod-liver oils, for example, they are not used in cooking. The terms fat and oil are often used interchangeably but to be accurate the term "fat" applies to substances that are solid at normal temperatures, whereas oils are liquid at these temperatures.

Food oils are made from olives, cottonseed, corn, peanuts, coconuts, palm nuts, soybeans, rapeseed, sesame seed, poppy seed, safflower seed, sunflower seed, walnuts, hickory nuts, almonds, beechnuts, and others. Generally it is cottonseed or corn oil which is used in making the widely available cooking, salad, and vegetable oils.

The principal uses of oils in cookery are:

(1) *To give richness and flavor,* as in the addition of oil to mayonnaise or French dressing. Olive oil is much prized for the latter, where its unique flavor is particularly prominent.

(2) *To sauté, pan-fry, or deep fry foods.* In choosing a fat for sautéing or frying the physical and chemical qualities of the fat are as important as the flavor. The oils are particularly well suited for both purposes since most of them have high smoking points and negligible flavor. An exception is olive oil which tends to spatter over high heat. Nevertheless it is often used, especially in Italian cooking, because its flavor is desirable and blends well with the food being cooked.

(3) *For shortening (tenderizing),* as in cakes, pies, muffins, biscuits, etc. Oils can be used with good results for shortening, but recipes specifying oil are necessary since the oils add more liquid. Oil is used in making chiffon cakes and is convenient for making tender, flaky pie crust.

Storage—Oils can be kept, tightly covered, on the kitchen shelf in a cool dry place away from foods with strong odors for 2 to 3 months. They should not be exposed to light as it fades them. When exposed to air they will become rancid if moisture is present. Cans are better for storage than bottles. If to be kept for longer periods of time, oils, with the exception of olive oil, should be refrigerated, tightly covered. They will keep this way on the refrigerator shelf for up to 1 year. Olive oil is an exception; it may solidify if refrigerated for long periods of time.

Nutritive Food Values—Oils are a highly concentrated form of food energy. One cup of pure oil yields about 2,000 calories. Fats and oils give a general satisfaction to food because they slow down the rate at which it is digested. They also contain certain fatty acids that are essential to good nutrition.
1 cup = 1945 calories
1 tablespoon = 125 calories

OKRA—A tall annual plant, *Hibiscus esculentus,* of the mallow family which yields an edible pod with a gooey, mucilaginous quality. Okra should be eaten when very tender; the pods, which grow extremely fast, should be cut often.

Okra, in America, is also often called gumbo since it is used mostly in the southern states to flavor and thicken the gumbos or soup-stews that are a specialty of the region.

Grown extensively in South America, the southern United States, and India, the plant is a native of tropical Africa, and is said to have come from the region that includes Ethiopia and the eastern, higher part of the Sudan. Okra is of considerable antiquity, but relatively little is known about it. It was mentioned by a Spanish Moor who visited Egypt in 1216. Very likely, it was introduced into the Arab countries through traders and slave raiders from Ethiopia and the Sudan. The Arabs grew very fond of it, calling it *bâmiya.*

From Arabia, okra was taken west to North Africa and the Mediterranean and east to southwestern Asia. It was brought to the New World, specifically, to Brazil and the West Indies, around the middle of the 17th century. How okra came to Louisiana and other southern states we do not know; it may have been introduced by the Spanish or French colonists, or by African slaves, or by both.

Okra was cultivated as far north as Philadelphia in 1748. Jefferson says that it was known in Virginia before 1781. Garden writers speak about it from 1800 on.

The ripe okra seeds yield an edible oil used in Mediterranean countries and in the orient. Sometimes they are ground and used as a coffee substitute or stretcher, like chicory.

Availability—Fresh okra is available year round in the southern United States and from April to November in the north. Peak months are June through October. Some varieties are long and thin. Others are short and chunky. The pods vary from whitish-green to green in color and may be smooth or ridged.

Okra is also available canned and frozen. It is an ingredient in canned chicken-gumbo soup.

Purchasing Guide—Look for young, tender, crisp, fresh pods, 2 to 4 inches in length. The pods should snap easily and be free from hard seeds.

Storage—Wash; store in a covered container in refrigerator.
Fresh, or canned and opened, refrigerator shelf or vegetable compartment: 4 days
Fresh, prepared for freezing; or frozen, refrigerator frozen-food compartment: 1 month
Fresh, prepared for freezing; or frozen, freezer: 1 year
Canned, kitchen shelf: 1 to 2 months

Nutritive Food Values—Fair source of vitamins A and C.
3½ ounces (about 8 pods), boiled and drained = 29 calories
Frozen, whole, boiled and drained, ½ cup = 35

Basic Preparation—Scrub pods. If pods are large, cut off stems and slice into ½- to 1-inch slices. Small pods may be left whole.

To Cook—Cook, covered, in ½ to 1 inch of boiling salted water for 10 to 15 minutes, or until tender. (If overcooked, okra may have a gummy consistency.) May also be steamed until just tender. Season with salt, pepper, and butter or margarine.

Boiled or steamed okra may be served with individual dishes of melted butter or margarine or hollandaise sauce. Pods are picked up by the stems and dipped into the butter sauce. Okra may be added to soups.

To Fry—Dip crosswise slices into a mixture of egg and 1 tablespoon water, then roll in seasoned flour, crumbs, or cornmeal. Panfry or deep fry for 2 to 5 minutes.

To Freeze—Wash; remove stems with a sharp knife. Blanch in boiling water, 2 or 3 minutes for small pods, 3 or 4 minutes for large pods. Chill in ice water for 3 to 5 minutes. Drain. Pack whole or slice crosswise. Pack into containers, leaving ½-inch headspace. Seal.

OKRA

by MARGARET M. THORNBURGH

People who like okra, and people who think they don't, are as violently partisan as candidates before election. In our family, we are all okra addicts. It shows, too, especially in our garden.

As gardeners, we have always been a little on the casual side, except for a neat plot that we plant with gusto and tend with care. In it grow four kinds of vegetables: okra, tomatoes, green peppers, and onions, the necessary ingredients for okra stew.

If you are a gardener, try a row or two of gumbo, as this delectable is sometimes called. It's a warm-weather plant, so wait until the winter's chill is out of the ground and all danger of frost is past. It will grow well in any good, well-drained garden soil, but prefers a rich, sandy loam.

Sow seed a half inch deep, and space rows three-and-a-half feet apart for the dwarf varieties; a foot or more farther apart if you try the mammoth, long-pod plants that reach a height of six or seven feet. When seedlings are about four inches tall, thin each row to provide one or two feet between plants.

Okra grows rapidly in warm temperatures, and in a little less than two months you will be harvesting the first pods. Watch for the plants to blossom, pale-yellow flowers, red at the throat, resembling the mallow or a small, single hollyhock bloom. Four to six days later, the pods should be about three inches long and ready for your table. Always cut them off promptly, for two reasons: young pods are tender and have the best flavor, and if they are not allowed to mature, the plant will continue to bear until frost.

It's surprising how quickly pods become tough and fibrous, so cut them every second day, at least. Cook them promptly, or if you must keep them a few days, store (spread out or pack very loosely) in refrigerator. Never cut into pods until you are ready to use them.

In buying okra, always choose pods that are crisp-looking and two to four inches long; avoid those that look limp and old or are streaked with brown.

Packaged frozen okra lends itself handily to combinations with other frozen vegetables. Such combinations are standard fare at our house for Sunday suppers and for early, hurry-up dinners that precede an evening out. Try frozen okra with frozen corn, cooked separately according to package directions. Transfer to casserole; pour a buttery cream sauce over the vegetables, and sprinkle with grated Parmesan cheese. Brown in preheated hot oven (425°F.) for 10 minutes.

A new canning method, in which freshly harvested pods are quickly placed in a precanning solution, results in okra that is tender yet firm. Of course, canned or frozen okra can be used in any recipe that calls for fresh okra.

Gumbo can be many things to a versatile and imaginative cook. It is delicious prepared whole. Just remove the little fringe of "beard," and cook, tightly covered, with very little water, until the pods can be cut with a fork—about 12 to 15 minutes. Season with butter, lemon juice if you like, salt, and pepper.

Or remove stems, dip pods in cornmeal, and fry.

For French-fried okra, dip pods in beaten egg and fine cracker crumbs; then fry in deep fat.

For a delicious chilled green salad, add cooked okra pods to tomato wedges; spoon finely diced radishes and celery over them, and serve on crisp salad greens with French dressing. We prefer a simple dressing of oil, red-wine-tarragon vinegar, salt, and black pepper.

Give okra a south-of-the-border touch with chili sauce. Just add ⅓ cup water and 1 teaspoon minced onion to a 15½-ounce can okra, and simmer for 10 minutes. Add 2 tablespoons chili sauce; heat.

Use okra in soups or stews, with chicken, with rice and tomatoes. Southern cooks recommend it as a seasoning in other vegetables—for instance, 3 or 4 pods in a batch of butter beans, in fried corn, or with purple-hull black-eyed peas. There are almost as many ideas for ingredients and preparation as there are good cooks in the South.

Don't overlook the possibilities of **Baked Okra.** To 2 cups cooked okra add 1 well-beaten egg, ½ teaspoon salt, 1 cup cream (or ½ cup each cream and milk), and 1 cup well-buttered, soft bread crumbs. Pour mixture into buttered pan or custard cups. Set in pan of water. Bake in preheated moderate oven (350°F.) until set, about 45 minutes. For a good variation, 1 cup drained, whole-kernel corn can be added. Makes 4 to 6 servings.

Our favorite **Okra Stew** is prepared without hard-and-fast rules. Proportions and ingredients vary according to the current stage of the garden. Sometimes we add bacon, sometimes we don't. You can prepare it to suit yourself. Here is a starter: Sauté chopped onion and green pepper in a little bacon fat or butter until tender. Add tomatoes, fresh or canned, and okra, whole (with stem end removed) or sliced, salt, and pepper. Simmer over low heat only until okra is tender. Top with bacon bits. Serve on triangles of buttered whole-wheat toast, or add croutons browned in butter. A thicker mixture may be topped with bread crumbs and browned in the oven. We like to season it with a little rosemary or thyme. You may prefer to season with chili powder, celery salt, or a hint of garlic. Serve with an ample supply of spoon bread (made, of course, with stone-ground cornmeal), followed by a light dessert and coffee, and there's a meal!

A similar combination can be the basis for a delicious **Chicken Gumbo.** First disjoint a medium-size hen, and simmer until tender. Remove chicken; dice meat, and return to broth. Add okra, cut in 1-inch pieces, tomatoes, celery, green pepper, onion, and parsley, all cut rather fine. Simmer until vegetables are tender. Season to taste with salt, black pepper, and a pinch each dried thyme and marjoram. Next, put cooked rice in a well-greased baking dish; pour the chicken gumbo over it; cover generously with buttered crumbs, and bake for 30 minutes in preheated moderate oven (350°F.).

Beef-and-Okra Stew makes a hearty main dish. For 6 servings: Melt ¼ cup fat in heavy pan. Add 1 pound lean beef, cut in small pieces (round steak is good), and 2 onions, chopped. Cook slowly, stirring, until onions start to brown. Add 2 tablespoons all-purpose flour, and blend. Add ½ cup beef broth or canned bouillon and 1 cup water, stirring until mixture thickens a little. Add 1 green pepper, chopped, 2 cups sliced carrots, 2 cups or 15½-ounce can okra, sliced, 1 teaspoon salt, black pepper, and 1 teaspoon Worcestershire. Simmer about 1 hour, stirring frequently. Serve over rice or with corn bread.

Vegetables, it seems to me, are the problem children of cookery. We serve them dutifully, and although we try to vary the cycle as much as possible, they do tend to become routine—a little monotonous, in fact. So why not try something new? Why not try okra?

OLIVE—The fruit of the evergreen tree *Olea europea* which, despite its botanical name, undoubtedly originated in Syria and the maritime parts of Asia Minor. The origin of the botanical name is obscure but its root is related to the Armenian word *eul,* meaning oil. The tree itself grows to heights of from twenty-five to forty feet and does best in poor, dry soil unsuited for other trees or crops. The ancient Roman scholar Pliny observed that olive trees grown in rich soil are more susceptible to disease and yield fruit that produces an inferior oil.

In their warm home countries, where the dairy products of temperate regions were not commonly available, olives provided the essential fat in human diets. Mediterranean man could not have lived without them. They are indeed the fruit of civilization. To this day, cookery in France, Italy, and Spain is divided into butter and oil cooking, and until fairly recently the twain seldom met.

Olive trees, which grow to a gnarled old age, do not start fruit until the age of eight years, so that an olive grove represented a considerable investment; thus, the ancients reckoned wealth by the number of olive trees owned. Cutting down olive trees was a serious crime; from this comes the origin of the olive as a symbol of peace, for war destroyed the sacred trees. Olive oil was held as sacred as bread, as we know from Egyptian records that go as far back as the 17th century B.C. The Sumerians used olive oil around 3,000 B.C. for cooking and for anointing their hair and bodies. The Bible mentions olives many times: the dove that announced the ebbing of the flood to Noah carried an olive leaf in its beak, but perhaps the most moving reference is found in Psalm 23 verse 5: "Thou preparest a table before me in the presence of mine enemies; thou anointest my head with oil; my cup runneth over."

In classical mythology the olive tree is said to have been created by Athena, the Greek goddess of wisdom. A new city in Greece was to be named, and Athena and Poseidon, god of the sea, competed for the honor of giving the city a name. The one who produced the best gift for the welfare of the new city was to be the winner. Poseidon offered a war horse, Athena an olive tree. The new city was named Athens.

OLIVE

There is no lovelier sight in the world than a grove of ancient, gnarled olive trees, thickly covered with silvery shimmery leaves, trembling in the breeze, seen against the deep blue of the water, as one can see in Spain, southern France, on Capri, and in the Greek islands. It is a sight to put the mind and senses at rest, in tune with the civilizations of the past.

Jesuit missionaries introduced olive trees into Mexico in the 17th century, and took them from there into southern California where they flourished.

In the United States olives are grown for their fruit but elsewhere they are grown primarily for oil. The olive itself is a hard-stoned fruit used as a condiment, for seasoning, and as an appetizer. Olives are also delicious when added to many meat dishes and stews. Because they are one of the prime foods of the Mediterranean, they are a frequent ingredient in many spicy dishes originating in these countries.

Olives, as they grow on the tree, are pale green. When they begin to turn straw-colored, they are picked and prepared in various ways for eating. Fresh olives are very bitter. The bitterness is removed in the preparation.

Green fermented olives, the well-known Spanish-style olives, are soaked in lye for a short time, washed, and then kept in barrels of salt solution for six to twelve months. This causes a lactic-acid fermentation and gives them their astringent taste. Sugar is added from time to time to keep fermentation going. When the olives are properly fermented, they are packed in a weak salt brine and bottled.

As the olive becomes riper it develops more oil. Ripe olives are either green or black. Both are picked later than the early light-green olives but before they turn jet-black, as they do when ready to be picked for their oil. These "ripe" olives are heated and soaked in lye, then packed in brine. The black color of the "ripe" olive is developed during the lye treatments. Between treatments they are exposed to the air to develop the characteristic dark color.

If the olive is left on the tree until it is fully ripe and ready to be pressed for oil, it turns jet-black. If used for eating, the olives are picked and mixed with salt. This removes some of the bitterness and most of the moisture. These olives, popular in France, Spain, Italy, and Greece, are wrinkled and shriveled and very nutritious. They are often packed in oil or eaten after being dipped in oil.

Availability and Purchasing Guide—Olives, available year round, are graded by size as small, medium, large, extra large, mammoth, giant, colossal, and super colossal. Green olives are sold in jars, pickled: pitted; unpitted; stuffed with pimientos, almonds, capers, onions, or celery.

Ripe olives are available in jars and cans, pitted or unpitted, whole, sliced, or chopped.

Dried and salt-cured olives, also known as Greek or Italian olives, are available canned and in bulk.

Olive condite, or salad, is available in jars and is also included with canned antipasto. Olive spread, or butter, made from green or ripe olives, is available canned. Chopped olives mixed with cream cheese and with process cheese spreads is available.

Storage—Olives in cans or jars can be stored unopened at room temperature indefinitely. Once opened they should be refrigerated in their own liquid and can be stored thus indefinitely. If any white scum forms on top of the liquid in which the olives are packed, rinse olives before using. They should not be used if they are no longer firm.

Caloric Values

Green, 1 large = 5 calories
Ripe, 1 large = 8 calories

OLIVE-AVOCADO APPETIZER

1 large ripe avocado
1 cup highly seasoned French dressing
⅓ cup chopped stuffed olives

Peel avocado. Cut into halves; remove seed. Cut into ¼-inch lengthwise slices. Immediately cover slices with French dressing and let stand in refrigerator for 30 minutes. Drain (reserve dressing for future salads). Sprinkle with olives. Makes 4 servings.

SPANISH MEAT LOAF

1½ pounds meat
1 cup drained canned chick-peas
¼ cup tomato sauce
¼ cup seedless raisins
¼ cup sliced stuffed olives
1 large onion, chopped
1 small green pepper, seeded and chopped
1 small garlic clove, chopped
2 eggs
Oregano, salt, and pepper

Toss together lightly but thoroughly meat, chick-peas, tomato sauce, raisins, olives, onion, green pepper, and garlic. Add eggs to bind and season with oregano, salt, and pepper to taste. Pack into loaf pan or 1½-quart casserole greased with bacon fat. Bake in preheated moderate oven (350°F.) for 1¼ hours. Makes 4 to 6 servings.

HAKE FILLETS WITH OLIVES

2 pounds hake fillets
Salt and pepper to taste
¼ cup butter or margarine, softened
1 small onion, minced
1 tablespoon cider vinegar
⅓ cup chopped olives

Season fish lightly with salt and pepper. Put in greased shallow baking dish. Combine remaining ingredients and spread on fish. Bake in preheated moderate oven (350°F.) for minutes, or until fish flakes easily with fork. Makes 4 servings.

OLIVE OIL—A product obtained by crushing tree-ripened olives, then extracting the liquid by pressing the pulp or by centrifugal separators. The first "crude olive oil" is obtained from this liquid by settling and skimming or by "washing" by a continuous flow of clear water. Refining produces the clear oil which we use for salads and cooking. The best olive oil is golden or straw-yellow in color. Greenish-colored oils are of an inferior quality. Olive oil is imported from France, Italy, Spain, and Greece. Fine quality California olive oil is also obtainable.

Olive oil should not be exposed to extremes of light or temperature. Light will fade its color and cold will cause it to congeal and separate. It is sold in bottles or cans by liquid measure.

Olive oil has a more distinctive flavor and a lower smoking point than other edible oils. It is used for salad dressings, seasoning vegetables, and sautéing over low heat where its special flavor is desired. Its use is characteristic of Mediterranean cookery.

OMELET—A combination of eggs, milk or water, and seasonings, cooked in a skillet until firm. Omelets generally are of two different types: puffy, in which the yolks and whites are beaten separately, resulting in a fluffier omelet; and French, in which the yolks and whites are beaten together, producing a firmer, less-fluffy omelet. All other omelets are variations of these basic types.

Success with an omelet depends primarily on the choice of pan. Special omelet pans are available, or use a medium-weight skillet with sloping sides, flat bottom and smooth surface. For a 2- or 3-egg omelet, use a pan with an 8-inch top and 6½-inch base. Pans with non-stick coating are especially good. (If omelet sticks to pan you are using, see To Season Pan, below.) Have ready a table fork or special omelet fork, standard measuring spoons, rubber spatula and regular-size metal spatula. Give the recipe your undivided attention. It is easier to make several small omelets of 2 or 3 eggs each, than a larger one.

Make omelets just before eating. Not more than 1 minute is required for an individual omelet—2 to 3 minutes if filled. Do not overcook; long cooking toughens eggs.

FRENCH OMELET I

3 eggs
1 tablespoon water
¼ to ½ teaspoon salt
Dash of pepper
1 tablespoon butter or margarine

Break eggs into medium bowl. Add water, salt and pepper. With fork, beat eggs briskly 25 to 30 seconds, or just enough to blend yolks and whites. Melt butter in pan over moderate heat until it begins to sizzle and foam (do not brown). Pour in eggs and scrape out bowl with rubber spatula.

Hold handle of pan in left hand and fork in right (or the reverse if left-handed). As edges of omelet crinkle and look firm, lift toward center with fork so that uncooked egg runs under firm portion. Tilt pan as necessary with left hand to hasten flow of egg. Continue lifting egg with fork until all uncooked egg has run under cooked portion. (Entire cooking time will be 3 to 4 minutes.) Smooth top of omelet with fork. (Edges should look firm; top, moist and creamy.) With metal spatula, lift edge of omelet; if not brown enough, increase heat slightly. With the spatula, fold one third of omelet toward center. Slide unfolded third of omelet onto center of serving plate. Invert pan, folding omelet over. Serve at once. Makes 1 or 2 servings.
NOTE: When filling omelet, have ingredients at room temperature; or heated through, if desired; put filling down center and fold first third over it. Proceed as above.

French Omelet II

Follow recipe for French Omelet I and pour eggs in pan as directed. Immediately slide pan back and forth over heat so that eggs will not stick. At the same time, using the fork in right hand, stir eggs in wide circular strokes smoothly and quickly, about 30 seconds. Keep uncooked egg spread evenly over bottom. As soon as a border around the edge is done to your liking, remove from heat, fill and fold as desired. Makes 1 or 2 servings.

To Season Pan. Cover bottom of pan with vegetable oil and heat slowly, turning pan occasionally to coat sides. When hot, remove from heat and cool; let stand overnight. Next day, heat again, pour off oil and wipe pan dry with paper towel.

Filling Suggestions

Sliced avocado and tomato
Sliced or diced pepperoni and diced Cheddar cheese
Flaked tuna, dairy sour cream and sliced black olives
Diced ham, sliced mushrooms and green onion
Drained crushed pineapple, cubed cream cheese and crumbled crisp bacon
Diced salami and cheese and chopped chives
Fried onions seasoned with salt and sage
Diced cooked ham and mushrooms and croutons or chopped cooked potatoes
Cooked chopped broccoli and diced cheese
Flaked salmon, chopped water chestnuts and dill
Cooked cut asparagus, diced ham and grated Swiss cheese
Curried chicken with chutney to taste
Any diced cooked meat and canned fried-onion rings
Shredded sharp Cheddar cheese and broken corn chips
Cooked vermicelli seasoned with minced garlic and mixed with drained minced clams and chopped parsley
Artichoke hearts and diced cheese
Chopped parsley with a pinch each of chervil and tarragon
Diced cooked chicken livers, mushrooms and water chestnuts; parsley
Diced cooked shrimps and water chestnuts
Cooked rice, chopped herbs and pine nuts
Finely chopped fresh herbs, such as parsley, chives, basil, cottage cheese seasoned with chopped parsley and chives
Dried beef. Cream and pour some over top
Creamed Spinach. Serve with sour cream

SPANISH OMELET

1 small onion, chopped.
½ cup canned tomatoes
1 small green pepper, chopped
1 small garlic clove, minced
2 tablespoons olive oil
Salt and pepper to taste
1 recipe for French Omelet, above

Put onion, tomatoes, green pepper, garlic, and olive oil in saucepan. Bring to boil and simmer for 10 minutes. Season with salt and pepper. Make French Omelet, filling it with half the mixture. Fold omelet, put on hot serving plate, and pour the remaining mixture around it. Makes 2 servings.

PUFFY OMELET

6 eggs, separated
½ teaspoon salt
⅛ teaspoon pepper
1½ tablespoons all-purpose flour
1 tablespoon water
2 tablespoons butter or margarine

Beat egg whites with salt until stiff but not dry. Beat egg yolks with pepper, flour, and water until fluffy. Fold yolk mixture into whites gently but thoroughly. Melt butter in 10-inch skillet. Tip skillet to spread butter over bottom. Pour in omelet mixture, level surface gently, and cover. Cook over very low heat until surface of omelet is dry and knife, when inserted, comes out clean. Fold and serve at once. Makes 4 servings.
NOTE: To cook in an electric skillet, heat butter at 320°F. and pour in omelet mixture. Reduce heat to 240°F. for cooking.

PUFFY HAM OMELET

1 cup minced cooked ham
½ teaspoon prepared mustard
1 teaspoon minced onion
1 recipe for Puffy Omelet

Mix ham, mustard, and onion. Make Puffy Omelet. Spread ham mixture on omelet before folding. Fold and serve at once. Makes 4 servings.

DESSERT OMELETS

Prepare French Omelet without pepper. Fill and top as suggested below.

Peanut Omelet

Sprinkle omelet with ¼ cup salted peanuts before folding. Serve finished omelet with Peanut-Honey Sauce: Mix 6 tablespoons honey, 2 tablespoons orange juice and ¼ cup creamy peanut butter until smooth and blended.

Peach-Cream Omelet

Before folding, spread half the cooked omelet with about 2 tablespoons dairy sour cream. Add drained sliced fresh or canned peaches. Fold over and turn out on plate. Spread top with a little sour cream and add a few sliced peaches. Sprinkle with toasted nuts.

Strawberry-Cream Omelet

Halve strawberries and sweeten with sugar. Add a little kirsch or Cointreau, if desired. Before folding, spread half the cooked omelet with a little dairy sour cream and top with drained berries. Fold and turn out on plate. Add additional strawberries.

Banana Omelet

Sprinkle sliced bananas with sugar and lemon juice. Fill omelet with fruit. Fold, sprinkle top with sugar and put under broiler to glaze. Or sift confectioners' sugar over top and omit broiling.

Frosted Omelet

Fill omelet with jam, jelly or any preferred fruit. Beat 1 egg white until foamy. Add 2 tablespoons sugar and ½ teaspoon vanilla and beat until stiff. Spread on folded omelet and sprinkle with sugar. Broil carefully until golden.

Ginger-Cream Omelet

Flavor omelet mixture with grated lemon rind and nutmeg to taste. Fill with dairy sour cream and chopped candied or preserved ginger to taste.

Mandarin-Orange Omelet

Fill omelet with dairy sour cream and drained canned mandarin-orange segments. Sift confectioners' sugar on top.

Fruit-Nut Omelet

Fill omelet with apple, peach or cherry pie filling and sprinkle folded omelet with chopped nuts. Or fill omelet with cranberry sauce and slivered almonds.

Cream-Cheese and Marmalade

Fill omelet with 1 package (3 ounces) cream cheese, softened and mixed with 3 tablespoons orange marmalade.

Flaming Omelet

Sprinkle folded omelet with sugar and pour ½ jigger brandy, warmed, over top. Ignite carefully and carry at once to table.

Five ways to fill an omelet: Avocado and tomato; Pepperoni and Cheddar cheese; tuna, sour cream and black olives; Ham, mushroom and green onions; Pineapple, cream-cheese and bacon.

ONION COOKBOOK

ONION—The underground bulb of the plant *Allium cepa.* There are many kinds of onions with different-colored skins, and in size they vary from the very small bulblets of the spring or green onions, also known as scallions, to the huge round red Italian onions. A pungent volatile oil, rich in sulphur, is the cause of the onion's strong smell and flavor, and the warmer the climate in which onions are grown, the milder and sweeter they tend to be.

Onions are a member of the lily family which includes such flowers as the tulip, hyacinth, and lily-of-the-valley as well as the edible leek, garlic, garlic chive, chive, and shallot. All have a bulb growing under the ground and a stalk, leaves, and flowers above.

The word "onion" comes through French from Latin, probably from the Latin word unus, meaning "one." Perhaps because the onion is a single bulb with a spherical shape it was considered a symbol of the universe by the Egyptians. Today we do not associate the onion with such symbolism, but it does have a practically universal use; much cooking would be flavorless without it.

The versatile onion, a native of western Asia, has been cultivated from earliest times. In the 4th millenium B.C., Egyptian slaves working to build the gigantic Great Pyramid at Gizeh are said to have subsisted largely on onions, radishes, and garlic. The children of Israel were loath to leave the onions they had enjoyed in Egypt and cried out bitterly when they were deprived of this delicacy, resisting even the substitution of manna. The American Indians ate a type of wild onion which was powerful to the taste, and also used it in cooking stews.

The ancient Greeks and Romans used onions medicinally as well as in cooking. Hippocrates, the Greek physician of the 3rd and 4th centuries B.C., declared onions to be good for the sight but bad for the body. In the Middle Ages onions were used to help cure dog bites, adder bites, and the bites and stings of "venomous worms."

A 14th-century Icelandic manuscript states: "It is good for them that have cold and wet natures, and it does good in the stomach, and gives good complexion. If one mixes onion's juice and paunch fat of chickens, it is good to rub on shoes that cut." Through the centuries onions and onion juice were recommended to cure earache, colds, fever, laryngitis, and warts: an onion, cut into halves, rubbed on a wart, tied together again and buried, was supposed to make a wart disappear while the onion decayed in the ground.

Availability—The more strongly flavored domestic onions, available year round, are globe-shape and have white, yellow, or red skins. The white-skinned onion has the mildest flavor in this group.

More mildly flavored still are the Bermuda, Spanish or Valencia, and Italian onions. Bermudas, large, flat, and white or yellow in color, are available from March to June. The very large Spanish onions, brown or yellow in color, are available from August through April. The large red Italian onions are available year round.

Green onions, or scallions, are available year round.

Available in cans or jars are boiled whole onions, pickled onions, onion juice, and onion soup.

Chopped onions, pearl onions mixed with peas, and creamed onions are available frozen.

Dried or freeze-dried onion products include instant onion, onion flakes, scallions, onion-soup mixes, onion bouillon cubes, and some onion-gravy mixes.

Onion powder, made by grinding dehydrated onion into a fine powder, and onion salt, a combination of onion powder and salt, are also available.

Purchasing Guide—Most onions are slightly dried before they come to market and this accounts for their characteristically dry paper-thin skin. They are sold by weight, but very large Bermudas or Spanish types often are sold by unit. They should be firm with a dry skin which is bright and smooth.

All types of green onions are sold in bunches. They should have fresh green tops and medium-size necks 2 to 3 inches in length. Necks should be young, tender, and crisp, and roots should not be too long.

Storage—Dry onions should be kept in a cool dry well-ventilated place in a single layer or in loosely woven or open-mesh containers. Green onions should have wilted parts and roots discarded. Wrap in moisture-proof wrapping and refrigerate.

Dry, room temperature, uncooked: 1 to 4 weeks
Green, refrigerator shelf or vegetable compartment, uncooked: 1 to 2 days
Refrigerator shelf, cooked: 4 to 5 days
Frozen, refrigerator frozen-food compartment: 2 to 3 months
Frozen, freezer: 1 year
Canned, kitchen shelf: 1 year
Dried instant onion, kitchen shelf: 6 to 8 months

Nutritive Food Values—Onions contain some vitamin C with small amounts of other vitamins and minerals. Green parts of the onion yield some vitamin A.

Raw, chopped ½ cup = 33 calories
Cooked, 1 cup = 60 calories
Green, 3½ ounces, raw, bulb
and entire top = 36 calories
Green, 3½ ounces, raw, bulb
and white portion of top = 45 calories
Green, 3½ ounces, green portion
of tops only = 27 calories

Basic Preparation

To Peel—Peel under running water to avoid tears. Onions can be more easily peeled by pouring boiling water over them and letting them stand for a few minutes.

To Chop—Cut into halves crosswise. With a sharp knife, cube the top cut surface of the onion, then cut onion crosswise to release all the cubes.

To Slice—To cut onion into rings, cut onions into crosswise slices and carefully separate the slices into rings.

To Cook Whole—Drop peeled onions into boiling salted water; cook for 20 to 35 minutes depending on the size of the onion, or until onion is transparent and can be easily pierced with a fork. Sliced onions can be cooked in the same way but require less time. Drain and season with salt and pepper to taste and add butter.

Odor can be removed from a knife by rubbing with a raw potato. Odor can be removed from the hands by rubbing with salt, lemon, vinegar or celery salt.

SOUPS

FRENCH ONION SOUP

1½ pounds onions (about 5 cups sliced)
¼ cup butter or margarine
6 cups beef bouillon
Salt and pepper
Toasted slices of French bread
Grated Parmesan cheese

Peel onions and slice thin. Brown lightly in butter. Add to bouillon and simmer, covered, about 30 minutes. Season to taste. Put into large casserole or individual casseroles. Top with toast and sprinkle with cheese. Makes 4 to 6 servings.

ONION AND CHEESE SOUP

1 cup chopped onion
2 tablespoons butter or margarine
2 tablespoons all-purpose flour
6 cups milk, scalded
Salt and pepper to taste
2 cups grated sharp Cheddar cheese
Paprika and minced chives

Sauté onion in butter until soft. Add flour and mix; add milk gradually, stirring all the while, and heat to just below boiling. Season and stir in cheese. Serve sprinkled with paprika and chives. Makes 2 quarts.

SOUTH AMERICAN ONION SOUP

6 onions, thinly sliced
3 tablespoons butter or margarine
2 quarts bouillon or 3 cans (10½ ounces each) condensed consommé with 3 cans water
1½ cups almonds, blanched and chopped fine
Salt and pepper to taste
Rounds of crusty bread, toasted
1 cup grated Gruyère cheese

Sauté onions in butter slowly until soft. Add bouillon and nuts and simmer for 30 minutes. Season and serve with toast rounds sprinkled with cheese. Makes about 2½ quarts.

MAIN DISHES

BEEF AND ONION PIE

3 pounds boneless beef chuck
2 tablespoons shortening
Salt and pepper to taste
Water
1 can (1 pound) cooked onions
¼ cup cornstarch
Beef-Pie Pastry

Cut meat into 1½-inch cubes. Brown meat in shortening in kettle. Sprinkle with salt and pepper. Add 2 cups water. Bring to boil, cover, and simmer for 2 hours, or until tender. Drain, reserving broth. Put meat in shallow baking dish. Measure broth and add onion liquid to make 3 cups. Add cornstarch blended with a little cold water. Cook until slightly thickened. Season to taste. Add onions and gravy to meat. Bake in preheated hot oven (425°F.) for 10 minutes. Reduce heat to moderate (350°F.) and bake for 20 minutes longer. Put baked Pastry on top of meat and serve. Makes 6 servings.

Beef-Pie Pastry

Sift 2 cups all-purpose flour and 1 teaspoon salt. Cut in ⅔ cup shortening until mixture resembles coarse cornmeal. Mix 1 egg yolk with 3 tablespoons water. Mix lightly into flour mixture. Roll ¼ inch thick. Cut into diamonds or other desired shapes. Put on ungreased cookie sheet. Prick tops with fork and brush with slightly beaten egg white. Bake in preheated moderate oven (350°F.) for 20 minutes.

PORK CHOPS WITH ONIONS

Salt
6 thick lean pork chops
1½ cups sliced onion
½ teaspoon dried thyme
1 can (10½ ounces) condensed beef consommé
¼ teaspoon pepper
Dash of cayenne
¾ cup dairy sour cream
2 tablespoons all-purpose flour
2 tablespoons water
12 cooked small potatoes
Parsley

In salted hot skillet brown chops; pour off any fat. Add onion, thyme, consommé, pepper, and cayenne. Cover and simmer slowly about 45 minutes. Remove chops and add sour cream; thicken with flour mixed with water; cook a few minutes, stirring. Season to taste and pour over chops. Garnish with potatoes and parsley. Makes 6 servings.

Chives
Leek
Red Globe Onions
Yellow Onions
Green Onions,
often called Scallions
White Onions
Shallots
Spanish Onions

FRENCH STUFFED ONIONS

6 Bermuda onions, peeled
½ pound ground veal or ham (if ham, substitute 2 tablespoons butter for bacon below)
2 bacon strips, diced
Salt and pepper
Cayenne
½ cup dairy sour cream
1 tablespoon finely chopped celery
2 tablespoons each chopped chives and parsley
1 cup soft bread crumbs
Butter or margarine
1 cup meat bouillon or consommé

Parboil onions for 10 minutes. Scoop out centers. Sauté chopped centers, veal, and bacon. Add remaining ingredients except butter and bouillon and stuff onions. Dot with butter. Set onions in shallow baking dish, pour bouillon into dish and bake in preheated hot oven (400°F.) for 45 minutes. Makes 6 servings.

ONIONS WITH CHICKEN

6 large mild onions, peeled
½ cup chopped mushrooms
½ cup chopped cooked chicken
2 tablespoons soft butter or margarine
½ cup soft bread crumbs
Salt and pepper
½ cup chicken bouillon
Paprika
½ cup dairy sour cream

Parboil onions for 30 minutes. Scoop out centers and make stuffing of chopped centers and remaining ingredients except bouillon, paprika, and sour cream. Stuff onions. Put in buttered baking pan. Add bouillon, sprinkle with paprika, cover, and bake in preheated hot oven (400°F.) about 30 minutes. Remove cover for last 10 minutes. Remove onions; add sour cream to pan; serve over onions. Makes 6 servings.

FRENCH ONION QUICHE

1 cup sliced mild onion
2 tablespoons butter or margarine
½ pound Swiss cheese, grated
Pastry for 1-crust, 9-inch pie, unbaked
3 eggs, beaten
1 cup each milk and light cream
1 teaspoon salt
¼ teaspoon pepper
Dash of ground nutmeg
3 crisp bacon strips, crumbled

Sauté onions in butter until golden and soft. Put with cheese in pastry-lined pie pan. Combine rest of ingredients and pour over cheese and onions. Bake in preheated moderate oven (375°F.) for 45 minutes, or until a knife blade, when inserted, comes out clean. Cool slightly. Makes 6 servings.

ACCOMPANIMENTS FOR MAIN DISHES

GLAZED ONIONS AMANDINE

36 tiny silver-skinned onions, peeled
2 tablespoons butter or margarine
½ cup slivered blanched almonds
2 teaspoons sugar

Cook onions in boiling salted water for 15 minutes. Drain. In a skillet melt butter and add onions and almonds. Add 1 teaspoon sugar and toss. Add remaining 1 teaspoon sugar and cook slowly until onions and almonds are glazed and browned, about 15 minutes. Toss or shake pan often. Delicious with turkey or chicken. Makes 4 to 6 servings.

CREAMED ONIONS

2 dozen small white onions, peeled
Water
¼ cup butter or margarine
¼ cup all-purpose flour
1½ cups light cream
Salt and pepper
Dash of cayenne
½ cup buttered soft bread crumbs, or grated sharp Cheddar cheese

Cook onions in water to cover until tender. Drain, reserving ½ cup liquid. Melt butter and blend in flour. Gradually add reserved liquid and cream, stirring constantly. Cook, stirring, until smooth and thickened. Add salt and pepper to taste and cayenne. Add onions and mix lightly. Pour into shallow baking dish, and top with crumbs. Cover, and bake in preheated moderate oven (350°F.) for 45 minutes. Uncover during last 20 minutes of baking to brown the top. Makes 6 servings.

FRENCH-FRIED ONIONS

Peel Spanish or Bermuda onions and cut into ¼-inch slices. Separate into rings, dip into evaporated milk, then into flour. Fry in hot deep fat. Drain on paper towels and sprinkle with salt.

SHALLOT GREEN BEANS

2 packages (10 ounces each) frozen green beans
4 shallots, sliced
1 can (10½ ounces) condensed cream of chicken soup
¼ cup milk or undiluted evaporated milk
Salt and pepper
1 tablespoon butter or margarine
Dash each of soy sauce and garlic salt
½ cup grated sharp Cheddar cheese

Cook beans, adding shallots for last 2 minutes of cooking. Drain and top with sauce made by mixing remaining ingredients. Good on rice or hominy. Makes 6 servings.

ONIONS, SWISS STYLE

2 mild onions, sliced thin
2 tablespoons butter or margarine
Salt and pepper to taste
2 cups grated Swiss cheese
1 can (10½ ounces) condensed cream-of-chicken soup
1 cup rich milk
1 cup buttered bread crumbs
Crisp toast

Separate sliced onion into rings and sauté in butter until golden; then cover pan and simmer for 10 minutes. Put in buttered baking dish, season, and cover with cheese. Dilute soup with milk and pour over cheese. Top with crumbs. Bake in preheated moderate oven (375°F.) for 30 minutes. Serve as a dunk with crisp toast. Makes 4 servings.

SPICED ONIONS AND BEETS

2 cups thinly sliced mild onions
2 cups sliced cooked beets
½ cup white vinegar
¾ cup water
1 cinnamon stick
4 cloves
1 tablespoon sugar
½ teaspoon salt
⅛ teaspoon pepper

Place all ingredients in saucepan. Bring to boil and simmer gently for 10 minutes. Serve cold as a relish or hot, with 1 tablespoon butter added, as accompaniment to meat. Improves with time and will keep for weeks in refrigerator. (Add just a touch of garlic salt for extra flavor.) Makes 4 servings.

GREEN HEAVEN IN A POT

1 box (9 ounces) frozen artichoke hearts
1 bunch of green onions
4 eggs
½ cup medium cream
Salt and pepper
Grated Parmesan cheese

Cook artichoke hearts as directed on the label. Drain and dice. Wash green onions and cut fine, including tops. Divide artichokes and onions among 4 greased small ramekins. Break an egg into each. Pour cream over eggs, season with salt and pepper to taste, and sprinkle with cheese. Bake in preheated moderate oven (350°F.) for 45 minutes, or until eggs are of desired doneness. Makes 4 servings.
NOTE: Good as a lunch dish with crusty French bread.

DANISH ONIONS

8 medium onions, peeled
¼ cup crumbled blue cheese
2 cups rich white sauce
Salt, pepper, and cayenne to taste

Boil onions in salted water until tender. Drain; mix with cheese in white sauce. Season; simmer for 5 minutes. Serve on potatoes. Makes 4 servings.

PEANUT CREAMED ONIONS

18 small white onions, peeled
½ cup salted peanuts, chopped fine
1 cup rich white sauce
Salt and pepper to taste
Dash of ground mace

Cook onions in salted water until tender. Drain and add with half of peanuts to white sauce. Season; top with remaining nuts. Bake in preheated moderate oven (375°F.) for 20 minutes. Makes 4 servings.

GARDEN RAGOUT

1½ cups diced scallions, including tops
2 medium cucumbers, peeled and diced
¼ pound mushrooms, sliced
2 tablespoons butter or bacon fat
Salt, pepper, and garlic salt to taste
Dash of soy sauce
1½ cups rich white sauce
1 egg yolk, beaten
Chopped chives
Hot cooked rice

Boil scallions and cucumber in salted water until tender; drain. Sauté mushrooms in butter, combine with vegetables, and season. Add to hot white sauce. Add some of sauce to egg yolk, then return egg mixture to sauced vegetables. Garnish with chives and serve with rice. Makes 6 servings.

SWEET-SOUR ONIONS, ITALIAN STYLE

1 pound small onions
2 ounces salt pork, chopped
1 tablespoon sugar
¼ cup cider vinegar
½ teaspoon salt
⅛ teaspoon pepper

Peel onions and soak in ice water 5 minutes; drain. Put salt pork in skillet and brown well. Pour off all but 2 tablespoons fat. Add sugar and vinegar to pork and fat and mix well. Add onions and seasonings, cover and cook slowly, adding a little water if necessary, 30 minutes, or until tender. Makes 4 servings.

GLAZED GREEN ONIONS

12 large green onions
Salt
2 tablespoons butter or margarine
2 tablespoons firmly packed brown sugar

Clean onions, leaving most of the green top on. Cook in boiling salted water to cover in skillet 8 to 10 minutes, or until tender. Drain off water and add butter and sugar. Cook over low heat 8 minutes, or until golden brown. Makes 2 to 3 servings.

SALADS

SCALLION AND BEAN SALAD

1 pound dried white beans
4 scallions, including tops, chopped
2 garlic cloves, peeled and pressed
¼ cup fresh lemon juice
½ cup olive oil
Salt and pepper to taste
Chopped parsley

Soak beans overnight, drain, and simmer in water to cover until done, about 2 hours. Drain and cool. Make dressing of scallions, garlic, lemon juice, olive oil, and salt and pepper. Pour over beans; top with parsley. Chill for several hours. Makes 3 servings.

ONION AND ORANGE SALAD

Peel oranges and slice about ½ inch thick. Peel red Italian onions and slice thin. Separate into rings. Arrange orange slices and onion rings on bed of salad greens and watercress. Pour French dressing over top.

MARINATED ONION AND BLUE CHEESE

½ cup olive oil
2 tablespoons fresh lemon juice
1 teaspoon salt
Dash each pepper and paprika
½ teaspoon sugar
¼ cup crumbled blue cheese
2 cups thickly sliced large red or yellow onion

Mix oil, lemon juice, seasonings, and sugar. Stir in cheese; pour over onions, cover, and chill for at least 2 days. Makes 6 to 8 servings.
NOTE: These are delicious with thin buttered slices of pumpernickel.

OTHER ONION DISHES

GOURMET RELISH

4 cups thinly sliced peeled Bermuda onion
1 teaspoon salt
⅛ teaspoon pepper
2 cups dry white wine
½ cup chopped parsley

Put onion and seasonings in wine and chill for several hours. Add parsley. Serve cold with rye-bread rounds and cheese for a late buffet. Makes 8 servings.

Onion and Orange Salad

SOUTHERN ONION BREAD

- 2 tablespoons butter or bacon fat
- ¾ cup white cornmeal
- 1 egg, beaten
- ¼ cup chopped onion
- 1½ cups buttermilk or sour milk
- ½ teaspoon baking soda
- 1 teaspoon salt
- ⅛ teaspoon pepper

Put butter in 1-quart casserole and heat in preheated oven. Mix rest of ingredients until smooth and put in hot casserole. Bake in hot oven (425°F.) for 30 minutes, or until barely set. Serve as you do spoon bread. Makes 4 to 6 servings.

ONION GRAVY

- 2 cups sliced onion
- ¼ cup meat fat and drippings
- ¼ cup flour
- 2 cups meat broth
- Salt and pepper
- Dash of garlic salt
- 1½ teaspoons Worcestershire
- Dash of bottled sauce for gravy

Sauté onion in fat until soft and golden. Add flour, stir, and add remaining ingredients. Stir, cover, and simmer for 5 minutes. Makes 3 cups.

OPOSSUM—A small marsupial animal found in the southern and midwestern United States, and increasingly in the central Atlantic states. The common, or Virginia, opossum is about the size of a cat, with grayish fur and black ears and feet. Opossum is often used for food, the flavor resembling young pig. It can be prepared in the same manner as roast suckling pig.

ORACHE, ORACH—An annual herb plant, *Atriplex hortensis,* native to the Tatary region of Asia, which is now extensively grown as a potherb in France. It is also known as Garden orache, Mexican spinach, French spinach, and sea purslane. Orache grows to a height of five to six feet. Its leaves vary in color from a pale yellowish-green to dark red, are arrow-shape, slightly crimped, and very tender. Orache is prepared for the table in the same way spinach is. The wild orache, commonly called mountain orache, is considered a weed, but is edible. In some English country districts it is known by the curious name fat hen.

ORANGE—This popular citrus fruit grows on an evergreen tree with shiny, rather narrow leaves and wonderfully fragrant white flowers. There are many varieties of oranges, but the three principal species are the sweet, common, or China orange, *Citrus sinensis;* the loose-skinned or "kid-glove" orange, *Citrus nobilis;* and the sour, bitter, Seville, or bigarade orange, *Citrus aurantium.*

The sweet orange is the most important species, and is the one from which most edible varieties have developed. The tree may reach a height of thirty-five or forty feet; the fruits are globular or oval, with a sweet and juicy pulp. Far and away most of the oranges grown in the United States are some variety of this species.

The best-known sweet oranges are the golden-yellow Valencia, or Spanish, heavy and juicy, with large coarse-grained fruit; Mediterranean oranges, which have a fine-grained fruit; blood oranges, with a red, or red and white streaked, pulp; and the seedless navel, or Washington navel oranges.

The trees producing the loose-skinned oranges are smaller, growing to perhaps twenty feet. Included among them are mandarins and king oranges, names often used to describe the entire species; the temple; and the tangerine. The flesh of these oranges divides easily into segments and they got the name "kid-glove" because of the ease with which their skins can be removed. They are grown extensively in Japan, southern Europe, and, in this country, in the Gulf states.

Sour orange trees seldom grow larger than twenty-five feet. The orange itself is large, with a rough, red-orange skin. Its pulp is too acid to be eaten raw. These trees are cultivated to a small extent in the United States for ornamental purposes. Spain grows them commercially: they are used for making marmalade; the peel is candied; the oil is used for food flavorings, in the liqueur Curaçao, and for medicinal and cosmetic purposes. The bergamot orange, probably a hybrid of the sour orange, is a golden-yellow pear-shape fruit, which grows on a spiny tree and is cultivated in the Mediterranean area, chiefly in Italy, where the peel is used to make oil of bergamot, for perfumes.

Oranges grew wild in great profusion in Florida. Columbus, on his second voyage to the New World, had planted the slips in the West Indies and from there they were brought to Florida. The Seminole Indians were quick to take advantage of the juicy fruit. John Bartram, an 18th-century naturalist, tells of the Indian custom of slicing off the top, filling the middle with wild honey, and then eating the delicious middle. John Bartram's son, William, reported of his journeys through Florida that a favorite dish was trout stewed in orange juice. This, he remarked "with boiled rice, afforded me a wholesome and delicious supper."

Benjamin Franklin had a special recipe for orange shrub: "To a Gallon of Rum two Quarts of Orange Juice and two pounds of Sugar—dissolve the Sugar in the Juice before you mix it with the Rum—Put all together in a Cask & shake it well—let it stand 3 or 4 weeks & it will be very fine & fit for Bottling." Franklin was so fond of this drink that he was careful to explain how to filter the dregs so "that not a drop may be lost."

Thomas Jefferson, the third American president, and a great experimenter, tried to grow orange trees, imported from Italy, at Monticello.

Today, of course, the United States is the largest orange grower in the world, producing half of the world supply.

Oranges can be grown on fertile and well-irrigated soil, wherever the climate is warm and dry. They do not tolerate frost. Oranges can be grown from seed, but commercially grown oranges are budded or grafted. Florida and California are leaders, followed by Texas, Louisiana, Arizona, and Mississippi. Orange growing in Florida and California is a most scientific enterprise. The maturing time, quality, and even the sweetness of the oranges is controlled. The oranges, to prevent bruising, are picked by gloved workers. They are washed and scrubbed in soap and water, borax solutions, and clean water. They are dried and often colored artificially, because many oranges, especially in Florida, are picked green although ripe, and do not have the glowing golden color we associate with them. The added coloring is entirely harmless.

Oranges are eaten raw, or used in cooking and for making candied fruit. The yellow part of the rind is often shredded or grated to add to both non-sweet and sweet dishes, for it gives a delicious flavor. But the majority of American oranges are consumed in the form of juice at breakfast. Orange juice, as distinct from orangeade, is an American custom, although oranges have been eaten all over the world for many centuries. The American custom of drinking orange juice has been taken up recently in Europe, but it is still thought of as rather dashing and "American." The peel of oranges is candied, for baking and confectionery. The essential oil pressed from the skins is used for cosmetics, medicine, and food flavorings. In Brazil, oranges are eaten in huge quantities, either by sucking or peeled, or, most deliciously, placed on a slice of fresh pineapple, and eaten with knife and fork. The skins are utilized as kindling wood for the kitchen stove. The oranges are peeled in one long strip which is left to dry on the backyard fence. When dried, the peel catches fire with great ease and fragrance.

Availability—A certain number of fresh oranges are available year round but they are at their peak during the fall and winter months. Among the sweet oranges available are: the *Hamlin,* a thin-skinned orange, good for juice and marmalade, in season from October to December; the *Indian River,* a thin-skinned variety with a rich juicy pulp, in season from December through April; the *navel,* or *Washington navel,* a large thick-skinned seedless orange, used for eating out-of-hand, for sections, slices, for crystallized peel, and marmalade, in season from October to December; the *Parson Brown,* a rough-skinned orange, good for eating, juice, and for marmalade, in season from October to December; the *Valencia,* a large and heavy golden-yellow orange, excellent for juice and flavor, easy to peel and section. It freezes well and makes a good marmalade, is in season from March to July. The Valencia variety accounts for about half the orange production of the United states.

Among the loose-skinned oranges available are: the *King* or *Satsuma,* a large thick- and rough-skinned orange, resembling the tangerine, which peels easily, is very sweet, and is best for eating out-of-hand, in season March to July; the *Ponkan,* a large tangerinelike variety, peels easily, best for eating out-of-hand, in season from December through March; the *tangerine,* easily peeled and segmented, sweet flavor, best for eating out-of-hand, in season from December through April; the *Temple,* a bright orange with a rough thick red skin, peels and segments easily, very sweet flavor, in season from December through March. A few *Mandarin* oranges, small, round, easily peeled and segmented, are grown in California. The *tangelo,* a cross between a loose-skinned orange and a grapefruit, is generally yellowish-orange in color and medium to large in size. Two of the most successful varieties differ considerably in shape (pear or round) and in peel (smooth and thin, or rough and thick). It is easy to peel and segment, its flavor is a pleasing and distinctive combination of the sweetness and tartness of its parents, and is in season December through March.

Chilled containers of orange juice and orange segments mixed with other fruits are available in food stores.

Canned orange juice, orange and grapefruit juice, tangerine juice, orange and grapefruit segments, and Mandarin orange segments are available. Available frozen are concentrated orange juice, orange juice blended with other juices, and tangerine juice; and frozen orange and grapefruit segments.

Other orange products available are orangeade, orange drinks, candied orange peel, orange-flavored gelatin desserts and puddings, orange-flower water, oil of orange, orange extract, and marmalades.

Purchasing Guide—Select fresh oranges that are firm and heavy for their size, free from soft spots or mold. Skin color does not indicate ripeness as regreening sometimes occurs in the ripe fruit. Russeting does not affect flavor, either. Sometimes oranges are artificially colored with a harmless dye to improve the appearance. Such fruits must be stamped "color added." Oranges are sold by the piece or by weight and are graded according to size.

Storage—Store in refrigerator or cool dry well-ventilated place. Oranges can be kept at room temperature if they are to be used in a very short time.

Fresh, refrigerator shelf: 1 to 2 months
Canned, kitchen shelf: 1 year
Canned, refrigerator shelf, opened: 5 to 6 days
Frozen, refrigerator frozen-food compartment: 3 weeks
Frozen, freezer: 1 year

Nutritive Food Values—**Excellent source of vitamin C with some vitamin A value. Fresh-squeezed orange juice may vary in vitamin C content according to variety and season, making canned juice higher in vitamin C than some fresh-squeezed juice. Juice from frozen concentrate is 12.5 percent higher in vitamin C than canned juice and compares favorably with the average for all fresh-squeezed Florida orange juice (California oranges are slightly higher), but any juice exposed to air loses its vitamin C value. The loss after 24 hours in a refrigerator is 20 percent; after 24 hours at room temperature, 60 percent.**

Peeled raw oranges, 1 cup sections (8½ ounces) = 118 calories
Orange juice, fresh, 1 cup = 110 calories
Orange juice frozen diluted with 3 parts water by volume, 1 cup = 120 calories
Orange juice, canned, unsweetened, 1 cup = 120 calories
Candied orange peel, 1 ounce = 90 calories

Basic Preparation—Wash before using. Serve peeled or unpeeled. Oranges may be cut into various shapes, slices, chunks, or sections.

ORANGE

To Eat Out-of-Hand—Cut into quarters. They may also be peeled by hand and spilt with the fingers into segments.

To Serve Whole—Slit the outer skin into 8 wedges cut from top to bottom. Carefully peel the skin away from the orange, leaving the skin attached to the bottom of the fruit. Tuck the skin points underneath the orange. (A tangerine may be prepared in the same way, snipping the skin with scissors at ½-inch intervals almost down to the bottom of the tangerine. The tangerine will then resemble a chrysanthemum.)

To Cut Sections—Remove the rind and the white inner rind with a sharp knife. Cut in between the membranes, releasing sections.

To Cut Shells—Cut fruit into halves and with a sharp knife cut out the pulp, leaving a shell about ½ inch thick. Cut up pulp and use with other fruits to refill shell. Shell edge may be scalloped by cutting diagonal slits into the fruit instead of cutting into straight halves.

To Squeeze—Leave them at room temperature to make them easier to squeeze.

To Grate Rind—Rub in short strokes across small area of grater and grate only the orange portion.

To Freeze—Use firm fruit. With a sharp knife peel fruit, removing fruit peel and white membranes. Section fruit, removing inner membranes and seeds. Pack fruit into containers. Cover with syrup. For every 4 cups water use 3 or 4 cups sugar, depending on sweetness of fruit. Allow ½-inch headspace. Cover.

MAIN DISHES

CHICKEN BAKED IN ORANGE SAUCE

1 frying chicken (about 3 pounds), cut into pieces
¼ cup olive oil
1 cup fresh orange juice
1 cup dry white wine
½ cup seedless raisins
½ cup blanched almonds, ground fine
1 tablespoon sugar
½ teaspoon ground ginger
1 teaspoon salt
½ teaspoon pepper

Brown chicken in hot oil. Place in shallow baking pan. Combine other ingredients and pour over chicken. Bake in preheated moderate oven (350°F.) for 45 minutes, or until tender, basting often. Makes 4 servings.

ORANGE-STUFFED VEAL

3 cups toasted bread cubes
1 teaspoon grated orange rind
1 cup chopped celery
1 teaspoon ground mace (optional)
½ cup chopped onion
¾ cup butter (about)
2 cups fresh orange juice
3 to 4 pounds breast of veal with pocket
Salt and pepper

Combine first 5 ingredients and ½ cup each butter and orange juice in large bowl. Blend thoroughly. Stuff meat and secure edges with small skewers or toothpicks. Rub meat with salt and pepper. Heat enough butter to cover bottom of skillet. Brown meat on all sides. Add remaining 1½ cups orange juice and cover tightly. Simmer gently on top of stove or bake in preheated moderate oven (325°F.) about 2½ hours, or until meat is tender. Check for dryness; if necessary, add hot water, 1 tablespoon at a time. Makes 4 servings.

ACCOMPANIMENTS FOR MAIN DISHES

FRESH BEETS IN ORANGE SAUCE

2 tablespoons grated orange rind
2 tablespoons fresh lemon juice
1 tablespoon fresh orange juice
¼ teaspoon salt
Dash of pepper
⅛ teaspoon ground nutmeg
¼ cup butter or margarine
4 cups sliced peeled cooked fresh beets

Combine orange rind, lemon juice, orange juice, salt, pepper, and nutmeg in top part of double boiler. Add butter and beets. Heat well. Makes 8 servings.

GLAZED ORANGES

6 seedless oranges
¾ cup sugar
½ cup water
3 tablespoons light corn syrup
6 cloves
One piece (2 inches) gingeroot (optional)

Peel oranges, remove all white membrane, and cut oranges into sections. Combine remaining ingredients and boil for 2 or 3 minutes. Add orange sections and simmer over low heat about 5 minutes. Before serving, remove cloves and gingerroot. Makes 6 servings.
NOTE: Good with cold roast duck, ham, or goose.

ORANGE RICE FOR DUCK OR HAM

3 tablespoons butter or margarine
⅔ cup diced celery with leaves
2 tablespoons chopped onion
1½ cups water
Grated rind of 1 orange
1 cup fresh orange juice
1¼ teaspoons salt
¼ teaspoon crumbled dried thyme
1 cup raw rice

Melt butter in heavy saucepan; add celery and onion, and cook until onion is soft and golden. Add water, orange rind and juice, salt, and thyme. Bring to a boil. Add rice slowly, stirring constantly. Cover; reduce heat and cook for 25 minutes, or until rice is tender. Makes 4 to 5 servings.

SALADS

ORANGE AND BELGIAN-ENDIVE SALAD

4 navel oranges
8 heads Belgian endive
¾ cup olive oil
¼ cup mild cider vinegar
1 teaspoon salt
2 teaspoons mild prepared mustard
¼ cup fresh orange juice
½ pound Swiss cheese, cut into ½-inch cubes (optional)

Peel oranges and remove all white membrane. Separate sections and remove seeds and membrane between sections. Chill. Cut Belgian endive into rounds and chill. Make dressing by combining remaining ingredients except cheese. Chill. At serving time, combine oranges, Belgian endive, and cheese. Stir dressing well and toss salad in it. Makes 6 servings.

ORANGE AND WATERCRESS SALAD

Rub a clove of garlic around inside of wood salad bowl. Combine sections from 2 or 3 oranges with leaves of 2 bunches of watercress. Toss in salad bowl with a plain French dressing. Makes 4 servings.

ORANGE-CHICKEN SALAD

4 cups diced cooked chicken (white meat only)
2 cups thinly sliced celery (white stalks only)
1 cup California walnuts, chopped
½ cup seedless green grapes
1 cup orange sections
Orange Cream Dressing
Salad greens

Combine all ingredients except dressing and greens, and chill. Toss with enough Orange Cream Dressing to moisten. Serve on a bed of greens. Makes 4 to 6 servings.

Orange Cream Dressing

Combine ¼ cup thawed frozen concentrated orange juice, ¼ cup mayonnaise, grated rind of 1 orange, ¼ teaspoon hot pepper sauce, and 1 cup heavy cream, whipped, just before serving. Makes about 2½ cups.

ORANGE FRENCH DRESSING

1¼ teaspoons salt
1 teaspoon celery seeds
½ teaspoon paprika
⅛ teaspoon white pepper
1 teaspoon finely chopped onion
1 garlic clove, crushed
2 tablespoons sugar
1 cup salad oil
⅔ cup fresh lemon juice
⅔ cup fresh orange segments, juice and all

Combine first 8 ingredients and let stand for 1 hour. Add remaining ingredients and mix well. Serve over apple salad. Makes 2 cups.

DESSERTS

ORANGES IN RED WINE

¾ cup sugar
1 cup dry red wine
1 cup water
2 whole cloves
½ teaspoon ground cinnamon
2 lemon slices
4 oranges

Mix sugar, red wine, and water in saucepan. Tie whole cloves, cinnamon, and 2 lemon slices in a small piece of cheesecloth. Put in saucepan. Bring to boil and simmer for 10 minutes, or until syrupy. Remove spice bag. Remove rind from oranges; reserve. Add segments to syrup. Chill. Serve with garnish of slivered orange rind. Makes 4 servings.

ORANGE FLUFF PUDDING

5 eggs, separated
½ cup sugar
Grated rind of 1 orange
1 envelope unflavored gelatin
Juice of 1 lemon
Juice of 1 orange
½ cup boiling water
⅛ teaspoon salt
Orange slices
Green grapes

Beat egg yolks until thick and lemon-colored; gradually beat in sugar and orange rind. Soften gelatin in fruit juices and dissolve in boiling water; add to egg-yolk mixture. Refrigerate until mixture just starts to set. Fold in the egg whites, beaten with salt until stiff. Pour into 2-quart ring mold. Refrigerate at least 4 hours. Unmold and decorate with orange slices and green grapes. Makes 6 to 8 servings.

ORANGE SOUFFLÉ

1 can (6 ounces) orange juice concentrate, thawed
¼ cup water
3 tablespoons butter
3 tablespoons all-purpose flour
4 eggs, separated
Dash of salt
Butter
Sugar
Rich custard sauce or whipped cream flavored with orange liqueur

Mix orange juice and add water. Melt butter and blend in flour. Slowly stir in orange juice. Cook over low heat, stirring constantly, until mixture thickens. Beat egg yolks until light and lemony and add to slightly cooled orange mixture. Beat egg whites with salt until they are stiff but still moist. Fold half of beaten whites into orange mixture rather thoroughly; then fold rest in very lightly. Butter a 2-quart soufflé dish and sprinkle bottom and sides lightly with sugar. Pour in orange mixture and bake in preheated moderate oven (375°F.) about 30 minutes. Serve with rich custard sauce. Makes 4 to 6 servings.

ORANGE VELVET ICE CREAM

2 egg yolks
1 cup light cream
¼ teaspoon salt
2 cups sugar
1 cup water
2 cups fresh orange juice
1 cup heavy cream, whipped
¼ cup finely diced or shredded candied orange peel

In top part of small double boiler beat egg yolks, light cream, and salt with rotary beater. Put over simmering water and cook, stirring constantly, until mixture is slightly thickened and coats a metal spoon; cool. Boil sugar, water, and juice for 5 minutes; cool. Combine mixtures and fold in cream. Partially freeze in crank-type freezer. Then add orange peel and finish freezing. Makes about 2 quarts.

ITALIAN ORANGE-RUM CAKE

3 eggs
1 cup sugar
2 teaspoons grated orange rind
3 tablespoons fresh orange juice
1 cup sifted all-purpose flour
1 teaspoon baking powder
Orange-Rum Topping
Orange slices, candied cherries, and whipped cream rosettes

Beat eggs until light. Gradually beat in sugar and continue to beat until mixture is thick and lemon-colored. Use an electric beater if possible, and beat at high speed for about 5 minutes. Stir in orange rind and juice. Sift flour with baking powder 3 times and fold into batter. Pour into buttered and floured 9-inch springform pan. Bake in preheated moderate oven (350°F.) for 30 minutes, or until cake tests done. Cool in pan. Pour Orange-Rum Topping over cooled cake and chill until serving time. Remove from pan. Decorate with oranges, cherries, and whipped-cream rosettes.

Orange-Rum Topping

1 envelope unflavored gelatin
¼ cup cold water
1 cup hot milk
¾ cup sugar
4 egg yolks, lightly beaten
⅔ cup dark rum
1 large orange, peeled and sectioned
1 cup heavy cream, whipped

Soften gelatin in cold water. Stir in hot milk and sugar. Cook over low heat until mixture is hot. Do not let boil. Gradually pour over egg yolks, stirring constantly. Add the rum. Set in bowl of cracked ice and stir constantly until cool and beginning to set. Fold in orange sections and whipped cream.

BRAZILIAN ORANGE CAKE

⅔ cup butter
2 cups sugar
Grated rind of 2 oranges
3 eggs, separated
⅔ cup orange juice
⅓ cup water
3 cups sifted cake flour
3 teaspoons baking baking powder
½ teaspoon salt
Orange Boiled Frosting

Cream butter, add sugar, and beat until fluffy. Add rind and beat in well-beaten egg yolks. Add orange juice and water alternately with mixed and sifted dry ingredients. Fold in stiffly beaten egg whites. Spoon into 2 greased paper-lined 9-inch layer-cake pans. Bake in preheated moderate oven (375°F.) for 25 minutes. Turn out on racks and cool. Spread Frosting between the layers and on top and sides of cake. Makes 8 to 10 servings.

Orange Boiled Frosting

1½ cups sugar
1 tablespoon light corn syrup
⅔ cup boiling water
¼ teaspoon salt
2 egg whites, stiffly beaten
Grated rind of 1 orange

Cook sugar, corn syrup, and water together until small amount of syrup forms a soft ball in cold water (242°F. on a candy thermometer). Pour gradually over salted egg whites, beating constantly until frosting has right consistency to spread. Fold in rind.

Orange Soufflé

FRESH ORANGE CHIFFON PIE

- 5 graham crackers
- 5 tablespoons sugar
- 2 teaspoons butter or margarine, melted
- 1 envelope unflavored gelatin
- 1½ cups orange juice
- 2 egg yolks
- ¼ teaspoon salt
- 1 tablespoon lemon juice
- 1 teaspoon vanilla extract
- 3 egg whites
- Fresh orange sections

Roll graham crackers into fine crumbs. Blend in 1 tablespoon sugar and melted butter. Save 1 tablespoon of crumb mixture to sprinkle over top. Sprinkle remaining crumbs over bottom and sides of buttered 9-inch pie pan. Bake in preheated moderate oven (375°F.) for 10 minutes. Remove from oven. Cool. Soften gelatin in ½ cup orange juice. Let stand for 5 minutes. Beat egg yolks lightly. Stir in remaining ¼ cup sugar and salt. Add remaining 1 cup orange juice and lemon juice. Mix well. Cook over hot water or low heat for 10 minutes, stirring constantly, or until thoroughly hot. Remove from heat and stir in softened gelatin and vanilla. Chill over ice water until mixture is about as thick as unbeaten egg whites. Beat egg whites until they stand in soft peaks. Fold into mixture. Turn into crumb-lined 9-inch pie pan. Chill until firm. Sprinkle remaining crumbs over top; garnish with fresh orange sections. Makes 6 servings.

ORANGE-AND-DATE TEA LOAF

3 cups sifted all-purpose flour
3 teaspoons baking powder
1 teaspoon salt
2 tablespoons sugar
1 cup sliced pitted dates
1 package (3 ounces) candied orange peel
1 egg, slightly beaten
1½ cups milk

Mix and sift dry ingredients. Add dates and orange peel. Combine egg and milk; stir into dry ingredients. Pour into well-greased loaf pan (9 x 5 x 3 inches). Bake in preheated moderate oven (325°F.) for 1 hour. Cool on rack; wrap in wax paper and store for 24 hours before slicing. Makes 1 loaf.

FLORENTINES

½ cup heavy cream
3 tablespoons butter
½ cup sugar
1¼ cups finely chopped almonds
⅓ cup sifted all-purpose flour
¾ cup finely chopped candied orange peel
Melted chocolate
Tiny colored candies

Combine cream, butter, and sugar in saucepan and bring to boil. Remove from heat and stir in almonds, flour, and orange peel. Drop by tablespoonfuls onto greased and floured cookie sheet, keeping cookies 3 inches apart. Bake in preheated moderate oven (350°F.) about 10 minutes. Cool for 5 minutes. Remove carefully with spatula to cake rack. Cool. Spiral melted chocolate over cookie tops and decorate with candies. Makes about 2 dozen 3-inch cookies.

OTHER ORANGE SPECIALTIES

SPICED ORANGE PEEL

1 quart orange peel, cut into strips ½ x 2 inches
Water
1¾ cups sugar
⅓ cup cider vinegar
1 tablespoon whole cloves
3 sticks cinnamon

Cover peel with water and let stand in refrigerator overnight. Drain, put in kettle, and cover with water. Bring to boil, drain, and again cover with water. Bring again to boil and drain. Cover with water, bring to boil for a third time, and simmer for 10 minutes, or until tender. Drain. Put peel and remaining ingredients in kettle and simmer for 5 minutes to form a thick syrup. Add peel and simmer, stirring frequently, for 5 minutes. Pour into hot sterilized ½-pint jars and seal. Makes about three ½-pint jars.

HONEYED ORANGE PEEL

Peel from 3 large oranges
Water
½ teaspoon salt
½ cup sugar
½ cup honey

Cover peel with water and add salt. Simmer for 30 minutes; drain. Cover again with water and simmer until tender; drain. Remove white inner portion of peel. Cut outer peel into strips. Bring sugar, honey, and ¼ cup water to boil. Add peel and simmer until clear. Cool in syrup for several hours. Reheat; then drain and spread out to dry on wax paper or foil. Roll in additional sugar if desired. Makes about ¾ pound.

JAMAICAN GOLD DOUBLOONS

½ cup (4 ounces) Jamaica rum
¾ cup fresh orange juice
Juice of 1 lime
1 teaspoon sugar
¼ cup orange liqueur
4 cups finely crushed ice
Mint sprigs

Mix all ingredients, except mint sprigs. Pour into 6 old-fashioned glasses. Decorate each with a mint sprig. Makes 6 servings.

ORANGEADE—Fresh, frozen, canned, or dehydrated orange juice mixed with water and flavored with sugar to taste. Lemon juice can be added to give the drink a tart-sweet flavor. Orangeade should be served chilled or with ice cubes. It can be garnished with a variety of fruits, mint leaves, etc.

Commercially made orangeade is available bottled and canned, with or without sugar; frozen concentrated, with or without sugar; and as a powder, also with or without added sugar.

ORANGEADE

Fill tall glasses half full of crushed ice. For each serving, prepare ¾ cup fresh orange juice, or use frozen orange juice concentrate and dilute according to directions on can. Add sugar syrup or lemon juice to taste and pour over ice. Stir well.

OREGANO [*Origanum vulgare*]—This popular herb, also called wild marjoram, is one variety of the aromatic plant origanum which is native to the Mediterranean region, but nowadays grows widely in northeast Canada and the United States. Oregano is a beautiful plant that grows in clumps with purplish, pink, lilac, or white flowers and reaches a height of two to three feet. it is the dark-green leaf, shaped like a roundish egg, that is used as a culinary herb. Leaves may be used fresh or dried. The tops of the plant may also be used.

The flavor is similar to that of sweet marjoram or thyme, all belonging to the mint family. Oregano is considerably more bitter and pungent, and should be used with discretion, Vegetable-juice cocktails and bean, beef, game, or tomato soups may be flavored with oregano. The herb adds pungency to beef, lamb, pork, veal, sausages, Swiss steak, poultry, fish, cheese spreads, or omelets, and it is essential to pizza. Oregano is often used as a seasoning in Mexican and Italian dishes. Fish, butter, cream, meat, spaghetti, or tomato sauces are improved by the addition of the herb, as are marinades for game. Oregano is good for seasoning many vegetables including broccoli, beans, carrots, Lima beans, mushrooms, onions, peas, potatoes, tomatoes, and aspic or potato salads. In short, like any other herb, it is to be used to taste, and with discretion. It is not only useful as a culinary herb for flavoring, but may be boiled alone as a potherb.

Oregano is sold in dried crumbled form, and is occasionally available ground. Fresh oregano, when in season, can be found in Italian, Spanish, and Greek neighborhood food stores.

MEXICAN MEATBALLS

1 pound ground beef
¼ cup white cornmeal
1 egg
1 garlic clove, minced
1 small onion, minced
½ teaspoon dried oregano
1¼ teaspoon salt
½ teaspoon pepper
Chili-Tomato Sauce

Mix all ingredients except sauce. Shape into tiny balls about ½ inch in diameter. Drop into boiling Chili-Tomato Sauce; cover and simmer for 5 minutes. Makes 4 servings.

Chili-Tomato Sauce

1 tablespoon shortening
1 small onion, chopped
1 garlic clove, minced
2 to 3 tablespoons chili powder
3 cups tomato juice
Salt

Melt shortening in large saucepan. Add onion and garlic and cook slowly until lightly browned. Add chili powder, tomato juice, and salt to taste. Cook for 10 minutes. Makes about 3 cups.

VEAL WITH MUSHROOMS

2 pounds veal steak, cut ¾ inch thick
½ cup red wine
2 tablespoons white vinegar
¼ cup chopped onion
1 garlic clove, mashed
1 teaspoon dried oregano
¼ cup olive oil
¼ cup butter or margarine
1 teaspoon salt
½ pound mushrooms, sliced

Cut meat into serving pieces. Mix red wine, vinegar, onion, garlic, oregano, and olive oil and pour over meat. Let stand in refrigerator overnight. Remove meat from marinade; reserve marinade. Brown meat on all sides in hot butter. Put meat in shallow baking pan and cover with marinade. Top with salt and sliced mushrooms. Cover. Bake in preheated moderate oven (350°F.) for 1 hour and 20 minutes. Makes 6 servings.

HAMBURGER PIZZA PIE

1 pound ground beef chuck or round
1 teaspoon instant seasoned meat tenderizer
1 small garlic clove, minced
1 can (8 ounces) tomato sauce
¼ teaspoon garlic salt
½ teaspoon sugar
¼ teaspoon Italian herb seasoning
1 sweet onion, thinly sliced
¼ pound Italian salami, thinly sliced
½ pound Mozzarella cheese, thinly sliced
1 can (6 ounces) chopped mushrooms, drained
¼ teaspoon dried oregano
¼ cup grated Parmesan cheese

Mix first 3 ingredients and pat into 12-inch pizza pan. Mix next 4 ingredients and spread on beef. Arrange onion and next 3 ingredients on beef in order given. Sprinkle with oregano and grated cheese. Bake in preheated very hot oven (450°F.) about 15 minutes, or until Mozzarella is bubbly. Makes 4 to 6 servings.

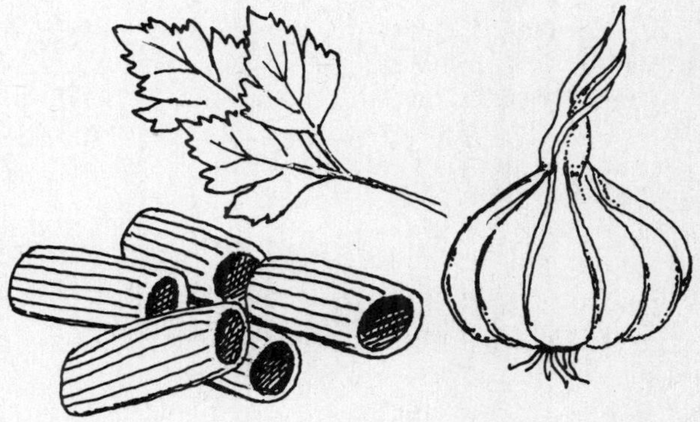

NEAPOLITAN RIGATONI

1 pound rigatoni
⅓ cup olive oil
1 garlic clove, minced
1 can (1 pound) stewed tomatoes
½ teaspoon salt
1 can (8 ounces) tomato sauce
¼ teaspoon coarse black pepper
1 teaspoon dried oregano
2 tablespoons chopped parsley

Cook and drain rigatoni; while pasta is cooking, make sauce. Heat olive oil in heavy saucepan. Add garlic and cook for 3 or 4 minutes. Add all other ingredients. Cook, stirring constantly, for 10 to 15 minutes. Makes 6 servings.

SAVORY MUSHROOMS WITH OREGANO

1 pound large mushrooms
3 tablespoons olive oil
1 garlic clove, mashed
1 teaspoon dried oregano
Salt and pepper

Cut mushrooms into thick slices, splitting the stems once. Heat olive oil in large skillet. When just below smoking, add mushrooms. Cook for 10 minutes, stirring frequently. Add garlic, oregano, and salt and pepper to taste. Serve as a vegetable, or as an entrée with buttered hot French bread and a tossed green salad. Makes 2 to 4 servings.

ORGEAT—A syrup used in France, Spain, Italy, and other Latin countries as a refreshing drink when mixed with water, or as a flavoring for frostings and fillings. Originally orgeat was made from barley mixed with almonds, but today the syrup is made from an emulsion of almonds and sugar with a little rosewater or orange-flower water added. The origin of the drink is probably Arabic or Persian.

Orgeat is imported and sold bottled in gourmet food stores.

ORTOLAN—A central and southern European bunting about six inches in length. The bird frequents orchards and its name is derived from the Latin *hortulanus* or "gardener." Although now almost extinct, the ortolan was long considered a great delicacy, and large numbers were netted and fattened for the table, with gourmets maintaining that the best method of preparation was to roast the birds in the oven or on a spit, and only in their own fat.

OSSOBUCO or **OSSO BUCO**—An Italian dish made with veal shanks, shin, or knuckle; white wine; olive oil; tomato purée; chopped anchovies; etc., and served on saffron-colored rice. The literal translation is "hollow bone."

OSSOBUCO

4 meaty veal shanks, about 2 inches thick
All-purpose flour
Salt and pepper to taste
¼ cup olive oil
1 garlic clove, minced
½ cup dry white wine
½ cup tomato purée
1 anchovy fillet, minced
Few sprigs of parsley, chopped
Grated rind of 1 lemon
Hot cooked rice
Pinch of saffron

Dredge veal shanks with flour seasoned with salt and pepper. Brown on all sides in hot olive oil. Add garlic, wine, and tomato purée. Bring to boil, cover, and simmer for 1 hour, or until meat is tender. Add anchovy, parsley, and lemon rind. Heat well, and serve on rice lightly mixed with the saffron. Makes 4 servings.

OUTDOOR COOKING AND EATING

by CRAIG CLAIBORNE

Everything tastes better out-of doors. If I have heard that once, I have heard it a hundred times within the past few months. For me "out-of-doors" is a little over 100 miles from New York City as the sea gull flies. It is light years away from the subway and Times Square and the oppressive heat of Manhattan. It is blue sky and a pebbly beach and good friends who love to cook both indoors and out.

"Out-of-doors" is in reality a small plot of ground less than an acre on which is set a somewhat small, prefabricated house that is far more endearing than a castle in Spain. It is a house surrounded by fruit trees, apples, wild cherry and pear, by cedar and an underbrush of bayberry and beach plum. The front lawn, so to speak, is Gardiners Bay, and with a small boat during the summer there is a constant harvest of sea bass and striped bass, blowfish, porgies, weakfish, mussels and clams. With a net we can haul in whitebait for dredging with flour and cooking in fat for the keenest first course imaginable.

In addition to myself, we are the Pierre Franeys and the Auguste Chardenets, good neighbors who enjoy good food and good fishing. In summer there is rarely a meal that doesn't begin with clams on the half shell or with steamed clams or mussels. During the summer when the Franey children are free from school the charcoal grill does yeoman work at least twice a day and sometimes more often if hungry guests drop by unexpectedly.

Since I am a professional food man whose closest friends have a professional interest in food, the meals in my house may run a fairly fancy gamut. When fancy city folk arrive for a weekend the kitchen may produce such elegant dishes as creamed sweetbreads in patty shells, fresh asparagus with hollandaise, or chicken with an egg-and-cream sauce supreme. Then there comes a time when the appetite cries for the simplicity of a grilled steak or hamburger, fresh corn on-the-cob, or a summer casserole with all the good things the small garden to the side of the house has to offer (tomatoes, Italian squash, green peppers, eggplant), and then, for a final touch, fresh watermelon dripping with honeyed sweetness. The refrigerator is stocked throughout the summer with an unending supply of iced tea, beer, cola drinks, and for serious occasions chilled white wine. A serious occasion can happen at almost any time. In late afternoon, for example, with fresh-caught sea bass cooked in a skillet on the beach.

Food is something to be treated seriously, or at least it should be if we are to believe Arnold Bennett who observed that "A man of 60 has spent more than three years of his life in eating." A hamburger or a sparerib is just as important as a soufflé and deserves as much care. All things should be done in moderation but if eat we must, then let us feast and enjoy it to the fullest. Pleasure is good for digestion.

Attractive service pieces, sparkling glasses, and decorative plates add to the pleasure, To me they are as important outdoors as they are at a formal dinner. I do not mind washing dishes. I do not mind washing them after breakfast, lunch, or dinner. Unfortunately, I am not for hire.

I am an addict of charcoal-grilled foods and always will be. Food rarely tastes better than when it is cooked properly over hot coals and part of it is because the open air and the whole atmosphere of cooking out-of-doors whets the appetite and sharpens the taste buds.

It is certainly not necessary to have elaborate equipment in order to use charcoal successfully. I happen to own a grill with a large fire basket that can be raised or lowered with the greatest of ease; it has a hood; it has an electric spit; it does the job.

Such a grill is a convenience but not essential. Food can be grilled with great success on an improvised one made of stones or bricks with a sturdy metal grill laid across. Ideally, it should be possible to raise or lower the grill from the fire or raise or lower the fire. The reason is obvious: to adjust the cooking temperature by altering the distance between the source of heat and the food being grilled. Some manufacturers of grills disagree with me that the amount of charcoal used in grilling is not of the essence. There are those who believe they do not enjoy the full flavor of smoke from a grill and I do. I believe in a full fire-basket of hot coals and by hot I mean that the coals should not be used for cooking until white ash forms. That is more or less standard procedure in all books. It may be commonplace to add that the smoked flavor of charcoal-grilled foods does not come from the taste of charcoal itself. White-hot charcoal is tasteless. The smoke and resultant flavor come from the fat that falls into the fire.

CASSEROLE BUFFET

If there is one single request that crosses my desk as a professional food writer, it is for dishes that can be made ahead and then reheated. Another that is commonplace is the request for dishes to be cooked for large gatherings. The best recipe that I know that meets both requirements is for a spaghetti casserole with chicken and *chorizos,* which are Spanish sausages. These sausages have a wonderful flavor and are available in Spanish markets in metropolitan areas. This spaghetti dish will require the better part of a morning to prepare, but it can be made several hours in advance, and rest assured that in this case the game is worth the candle. For those who do not have access to the sausages, it may be made without them.

MENU

Shrimps with Anchovy Butter
Chicken and Chorizo Spaghetti
Garlic Olives
Tossed Green Salad
with French Dressing
Parsley and Green-Onion
Stuffed Bread
Lotus Ice Cream
Iced Tea

SHRIMPS WITH ANCHOVY BUTTER

5 pounds raw shrimps
2 cups butter, melted
3 tablespoons anchovy paste
Juice of 1 lemon
Cayenne to taste

Using a pair of kitchen shears split shrimps down the back shell but do not cut through the last tail segment. Peel off the shell but leave the last tail segment intact. Rinse and dry shrimps. Arrange them on 6 skewers and place over charcoal. Brush lightly with butter and broil about 3 minutes to a side. Cooking time will depend on size of shrimps, heat of coals, and distance of shrimps, from coals. Turn once; brush with butter. To the remaining butter add remaining ingredients. Beat lightly with a fork to blend. Serve as a dip for the shrimps. Makes 16 servings.

CHICKEN AND CHORIZO SPAGHETTI

2 roasting chickens (about 4 pounds each)
2 onions
1 large carrot, cut into 1-inch lengths
2 celery stalks with leaves, halved
Salt
3 parsley sprigs
10 peppercorns
Water
1 can (2 pounds 3 ounces) tomatoes, preferably Italian plum variety
¾ cup butter
2 cups finely chopped celery
2 cups finely chopped green peppers
3 cups finely chopped onions
8 to 10 garlic cloves, finely minced
1 pound mushrooms, thinly sliced, or 1 cup drained canned button mushrooms
7 chorizos (about 1½ pounds)
1 pound ground round steak
1 bay leaf
½ teaspoon crushed red pepper
¼ teaspoon dried thyme
Freshly ground black pepper
1 cup all-purpose flour
6 cups chicken broth
½ cup heavy cream
2 pounds thin spaghetti
1 pound shredded sharp Cheddar cheese
2 or more cups grated Parmesan or Romano cheese

Place chickens in a kettle and add onions, carrot, celery stalks and leaves, salt to taste, parsley, peppercorns, and water to depth of about 1 inch. Bring to boil and simmer until tender, 1 to 1½ hours. (If stewing chickens are used, it will take longer.) Let chickens remain in broth until ready to use.

Put tomatoes in a large kettle. Melt 2 tablespoons butter in a large skillet and add chopped celery, chopped green peppers, chopped onions, and garlic. Cook, stirring, until onions are translucent. Add to tomatoes. Melt 2 tablespoons butter in same skillet and cook mushrooms; add to tomatoes.

Slice chorizos and cook them in skillet until they are slightly browned. Pour off most of the fat and add chorizos to tomatoes. Cook ground meat in same skillet until it loses its red color. Add bay leaf, crushed red pepper, thyme, and salt and pepper to taste. Add to tomatoes. Simmer for 20 to 30 minutes, stirring occasionally so it will not stick to the skillet.

Melt remaining ½ cup butter in saucepan and add flour, stirring preferably with a wire whisk. Add 6 cups broth in which the chicken cooked. When mixture is thickened and smooth, continue cooking, stirring, for 5 minutes or longer. Stir in heavy cream and combine with tomato sauce. Add a little more salt if necessary.

Meanwhile remove skin and bones from chicken and tear or cut into large bite-size pieces. Cook spaghetti in a large container of boiling salted water. The water should be boiling vigorously and the spaghetti should be immersed in it. Stir with a 2-prong fork until all strands are wilted and under water. Continue stirring until a roaring boil is reached again. This is important: cook the spaghetti only until it is barely tender. Do not cook as long as the package directions say because the spaghetti will be reheated later. Drain spaghetti and rinse it to prevent strands from sticking together.

To assemble the dish, cover the bottom of greased large heatproof casserole or roasting pan with a little sauce. Add a layer of spaghetti, then of chicken, Cheddar cheese, and more sauce. Continue building up layers until all the ingredients are used, ending with a final layer of cheese. It may be necessary to add more broth if, as the casserole stands, it seems to become dry. The sauce should be a little, but not too, soupy. Set aside until ready to serve.

When ready to serve, preheat the oven to hot (400°F.). Place casserole in oven and bake without cover until spaghetti is piping hot and bubbling on top. Do not overcook or spaghetti will become mushy. Serve with grated Parmesan on the side. Makes about 16 servings.
NOTE: The chorizo can be omitted or pepperoni can be substituted.

GARLIC OLIVES

1 jar (1 pound 5 ounces) large green olives
1 can (1 pound) black olives
3 tablespoons wine vinegar
Juice of ½ lemon
1 to 3 garlic cloves, crushed
¾ cup olive oil
10 peppercorns, crushed
Crushed red pepper (optional)

Drain olives and crush them slightly. Put them in a mixing bowl or other container. Add remaining ingredients and stir well to coat all the olives. Chill, stirring occasionally, for several hours or overnight. Serve as an appetizer. These olives keep well in the refrigerator. Makes about 3 pounds.

TOSSED GREEN SALAD

There is a lot of nonsense at large about salad making. Some say the greens should be torn apart with the fingers. I say it bruises the lettuce. Preferably, the greens should be cut into bite-size pieces with a knife or scissors. In the same vein, salad dressing should never be made far in advance and refrigerated, particularly if it contains a garlic clove. Overnight the garlic loses its freshness and gives indigestion. It is also true that salad bowls should not only be washed, they should be scrubbed after each use. An unwashed salad bowl becomes rancid and the subsequent salads not only have a questionable taste but a questionable odor.

FRENCH DRESSING FOR SALAD

This is the best standard recipe for a French dressing I know.

Salt
1 garlic clove (optional)
2 tablespoons prepared mustard, preferably Dijon or Düsseldorf
3 tablespoons wine vinegar
2 tablespoons finely chopped shallots or green onions
¾ cup olive or salad oil
Freshly ground black pepper to taste

Sprinkle the bottom of a salad bowl with salt and rub it with a garlic clove. Add mustard and stir in vinegar with a fork. Add shallots and oil and salt and pepper to taste. Stir well before adding crisp greens. Makes about 1 cup.

PARSLEY AND GREEN-ONION STUFFED BREAD

3 long crusty loaves of French or Italian bread
1 cup butter or margarine
¾ cup finely chopped parsley
¾ cup finely chopped green onions (green part and all)

Split loaves lengthwise but do not cut through both sides of the bread. Leave one side as a "hinge." Melt butter and stir in parsley and onion. Spoon the mixture into the center of split loaves. Wrap each loaf in heavy-duty aluminum foil and place over hot coals until heated through. Or bake in preheated hot oven (400°F.) about 10 minutes. Slice bread and serve piping hot. Makes about 16 servings.

LOTUS ICE CREAM

12 lemons
6 cups sugar
12 cups light cream
6 cups milk

Slice away and discard the ends of 3 lemons. Cut into thin, almost transparent slices. Remove seeds and cut slices into halves to make crescent shapes. Squeeze remaining lemons and combine juice with sugar. Add lemon slices, cover, and refrigerate overnight. Stir.

Combine cream and milk and pour into the churn of an ice-cream freezer. Cover and if possible place the churn in an electric freezer about 10 minutes. Do not freeze at this point. Add lemon mixture to the cream and place churn in the ice-cream freezer. Freeze according to the directions and keep frozen until ready to use. Makes 18 servings.

FISH PICNIC

My dear friend Pierre Franey is probably the greatest chef alive, although I may be prejudiced since I have been for years almost part and parcel of his family. He was chef at Le Pavillon for twenty-five years and is now a vice president of Howard Johnson's. He is the one who first introduced me to the pleasures of fish with rosemary, a splendid combination particularly if the fish are straight from Gardiners Bay and if they are cooked over an open fire on the beach.

MENU

Cocktail Sausages
with White Wine
Grilled Fish
with Mushrooms and Rosemary
Corn on-the-Cob
with Pepper Butter
Cucumbers with Sour Cream
Pickled Beets
Tomatoes Vinaigrette
Rolls
Fruit with Cheese
Beer Cola Coffee

COCKTAIL SAUSAGES WITH WHITE WINE

24 cocktail sausages
2 tablespoons butter, melted
Dry white wine

Put sausages on skewers and brush with melted butter. Place over charcoal and brown lightly. Brush with a little dry white wine. Do not overcook. Serve immediately with assorted hot mustards including English Mustard. Makes 6 to 8 servings.

English Mustard

Spoon 2 tablespoons dry mustard into a small mixing bowl and add beer, milk, or water, a little at a time, to make a smooth paste. Thin the mustard to the consistency of heavy cream. Cover and let stand for 10 minutes to develop flavor.

GRILLED FISH WITH MUSHROOMS AND ROSEMARY

6 small whole sea bass or other fish suitable for frying
Sprigs of fresh rosemary or 6 teaspoons dried rosemary
Salt and pepper to taste
All-purpose flour
Peanut oil
¾ cup butter or margarine
1 pound mushrooms, thinly sliced
Juice of 1 lemon
Lemon wedges
3 tablespoons chopped parsley

Clean the fish and rinse under cold water. Dry inside and out. Put 1 sprig of fresh rosemary or 1 teaspoon dried in the cavity of each fish. Sprinkle fish inside and out with salt and pepper and dredge with flour. Heat ¼ inch of oil in a large skillet. When it is hot, brown the fish quickly on one side, then on the other. Do not overcook. Immediately transfer fish to a hot serving platter or another skillet and wipe out the skillet with a cloth or paper towel. Quickly add the butter to the skillet, heat quickly, and add mushrooms. Stir; when the mushrooms are wilted, sprinkle with lemon juice. Do not burn the butter. Pour the mushrooms and sauce over the fish. Garnish with wedges of lemon sprinkled with chopped parsley. Serve immediately. Makes 6 servings.

CORN ON-THE-COB

12 ears of fresh corn on-the-cob
Water to cover
Pepper Butter

Do not shuck the ears until they are ready to be cooked. Bring enough water to cover the corn to a boil in a large kettle and when it is boiling vigorously add the shucked ears of corn, one by one. When the water returns to the boil, cover the kettle and turn off the heat. Let the corn rest in the water for 5 to 10 minutes and serve immediately with Pepper Butter. Makes 6 servings.

Pepper Butter

½ cup butter
Coarsely cracked black pepper to taste

Cream butter with pepper, roll into a sausage shape in wax paper, and chill until ready to use. Unwrap and serve with hot corn on-the-cob.

CUCUMBERS WITH SOUR CREAM

2 large cucumbers, washed and dried
1½ cups dairy sour cream
1 tablespoon wine vinegar
Salt and pepper to taste
¼ cup chopped chives, green onion, or dill, or any combination of these

Run the tines of a fork down the sides of the cucumbers. Slice them thin. Combine remaining ingredients in a mixing bowl and toss gently with cucumbers. Chill. Serve sprinkled, if desired, with additional chopped herbs. Makes about 6 servings.

PICKLED BEETS

8 to 12 medium-size beets (1 quart sliced)
Salt
1 tablespoon pickling spices
2 tablespoons sugar
Freshly ground black pepper
1 cup wine vinegar

Cut tops from the beets but leave 1 inch of stem. Wash beets and put them in a kettle. Add water to cover to the depth of 1 inch and salt to taste. Bring to the boil and cook for 1 to 2 hours depending on size and age of beets, until beets are tender. Drain; when cool enough to handle, peel them. Slice the beets and put them in a mixing bowl. Add remaining ingredients, and chill. Serve cold. The beets will keep for several days in the refrigerator. Makes 8 or more servings.

TOMATOES VINAIGRETTE

3 to 6 red tomatoes, depending on size
Salt and pepper
¾ cup finely chopped sweet onions (Bermuda or Italian)
½ cup finely chopped parsley
¼ cup wine vinegar
½ cup olive oil

Wash and dry tomatoes and pare away the cores. Peel them, if desired, and cut them into fairly thick slices. Arrange them on a serving dish and sprinkle liberally with salt and pepper. Scatter the onions and parsley over the tomatoes and sprinkle with vinegar and oil. Serve immediately. Makes 6 servings.

CHICKEN DINNER

Perhaps it is because I am a child of the South (Mississippi) or a child of the Depression, but I have an absolute passion for chicken in almost any form. During my early youth chicken appeared on the table once a day and more often than not twice a day. I like cold fried chicken and hot fried chicken. Even more (a taste developed perhaps during a period when I studied in France), I have a boundless appetite for roast chicken, either hot or cold. They will never invent the dish, perhaps, more delicious than cold roast chicken for a picnic. A loaf of bread, a bird, and a bottle and that is paradise, now.

MENU

King's Point Pâté
Cold Roast Chicken on Bed of Chicory
Gardiners Bay Potato Salad
Hard-Cooked Eggs
French Bread
Watermelon
Espresso

KING'S POINT PÂTÉ

2 pounds salt pork
2 pounds chicken livers
1 pound lean pork
1 pound lean veal
Boiling water
1 cup dry white wine
2 tablespoons brandy
¼ teaspoon each ground allspice, bay leaf, and thyme
2 teaspoons salt
2 black truffles, coarsely chopped
1 cup heavy cream
4 egg yolks, lightly beaten
Sliced red pepper
Parsley or watercress

Remove rind from salt pork and tough membranes from chicken livers, pork, and veal. Cut all the meats into 1½-inch cubes. Place salt pork in a pan, cover with boiling water, and bring to the boil. Simmer for 5 minutes, drain, and add to livers, pork, and veal. Combine wine and brandy, allspice, bay leaf, thyme, and salt and pour mixture over the meats. Let stand for 1 day, covered, in the refrigerator. Turn the meats occasionally to marinate on all sides. Preheat the oven to slow (325°F.). Drain meats, reserving marinade. Grind meats twice, using first the coarsest and then the finest blade of food grinder; then add the marinade and truffles. Add cream and egg yolks and blend well.

Turn mixture into 2 bread pans, 9 x 5 x 3 inches. Place them in a pan of hot water and bake for 2 hours, or until done. Remove pans from water and let stand at room temperature for 2 hours. Loosen the loaves with a sharp knife, cover with a platter, and invert to unmold. Chill. Garnish the top with sliced red pepper and the base of the loaves with parsley or watercress. Slice and serve with French bread or buttered toast. Makes 2 loaves, or about 30 servings.

COLD ROAST CHICKEN

3 frying chickens (3 pounds each)
Salt and pepper
3 small onions
1½ bay leaves
Dried thyme
½ cup butter or margarine
3 celery stalks, coarsely chopped
3 carrots, coarsely chopped
2 parsley sprigs

Preheat oven to very hot (450°F.). Sprinkle chickens inside and out with salt and pepper. Place 1 onion, ½ bay leaf, pinch of thyme, and approximately 1 teaspoon butter in the cavity of each. Tie legs of chickens together securely. Heat remaining 7 tablespoons butter in a large open heatproof skillet or roasting pan and place chickens in it on their sides. Scatter vegetables around them and place the skillet in oven. Cook for 15 minutes; baste with a large spoon. Turn chickens to the other side and baste. Cook for 15 minutes longer and place the chickens on their backs. Continue basting and cooking for about 30 minutes, or until done. The chickens, when done, should be golden-brown and when the thigh is pierced with a fork the liquid should run clear. Remove chickens from the oven and cool slighty. Chill until ready to serve. Cut into halves. Makes 6 servings.

GARDINERS BAY POTATO SALAD

3 pounds raw potatoes
Water
Salt to taste
½ cup oil and vinegar dressing
¾ cup finely chopped seeded peeled cucumber
3 shallots or green onions, finely chopped (green part and all)
1 cup mayonnaise
1 teaspoon celery seed
3 tablespoons fresh lemon juice
3 tablespoons chopped fresh basil
Freshly ground black pepper to taste

Wash potatoes and place in a small kettle or saucepan. Add water to cover, salt, and simmer until done, 20 minutes or longer depending on size. Drain and peel the warm potatoes and slice into a mixing bowl. Pour oil and vinegar dressing over them, and chill. Before serving add remaining ingredients and toss lightly; garnish with hard-cooked eggs and parsley, if desired. Makes 6 servings.

STEAK PARTY

One of my favorite quotations belongs to Alice B. Toklas, best known as the companion of Gertrude Stein. A resident of Paris, she is highly knowledgeable about fine cuisine and when someone once asked, "How many does this recipe serve?", she answered with admirable candor,

Steak Party

"How should I know how many it serves? It depends—on their appetites—what else they have for dinner—whether they like it or not."

The thought could be turned to good purpose to answer those who ask how to charcoal-grill a steak. How thick, for example, is the steak? How close will it be to the coals? How hot are the coals and is the steak at room temperature or is it chilled from the refrigerator? Is there a breeze blowing?

There is no one on earth who could formulate an inviolate rule of thumb for grilling steak because there are so many variables involved. For those who insist, however, this is as good as any. With a hot fire to cook a 1-inch-thick steak very rare, try 3 or 4 minutes to a side. For well done, 10 minutes to a side or more. If the steak is nearly 3 inches thick, cook it for 10 to 15 minutes to a side for rare, and for well done for 20 to 25 minutes to a side, but not according to conscience. Anyone with a conscience would have no appetite for a well-done steak. In the end, the best timetable to use is personal judgment if not trial and error. Let us profit, praise be, by yesterday's mis-steaks.

MENU

Big 3-Inch-Thick
Sirloin to Slice
Three Sauces:
Mustard, Shallot or
Green-Onion, and Mushroom
Baked Potatoes with Coriander
Fireplace Road Succotash
Twisted Bread or Hard Rolls
Strawberry and
Almond Cheesecake
Coffee

MUSTARD SAUCE

1 tablespoon dry mustard
Water
2 tablespoons finely chopped shallots or onion
3 tablespoons butter or margarine
¼ cup dry white wine
1 cup brown sauce or canned beef gravy
Salt to taste
Freshly ground black pepper to taste
1 tablespoon lemon juice

Place mustard in a cup and add enough water to make a thin paste. Let stand for 10 minutes to develop flavor. Cook shallots in 2 tablespoons butter, stirring, for about 1 minute. Add wine and cook until liquid is reduced by half. Add brown sauce and salt and pepper and simmer for about 15 minutes. Add lemon juice and remove sauce from the heat. Stir in mustard and swirl in remaining 1 tablespoon butter. Do not cook after mustard is added. Serve hot. Makes about 1 cup.

SHALLOT OR GREEN-ONION SAUCE

¼ cup finely chopped shallots or green onions
Butter or margarine
2 tablespoons tarragon vinegar
½ cup dry white wine
1 tablespoon bottled steak sauce
Salt and freshly ground black pepper

Cook shallots in ¼ cup butter, stirring frequently, over moderate heat for about 1 minute. Add vinegar and continue cooking about 2 minutes. Add wine and simmer for 5 minutes. Add steak sauce and salt and pepper to taste. Remove from heat and swirl in 1 tablespoon butter. Serve immediately. Makes about 1 cup.

MUSHROOM SAUCE

1 tablespoon chopped shallots or green onions
¼ pound mushrooms, sliced thin
3 tablespoons butter or margarine
1 teaspoon fresh lemon juice
1½ cups brown sauce or canned beef gravy

Cook shallots and mushrooms in butter for 5 minutes, stirring occasionally. Add lemon juice and brown sauce and blend well. Bring to boil and serve hot. Makes about 2 cups.

BAKED POTATOES WITH CORIANDER

12 large potatoes for baking, washed and dried well
Bacon fat or shortening
¾ cup butter
Salt and freshly ground black pepper to taste
About 20 coriander seeds, crushed in a mortar with pestle or under a heavy skillet

Preheat oven to hot (425°F.). Rub outside of potatoes with bacon fat and place on a rack in the oven. Bake for 40 minutes to 1 hour, depending on the size. To test for doneness, press fingers into the sides of potatoes, guarding fingers with a heavy cloth. Make a large deep gash down the center of potatoes, loosen pulp with a fork, and fill opening of each with 1 tablespoon butter. Sprinkle with salt, pepper, and coriander and serve immediately. Makes 12 servings.

NOTE: Other ground spices such as cuminseed and nutmeg are also good in baked potatoes.

FIREPLACE ROAD SUCCOTASH

⅓ cup olive oil
3 garlic cloves, peeled and chopped
2 cups thinly sliced onions
1 medium-size eggplant, peeled and cut into large cubes
¼ cup all-purpose flour
6 zucchini (about 2 pounds), scrubbed and cut into 1-inch slices
3 green peppers, seeded and cut into strips
Salt and freshly ground black pepper
5 red ripe tomatoes, peeled and chopped
2 cups fresh corn, cut from the cob

Heat oil and cook garlic and onion until onion is translucent. Transfer garlic and onion to a flameproof casserole. Dredge eggplant with flour and brown it lightly in same skillet. It may be necessary to add more oil. Add zucchini and green peppers. Stir them around in the skillet and add salt and pepper to taste. Pour mixture into greased casserole, cover, and simmer gently about 1 hour; add a little water if necessary. Add tomatoes, stir gently, and simmer, uncovered, until thickened, 20 to 30 minutes. Ten minutes before the dish is done, stir in the corn. Makes about 12 servings.

STRAWBERRY AND ALMOND CHEESECAKE

2 cups graham-cracker crumbs
⅓ cup melted butter
11 ounces cream cheese, softened
2 eggs
¾ cup sugar
½ teaspoon vanilla extract
2 cups dairy sour cream
¼ cup toasted whole almonds
Whole strawberries
¼ cup currant jelly
1 tablespoon water

Combine crumbs and butter and press into 9-inch pie pan. Preheat oven to moderate (350°F.). Place cream cheese in a large mixing bowl and blend slowly with an electric mixer. When cream cheese is fairly smooth, add eggs, one at a time, beating mixture well after each addition. Continue beating on low speed. Gradually add ½ cup sugar and vanilla. Pour mixture into prepared crust. Bake for 20 minutes. Blend sour cream with remaining ¼ cup sugar and almonds. Spread mixture evenly over top of pie. Turn off oven heat. Return pie to oven for 4 minutes. Cool pie briefly, then chill until set. Before serving garnish top with whole strawberries. Glaze with currant jelly melted with water and heated to dissolve. Makes 6 servings. Make 2 pies for 12 servings.

HAMBURGERS SUPREME

Whether you are thinking of a backyard cookout or have a picnic site in mind by some secluded stream, hamburgers are always good. Here is a menu which is supreme.

Again, harkening back to my childhood, one of the delights of youth was driving to a combination service station and sandwich shop. This was, in fact, a principal diversion for the entire town: going to "Charlie Labella's for a hamburger and a Coke." One of the great mysteries of the town was how Labella made anything as delicious as those hamburgers, served with a sauce containing chili powder. Years later in doing research on Romanian cuisine I found a recipe for a grilled meat dish with garlic and discovered what I believe to be the closely guarded secret of the Labella family. It was the simple addition of garlic to the meat before it was grilled, rather than to the sauce.

In any event, garlic hamburgers are delicious for those who enjoy garlic. And chili is good anytime.

MENU

Hot Clam-Juice Cocktail
Garlic Hamburgers
on Toasted Buns
Chili con Carne Sauce
Shaved Lettuce
Mexican Potato Chips
Pickles
Anise Fruit Cup

HOT CLAM-JUICE COCKTAIL

Bring 4 to 6 cups fresh or bottled clam juice to the boil and sprinkle with celery salt. Ladle into 6 hot cups or mugs and sprinkle a little fresh lemon juice over each serving. Makes 6 servings.

GARLIC HAMBURGERS ON TOASTED BUNS

2 pounds ground round steak or sirloin
1 garlic clove, finely minced, or more to taste
Salt and pepper to taste
6 to 8 toasted buns
6 to 8 pats of butter
2 cups Chili con Carne Sauce
Shaved lettuce

Place meat in mixing bowl and add garlic salt, and pepper. Mix lightly but thoroughly and shape into 6 to 8 patties. Grill to the desired degree of doneness and place each on a hot toasted bun. Top each with a pat of butter and shaved lettuce. Serve sauce separately. Makes 6 to 8 servings.

Chili con Carne Sauce

½ pound twice-ground pork or veal
½ cup minced onion
½ garlic clove, finely minced, or more to taste
2 tablespoons olive oil
1 cup tomato purée
½ cup water
3 tablespoons tomato paste
½ teaspoon ground cuminseed
½ bay leaf
Salt to taste
1 tablespoon chili powder, or more to taste

Cook meat, onion, and garlic in olive oil until meat loses color. Add remaining ingredients and stir to sauce consistency. Simmer, stirring occasionally, about 30 minutes. When finished, the sauce should have the consistency of thick soup. If necessary, thin with additional tomato purée. Makes about 2 cups.

MEXICAN POTATO CHIPS

Use enough potato chips to fill a 2-quart bowl. Sprinkle the chips lightly with juice of 1 lime, tossing gently. Sprinkle with hot pepper sauce, salt, and steak sauce to taste. Serve immediately. Makes 6 servings.

ANISE FRUIT CUP

½ cup sugar
¾ cup water
2 tablespoons fresh lemon or lime juice
½ teaspoon aniseed
Dash of salt
2 cups fresh orange sections
2 cups fresh strawberries
1 cup diced pears
1 cup seedless grapes

Combine sugar, water, lemon juice, aniseed, and salt in a saucepan and cook for 2 minutes. Bring to the boil and simmer for 10 minutes. Cover; leave for 10 minutes. Chill. Prepare fruits. Place in bowl; pour syrup over. Chill. Makes 6 servings.

OUTDOOR MEALS

TIPS FOR OUTDOOR EATING

A small sharp paring knife is a handy item to take to a picnic. For safety's sake, carry knife in a plastic toothbrush holder.

Stack paper plates for a picnic with a sheet of waxed paper between plates. Serve the first course on the paper, which keeps food from soaking into the plate, and after the first course remove the paper and use the plate for dessert (saves work and paper).

Carry unpeeled hard-cooked eggs and soft fruits such as plums in egg cartons.

Empty plastic pill bottles make good containers for dressings, catsup, mustard, etc. Wash thoroughly before using.

Put salt in an empty seasoning or tenderizer jar. This will give you a handy shaker and the screw top will keep salt from spilling.

Freeze individual cans of flavored bouillon (or fruit or vegetable juice) and pack them frozen. By lunchtime, they'll be the right temperature for drinking. Pack miniature can openers.

For easier eating, make meat sandwiches with several thin slices of meat rather than a single thick one.

Pack cubes of cold cuts on toothpicks for dunking in catsup or mustard.

Fill wide-mouthed vacuum containers with ice cream, refreeze, wrap in foil or pack with canned ice and they'll keep until lunchtime. Put gelatin desserts and frozen puddings in these containers too.

SOUPS

CHILLED CLAM AND TOMATO SOUP

Mix 2 chilled cans (10½ ounces each) condensed tomato soup, 1 bottle clam juice and 2⅓ cups cold water. Add lemon juice to taste and garnish with sliced lemon and chopped parsley. Makes 6 servings.

TUNA-CORN CHOWDER

2 cans (6½ or 7 ounces each) tuna
2 tablespoons instant minced onion
1 cup water
2 cups diced peeled raw potatoes
1 can (1 pound) cream-style corn
3 cups milk
2 teaspoons salt
2 tablespoons parsley flakes
¼ teaspoon hot pepper sauce

Drain 2 tablespoons oil from tuna. Sauté onion in oil, stirring, a few minutes. Add water and potatoes, cover and cook 10 minutes over low heat until potatoes are tender. Add tuna and remaining ingredients and heat thoroughly, about 10 minutes longer. Makes 6 generous servings.

MAIN DISHES

MEAT-VEGETABLE BUNDLES

Rehydrate 1 tablespoon instant minced onion in ¼ cup cold water 10 minutes. Mix thoroughly with 2 pounds meat-loaf mix. Shape mixture in 6 patties. Arrange enough carrot sticks, onion slices, potato wedges and green and red pepper rings with each patty to make one serving on large square of foil. Sprinkle with salt, pepper and oregano. Fold each packet to seal. Cook over hot coals 1 hour, or until meat and vegetables are done (check one packet). Sprinkle carrots and potatoes with chopped parsley (fresh or dried). Makes 6 servings.

Meat-Vegetable Bundles
Barbecued Beans

GRILLED MINTED LAMB CHOPS

6 double loin lamb chops
Salt, pepper and dried rosemary
¼ cup butter or margarine, melted
½ cup dry white wine
1 teaspoon Worcestershire
¼ cup mint jelly
2 tablespoons finely chopped fresh mint

Sprinkle chops with salt, pepper and rosemary. Put on grill 6 inches above gray coals and cook, turning occasionally, 15 minutes. Mix remaining ingredients and heat in saucepan on grill until jelly is melted. Brush chops with mixture and cook 15 minutes, or until chops are done, brushing with glaze every few minutes. Makes 6 servings.
NOTE: Chops can also be cooked in broiler indoors.

GLAZED PORK CHOPS WITH FRUIT

½ cup honey
½ cup lime or lemon juice
¼ cup dark corn syrup or 2 tablespoons firmly packed brown sugar
2 tablespoons soy sauce
½ teaspoon ground cloves
½ teaspoon grated lime or lemon rind (optional)
½ teaspoon salt
6 loin pork chops, 1 to 1¼ inches thick
2 large oranges, peeled and sliced
½ medium cantaloupe, peeled and cut in chunks
½ medium honeydew, peeled and cut in chunks

Combine first 7 ingredients in saucepan, mix well and heat. Put chops on greased grill about 5 inches above low heat and grill 15 minutes, or until well browned on one side. Turn and grill, brushing occasionally with glaze, 12 to 15 minutes, or until well done. Thread fruit on skewers, brush with glaze and warm on grill 3 to 5 minutes. Makes 6 servings.
NOTE: Fruit can be omitted, if preferred.

GRINDERS

½ pound chopped bologna, ham or luncheon meat
1 cup shredded process American cheese
3 tablespoons mayonnaise
⅓ cup pickle relish
6 pimiento-stuffed olives, chopped
Butter
6 hamburger buns

Combine first 5 ingredients. Butter buns and divide cheese-bologna mixture among them, using a heaping ⅓ cup on each. Wrap separately in heavy-duty foil, twisting ends to seal. Grill over hot coals, turning occasionally, 5 minutes per side. Makes 6 servings.
NOTE: Can also be baked at 350°F. 10 to 15 minutes.

SMOKY LINKS WITH BEANS AND APRICOTS

¾ cup finely chopped dried apricots
1 package (12 ounces) smoky links
1 can (28 ounces) pork and beans in tomato sauce
2 tablespoons firmly packed brown sugar

Cover apricots with boiling water and let stand 5 minutes; drain. Cut links in bite-size pieces. Combine all ingredients, bring to boil and simmer over fire or low heat 20 minutes, or until apricots are tender. Makes 6 servings.

MEDITERRANEAN GRILLED CHICKEN

½ cup olive oil
½ cup white wine
¼ cup honey
¼ cup white-wine vinegar
2 teaspoons dried oregano
1 lemon, thinly sliced
1 orange, thinly sliced
2 broiler-fryers, split

Mix thoroughly all ingredients, except chicken. Pour over chicken in glass bowl and refrigerate overnight. Warm to room temperature before grilling. Grill over hot coals, basting frequently with marinade, 45 minutes, or until done. Add fruit slices the last few minutes of cooking to heat through. Makes 4 servings.
NOTE: Chicken can also be cooked in broiler indoors.

BACKPACKER'S ALL-IN-ONE

5 cups instant cereal such as grits or oatmeal (any combination)
4 cups dry nonfat milk powder
1 cup wheat germ
2 cups sesame-seed meal
½ cup ground or minced filberts, almonds, pecans or Brazil nuts
½ cup dehydrated date nuggets, packaged chopped dates, dry seedless currants or finely chopped figs or seedless raisins
2 cups firmly packed dark-brown sugar
½ cup brewer's yeast
2 teaspoons ground cinnamon

For toasty flavor, spread cereals on baking sheet and heat in preheated very slow oven (250°F.) about 20 minutes. Mix with remaining ingredients. To prepare, put ¾ cup mix in serving bowl or cup and stir in enough boiling water to make of cereal consistency. Let stand in warm place about 5 minutes and serve plain or with reconstituted whole milk. Makes 12 cups firmly packed mix.
NOTE: Sesame-seed meal and brewer's yeast can be bought in health-food stores, date nuggets in mountaineering or sporting-goods stores. Crumbled bacon bar can be sprinkled on top of prepared cereal, if desired.

VEGETABLES

BARBECUED BEANS

2 cans (21 ounces each) pork and beans in tomato sauce
2 tablespoons instant minced onion
¼ cup bottled barbecue sauce
¼ cup chili sauce
¼ cup molasses
8 slices cooked bacon
Chopped green onion (optional)

Combine all ingredients, except last 2, in pot. Bury bacon slices in beans. Heat over coals or low heat until bubbly. Sprinkle with green onion, if desired. Serve in bowls with spoons. Makes 6 to 8 servings.

CORN SALAD

1 package (10 ounces) frozen cut corn
1 cup sliced celery
1 tomato, diced
⅓ cup chopped green pepper
⅓ cup sliced green onions
½ cup sliced pitted black olives
¼ cup bottled creamy dressing

Cook corn according to package directions. Drain and mix with remaining ingredients. Chill thoroughly. Makes 4 to 6 servings.

ONIONS IN THE COALS

Count 1 sweet Spanish onion per serving. Put, unpeeled, at edge of hot coals. Roast, turning occasionally, 45 minutes to 1 hour. To serve, remove charred outer layer, dot with butter and sprinkle with salt and pepper. Good with spit-turned roasts or sizzling steaks.

HERBED POTATOES

4 medium potatoes, thinly sliced
¼ cup butter or margarine, melted
1 tablespoon each chopped parsley and chives
1 teaspoon dill seed
½ teaspoon salt
¼ teaspoon monosodium glutamate

Mix all ingredients together and wrap tightly in 15-inch length of heavy foil. Cook on grill, turning occasionally, 15 to 20 minutes, or until tender. Makes 4 servings.

SWEETS

STRAWBERRY-MANDARIN-CHEESE DESSERT

1 pound (2 cups) creamed cottage cheese
1 pint strawberries, washed, hulled and sliced
2 tablespoons confectioners' sugar
Grated rind of 1 orange
1 can (11 ounces) mandarin oranges, drained

Make a layer of cottage cheese in serving dish. Carefully mix remaining ingredients and spoon on top. Chill at least 1 hour. Makes 4 to 6 servings.

WINE-FRUIT KABOBS

2 ripe peaches or nectarines, cut in large chunks
1 pear, cut in large chunks
1 banana, cut in 6 pieces
½ small cantaloupe, peeled and cut in 2-inch chunks
¼ cup butter or margarine, melted
¼ cup red dessert wine
¼ teaspoon ground ginger
Grated rind and juice of 1 small orange

Push fruit chunks onto skewers. Mix remaining ingredients and brush on fruit. Put skewers 8 inches above gray coals on greased grill. Cook, brushing with wine mixture, about 5 minutes. Makes 6 servings.
NOTE: Fruit can also be heated in broiler indoors.

CHOCOWICHES

For each serving, spread a slice of bread with peach or apricot jam, then sprinkle with flaked coconut and semi-sweet chocolate pieces. Top with second slice of bread and wrap in foil, leaving ends open. Put on grill and heat, turning, until bread is toasted and chocolate melted.

GRILLED PINEAPPLE

Cut a ripe fresh pineapple in 6 or 8 (depending on size) lengthwise wedges, cutting through leaves. Brush with melted butter and broil over medium fire until hot and slightly browned. Serve at once. Canned pineapple can be substituted. Makes 6 to 8 servings.

BAKED APPLES

Core cooking apples and fill with mixture of cut-up dates, finely chopped nuts, cut-up marshmallows and cinnamon-sugar mixture. Place each apple on square of foil, gather up sides and twist together. Bake on coals 45 minutes to 1 hour, turning occasionally.

STRAWBERRIES IN FOIL

Wash 1 quart fresh strawberries, remove hulls and slice in bowl. Sprinkle with ¾ cup superfine sugar and let stand ½ hour. Divide berries among 6 squares of double foil, add 2 teaspoons Cognac to each and seal well. Put packages on preheated grill and cook over slow fire 7 to 8 minutes. Serve warm over ice cream, or top with cold whipped cream. Makes 6 servings.

OVEN—In simplest terms, an oven is a box which can be heated. It may be part of a range, built into a wall, or portable. It may use gas or electricity as its source of heat. It has one, or sometimes two, doors, shelf supports, and racks which are usually movable, varying degrees of insulation, as well as different combinations of controls, timers, thermostats, and thermometers. It may have a vent and/or a hood and fan. It is used to broil, bake, roast, or cook (as in casseroles).

Electronic or microwave ovens are exceptional in that, although they use electricity, no heat is created in the oven except in the food to be cooked. Since it is a rapid method of cooking it is used to cook the foods more frequently cooked on the top of the range in addition to being used to prepare the conventional oven foods.

A Dutch oven is a heavy saucepot with tight-fitting lid used for cooking pot roasts, stews, soups, or other dishes which require long cooking.

OXFORD SAUCE—An English sauce, also known as Cumberland sauce, which is traditionally served with cold venison. It can be used with other game and meats.

OXFORD SAUCE

3 shallots, minced
1 orange
1 lemon
¼ teaspoon sugar
Dash of cayenne
⅓ cup red currant jelly, melted
⅓ cup port wine
½ teaspoon prepared mustard
Dash of ground ginger

Cook shallots in a little water for 1 or 2 minutes. Drain. Cut off thinnest possible peeling from the orange and lemon. Cut peeling into fine julienne strips, and simmer in water to cover for 10 minutes. Drain. Put shallots, orange and lemon peelings, juice from the orange and from half the lemon, and remaining ingredients in bowl. Mix well. Makes about 1 cup.

OXTAIL—A beef tail, weighing one-and-a-half to two pounds. This is an extremely bony cut, but it is very flavorful when braised or used as the basis for oxtail soup, a favorite of English cookery.

OXTAIL AND VEGETABLE SOUP

2 oxtails
All-purpose flour
3 tablespoons shortening
2 quarts water
1 teaspoon salt
½ teaspoon peppercorns
Dash of cayenne
1 bay leaf
1 celery stalk, diced
1 medium onion or leek, chopped
1 carrot, diced
½ cup tomato purée
1 teaspoon Worcestershire
Chopped parsley
Salt and pepper

Have oxtails cut into pieces; roll in ½ cup flour. Brown in 2 tablespoons shortening in large kettle. Add water, salt, peppercorns, cayenne, and bay leaf. Bring to boil; skim; cover and simmer for 3 hours, or until meat is tender. Strain broth; cool, and remove fat. Separate meat from bones. To broth and meat add celery, onion, and carrot. Bring to boil and simmer for 30 minutes. Add tomato purée and simmer for 10 minutes. In skillet brown 2 tablespoons flour; blend in remaining 1 tablespoon shortening. Add to soup and bring to boil. Add Worcestershire, parsley, and salt and pepper to taste. Makes 6 servings.

OYSTER—A bivalve mollusk of the family Ostreidae, found mainly between the tidal levels or in shallow waters along the coasts of all continents except those bordered by polar seas. The common oysters of Europe are the Flat or Plate oyster *(Ostrea edulis)* and the Portuguese oyster *(Crassostrea angulata);* on the eastern and Gulf coasts of the United States we have *Crassostrea virginica;* on the Pacific coast the Olympia oyster *(Ostrea lurida)* and the introduced Japanese oyster *(Crassostrea gigas).* Many varieties of each species exist, with different sizes, shapes and flavors, according to the habitat and food supply of the place where they grow.

Oysters have an irregular, two-part shell, held together at the hinge by an elastic ligament. The oyster itself is found in the concave lower half of the shell, protected by a thin membrane, called a mantle, which lies against the inner side of the shell.

Oyster fishery is an important industry in the United States, France, the Netherlands, the United Kingdom, and Australia, with the United States leading in the quantity grown for market and the value of the product. Many famous oyster varieties come from Chesapeake Bay; others from New York, Mississippi, Louisiana, and all the seaboard states. At one time, such names as Blue Point, Lynnhaven, and Cape Cod meant oysters from those specific regions. To some, they still do. But to market experts, Blue Point now indicates any oyster from two to four inches long and from two to two-and-a-half inches wide, no matter where it is produced. Lynnhaven has become a general name for any larger, angular-shape oyster. On the Pacific coast, the supply is chiefly of the native oyster, the Olympia *(O. lurida),* generally much smaller than the eastern, and the eastern type grown from baby or "seed" oysters shipped from eastern beds. The three chief sizes recognized in the oyster trade are "half-shells," the smallest, usually preferred for eating raw; "culls," of medium size, for eating raw and for stewing, etc.; and "box," the largest, generally used for frying.

Availability—Fresh oysters are available from September to April in the shell or shelled. Eastern oysters are graded as:

Counts or Extra Large—Not more than 160 per gallon, or 44 in a quart.

Extra Selects or Large—From 161 to 210 per gallon. A quart of the smallest oysters from this gallon contains 36.

Selects or Mediums—From 211 to 300 oysters per gallon. A quart of the smallest oysters from this gallon may have 83 oysters and a quart of the largest has over 46 oysters.

Standards or Small—From 301 to 400 oysters per gallon, and a quart of the smallest of these cannot contain more than 138 oysters; a quart of the largest hold more than 68.

Very Small—Over 500 to a gallon, and a quart of the larger of these oysters contains more than 112.

Pacific oysters are generally larger than the eastern variety, with the exception of the Olympia (*Ostrea lurida*) which is often identified as such, and is much smaller. Other Pacific oysters are graded as:

Large Pacific—Under 65 per gallon.

Medium Pacific—From 65 to 96 oysters per gallon.

Small Pacific—From 97 to 144 oysters per gallon.

Extra Small Pacific—More than 144 oysters per gallon.

Canned oysters are sold packed in water or oyster liquor, whole or in pieces. Frozen oysters and oyster stew are available.

Purchasing Guide—If buying fresh oysters in the shell, make sure oysters are alive, with shells tightly closed. Shucked oysters should be plump, with no shell particles, and with clear liquor. Oysters should have a grayish color and a fresh sea odor.

Storage—Refrigerate fresh oysters and plan to eat or cook as soon as purchased.

Fresh, cooked; or canned, opened, refrigerator shelf: 1 to 2 days

Canned, kitchen shelf, unopened: 1 year

Frozen, refrigerator frozen-food compartment: 2 months

Frozen, freezer: 1 year

Nutritive Food Values—Oysters are a good source of protein, high in calcium, niacin, and iron, a fair source of thiamine and riboflavin, and low in fat.

Eastern, raw, 1 cup (8½ ounces) meat only = 160 calories

Pacific and Western (Olympia), 4 ounces, raw, meat only = 103 calories

Canned, 4 ounces, solids and liquid = 86 calories

Oyster stew, homemade, 1 cup (8½ ounces), prepared with 1 part oysters to 2 parts milk by volume = 245 calories

Oyster stew, commercial, 1 cup (8½ ounces), prepared with equal volume of water = 122 calories

Oyster stew, commercial, 1 cup (8½ ounces), prepared with equal volume of milk = 202 calories

Basic Preparation

To Open Oyster in the Shell—Scrub shells well and rinse in cold water. Insert point of sharp thin knife into hinged end of oyster and push blade between shells until muscle at center is cut and valves begin to separate. Run knife around shell, separate valves, and loosen oyster from shell.

THE DELECTABLE OYSTER

by JAMES A. BEARD

The author of *Gulliver's Travels* said some two centuries ago: "He was a bold man that first ate an oyster." We can only wonder now how it happened. Was it on a dare? By mistake? Out of curiosity? Once in an old copy of *Harper's Weekly* I saw a cartoon of a prehistoric man tackling an oyster. The expression on his face was dazed, frightened.

There is a legend that the first prehistoric eater of oysters got his taste for the bivalve as follows: He was strolling on the shore and spied an oyster, shell open, gaping at the world. On impulse, the caveman stuck his fingers into the opening. As the shell snapped shut he pulled his hand away and with his fingers dragged the oyster out. Naturally he put his fingers to his mouth and, mm-m! What flavor!

My own theory is that the Chinese were the first, or surely among the first, oyster eaters. Long ago they perfected a method of drying the bivalve and stringing it on bamboo sticks to keep for future use. Chinese cuisine includes scores of dishes using oysters and delectable oyster sauces. As for the Romans, we know from Apicius that they cherished the oyster and served it in many ways. One Roman recipe called for stewing oysters in honey! This I don't recommend. The ancient Greeks, who had more conservative tastes than the Romans, were particularly fond of oysters baked in their shells in charcoal or coals just until the shells opened. These they seasoned lightly with lemon and butter. This is still one of the choice ways to cook oysters. Modern cooks sometimes serve baked oysters with Béarnaise sauce, a thoroughly delicious combination.

The French, Spanish, and Portuguese, all living near the sea, learned to appreciate oysters in ancient days. The English also loved oysters but, sad to say, served these delicate morsels with vinegar. Dickens in *Pickwick Papers* tells how Sam Weller's wife consumed a half pint of vinegar with a plate of oysters. This mistreatment is doubly horrifying since English waters produce two of the finest oysters in the world, Colchesters and Whitstables. These, along with the French Marennes, are greatly prized by connoisseurs.

Oysters vary in size, looks, and taste because the water, climate, and even the exact location of an oyster bed have profound effects on their growth. They range from plump and grayish with a bland taste, to greenish or even coppery with a definite metallic taste. Some are as small as your fingernail and others, such as the Japanese or the Malpeques from Prince Edward Island, as big or bigger than the palm of your hand. The Pacific Northwest, where I grew up, is noted for its tiny Olympia oysters from Puget Sound. These delectable tidbits, not fatty but coppery in flavor, are such midgets that it takes over 2,000 of them to make a gallon. An oyster lover can consume at least 250 at a sitting. Olympias command a premium price. Shucking them is a tedious job. Also, as with much of our finest seafood, the harvest grows less each year. We greedy eaters have helped to deplete the beds, and the pollution of our waters has taken its toll.

On the East Coast, the Chincoteagues are the nearest to the Olympias. The Cape Cod oysters were probably the first to attain popularity in America. They were an important food for the Pilgrims. The small oysters from Delaware Bay pleased William Penn and other Quakers of the Pennsylvania colony. Philadelphians are great oyster fans to this day. Elizabeth Robins Pennell wrote in her delightful book *A Guide for the Greedy:* "But the glory of Penn's town is the oyster croquette—from Augustine's by preference. A symphony in golden brown and soft fawn grey, it should be crisp without, within of such delicate consistency that it will melt in your mouth like a dream. Pyramidal of shape, it is of itself so decorative that only with the rarest blue and white china, or the most fairy-like Limoges, will it seem in perfect harmony."

The famous Lynnhavens from Virginia are no longer easy to come by. Man has stripped the beds. Nearby are ancient kitchen middens containing over three million shells, a testimonial to the quality of these great bivalves.

New Orleans oysters have been famed since the city was founded, and the local cuisine boasts many oyster specialties, among them the well-known Oysters Rockefeller.

When I was young, a family friend in the west transplanted several well-known eastern varieties to the Toke Point area in Washington. We summered at the coast, and each week we received a great sack of these oysters. I can remember the wonderful pyramids of fried oysters my mother used to make with them. This was a breakfast specialty on the mornings when we went clamming and crabbing at dawn. Back we would come, tired, hungry, and cold. My mother was always in the kitchen ready for us. On the stove were two huge iron skillets partly filled with melted sweet butter, bubbling but not the least bit colored. The oysters, about a dozen to a person and a few for the pot, were opened and lined up. The moment we came in, the first lot would be quickly rolled in flour, dipped into beaten egg and milk, and then rolled in freshly crushed cracker crumbs. Then the oysters were slowly lowered into the hot butter and allowed to turn a golden-brown, no more. They were whisked to the table to be eaten with hot buttered toast and plenty of hot coffee. We bit through the crisp outside into the soft rich center. The coating of crumbs insulated the flesh so that these oysters were always delicate and tender, never tough.

This to me is still a great breakfast dish. Of course, most oyster fans insist that the delicacy is at its best served raw on-the-half-shell. Generally I agree. And in this form they need little or no embellishment. A dash of lemon juice and maybe a touch of freshly ground black pepper. But no vinegar, no chili sauce, and no cocktail sauce. With oysters on-the-half-shell serve thin sandwiches of rye bread lavishly buttered and a good wine or beer or stout. Dry white wines such as Chablis or Pouilly-Fuissé have a strong affinity for oysters.

Here are some ways to vary oysters on-the-half-shell:

Serve them with lemon juice and black pepper and piping-hot grilled or sautéed pork sausages; or with slices of garlic sausage. Be sure the sausages are hot and served on a hot plate and the oysters freshly opened and well chilled.

For a glamorous party dish, serve oysters on a bed of ice with a dab of fresh caviar and a squirt of lemon juice atop each one. Don't forget the rye-bread sandwiches with plenty of unsalted butter.

Serve oysters-on-the-half-shell and pass bowls of chopped chives and parsley. Lemon juice and black pepper go along too. You'll find the tang of these fresh herbs an interesting variation.

Serve oysters-on-the-half-shell with cocktails. Pass large trays of the oysters with lemon quarters, caviar if you like, and piping-hot tiny sausages.

OYSTER STEW

If there is any traditional Christmas Eve dish in this country, I guess it is probably oyster stew. Surely it is one of the more delicious morsels when hot and rich and served with piles of crisp, buttered toast.

You may go as rich as you please here. Try it with milk, with milk and cream, or, to be utterly fabulous, with heavy cream.

5 tablespoons butter
1 cup milk
2 cups heavy cream
1½ pints oyster liquor and oysters
Salt, pepper, cayenne to taste
Chopped parsley or paprika

Heat your bowl first. Add a good pat of butter to each bowl. Keep them piping hot. Heat milk, cream, and oyster liquor to the boiling point. Add oysters and bring again to the boiling point. Season with salt, pepper, and cayenne. Ladle into the hot bowls and add a little chopped parsley. Makes 4 to 6 servings.

OYSTERS EN BROCHETTE

This is a most picturesque and delicious way to serve oysters. It can be varied in many different ways.

For each brochette or skewer:
1 slice of bacon
4 mushroom caps
4 oysters
Lemon juice
Freshly ground pepper
Butter

Run the skewer through one end of the bacon, then skewer a mushroom cap, then an oyster, then bacon, mushroom, oyster, until you have the skewer filled and the bacon laced through it. Sprinkle with lemon juice, give the whole thing a grind of pepper, and brush with butter. Broil over charcoal or in preheated broiler until the oysters are curled at the edges and the bacon crisp and done. It is practical to cook the bacon for a few minutes and cool it before using on the skewers. These delectable morsels are delicious served with hollandaise sauce.

Variations—Alternate small cubes of beef tenderloin and tiny mushroom caps with the oysters. Brush well with butter and sprinkle with salt and pepper before broiling.

Alternate small cubes of precooked ham with oysters. Broil as above and serve with Béarnaise sauce.

Alternate oysters, scallops, and chunks of lobster meat laced with bacon strips on skewers, and broil. Serve with lemon or with hollandiase sauce.

OYSTER PAN ROAST

These are particularly popular on the west coast. They are oysters poached in butter with high seasoning and look well when served in small copper skillets or in a large oval au gratin dish.

½ cup butter
1 pint drained oysters
Salt, pepper, cayenne, lemon juice

Melt butter in a skillet or in individual skillets; when it is hot and bubbly, add oysters and poach until they are plumped and curled at the edges. Add salt, pepper, cayenne, and a good squirt of lemon juice. Serve at once on fried toast or on crisp well-buttered toast with chopped parsley and chives. Makes 4 servings.

Variations

Piquant—Poach the oysters in butter. Season to taste and add a goodly dash of Worcestershire and a dash of catsup or chili sauce. Serve on buttered toast.

Western—Poach oysters in butter. Season with salt and a dash of cayenne. Add ¼ cup sherry and a little oyster liquor and bring to the boiling point. Serve on buttered toast points with chopped parsley.

HARRY HAMBLET'S GOLDEN-FRIED OYSTERS

Butter
3 eggs, lightly beaten
3 tablespoons heavy cream
36 to 48 oysters
Flour
Freshly rolled coarse cracker crumbs
Salt and pepper

Melt plenty of butter in a heavy skillet. It should be lavishly done for this preparation. (If you wish to be safe you may add part oil to the butter so as to be certain there will be no burning of the butter.) Combine eggs with cream. Dust oysters lightly with flour, dip into egg mixture, and then roll in cracker crumbs (the crumbs of soda crackers or saltines are by far the best). Let dipped and crumbed oysters stand for a few minutes before cooking. Cook quickly, just long enough to brown the oysters nicely on both sides. Season with salt and pepper to taste when they are browned. Serve on a very hot platter with lemon wedges and coleslaw. Makes 6 servings.

OYSTER OMELET

Fold freshly fried oysters into individual omelets and serve with a dusting of chopped parsley and a dash of fresh lemon juice. This is a most attractive and picturesque brunch or luncheon dish which is quick and easy for a small group.

OYSTERS CASINO

24 oysters on the half shell
4 pie pans filled with rock salt
1 cup butter
½ cup chopped green onion
⅓ cup chopped parsley
3 tablespoons chopped green pepper
Fresh lemon juice
Salt and pepper
6 to 8 bacon strips, partially cooked

Arrange the oysters, 6 to a serving, on the rock salt in pie pans. Cream butter, and blend in onion, parsley, and green pepper, spike with a little lemon juice, and salt and pepper to taste. Spoon butter mixture onto oysters and top each oyster with a small strip bacon. Bake in preheated very hot oven (450°F.) until the bacon is crisp and oysters curled at the edges. Serve with additional lemon juice. Makes 4 servings.

HANGTOWN FRY I

This is a recipe which supposedly started in the west and for which there seem to be dozens of different versions.

6 to 8 fried oysters
6 eggs, well beaten
2 tablespoons water
Salt and pepper to taste
Crisp bacon

Fry oysters, according to the recipe for Golden-Fried Oysters, in plenty of butter until golden-brown. Pour well-beaten eggs mixed with water and seasonings over oysters and cook as you would an omelet. Pull eggs from the sides of the pan with a spatula; when the omelet is cooked but not dry, roll it onto a hot platter and garnish with strips of crisp bacon. A perfect Sunday breakfast or dinner entrée. Makes 6 servings.

HANGTOWN FRY II

8 large oysters
All-purpose flour
6 tablespoons butter
6 eggs
3 tablespoons cream
¼ cup grated Parmesan cheese
¼ cup chopped parsley
Salt and pepper

Dip oysters into flour and sauté lightly in hot butter. Blend eggs, cream, cheese, and parsley. Add salt and pepper to taste, pour over oysters in pan, and cook over low heat until eggs are set. Place under a broiler to brown lightly. Serve from the skillet or slip onto a hot platter. Makes 4 to 6 servings.

DEVILS ON HORSEBACK

Wrap oysters in rashers of bacon and broil under a hot broiler unit until bacon is crisp. Turn once during cooking. Serve on toast.

ANGELS ON HORSEBACK

Marinate 24 oysters in white wine to cover. Add 1 garlic clove, chopped, and 2 tablespoons chopped parsley. Remove oysters, and wrap in thin strips of ham. Broil until ham is nicely browned and serve oysters on toast with hollandaise sauce.

SCALLOPED OYSTERS

This is a traditional New England dish which has somehow or other worked its way into some Thanksgiving menus.

Butter
2 cups freshly rolled cracker crumbs (they should be coarse)
1 pint oysters
Salt, pepper, ground nutmeg to taste
½ cup heavy cream
Buttered cracker crumbs

Butter a baking dish well and cover with a layer of cracker crumbs. Cover with a layer of oysters, seasonings, and a little cream; dot with butter. Cover with buttered crumbs. Add another layer of oysters and seasonings and more cream. Top with additional cracker crumbs, dot heavily with butter, and season. Add a touch more cream and bake in preheated hot oven (425°F.) for 20 to 25 minutes. Makes 4 to 6 servings.

Oyster Stew

Oysters en Brochette

Hangtown Fry

OYSTER BISQUE

$2/3$ cup raw rice
1 pint oysters
1 small onion, stuck with 2 cloves
1 cup oyster liquor or chicken bouillon
Brandy
1 pint cream
Salt and pepper
Paprika (optional)
6 poached oysters (optional)

Cook rice in boiling salted water until very soft. Chop oysters very fine and save all the liquor. Combine oysters and liquor, onion, and about 3 tablespoons of brandy. Bring to the boiling point and simmer gently for 10 minutes. Remove onion and add drained rice. Put through a fine sieve or food mill. Add cream, and season to taste with salt and pepper. Return to the stove and heat almost to the boiling point. Or keep hot over hot water until time to serve. Serve with a dash of paprika and a poached oyster for garnish if you wish. Makes 6 servings.

Some Oyster Hints Which Are Delicious and Unusual:

When you make a beefsteak-and-kidney pie, combine 12 oysters with the usual ingredients you use for such a pie. Poach them in their own liquor or in a little beef or chicken bouillon before adding to the pie.

Oysters added to your favorite chicken pie recipe give it an entirely new twist and a really most exciting flavor and texture experience.

Crisp-fried oysters combined with a broiled steak is a wonderful experience in gastronomy. Or poached oysters with a steak are delicious.

Time was when a Pocketbook Steak meant a filet of beef cut in a thick steak with a pocket to be filled with fried oysters just before serving.

Of course you know that oysters added to your favorite stuffing give it something completely new and different. Try it with a stuffing of bread crumbs, butter, onions, loads of tarragon, and oysters. Superb.

Serve double chicken consommé boiling hot with one or two oysters poached in a little of the consommé in each cup; it is a sensational clear soup.

Beef consommé with an oyster or two added to each cup is another rare change from the regular diet of consommé.

Blanquette of veal or veal fricassee is one and the same thing. Combine a few oysters with the next one you do and see what a difference there is.

OYSTER PLANT or SALSIFY—A biennial herb, *Tragopogon porrifolius,* which is native to southern Europe, but will nevertheless thrive in cool climates. It has been cultivated in the Mediterranean and in Asia Minor for some 2,000 years, both as a food plant and for ornamental purposes. Oyster plant grows to a height of about four feet and is sometimes called "goatsbeard" because of its thin tufted grasslike leaves. Because its purple flowers close around midday it is also known in England as John-go-to-bed-at-noon.

The root, for which it is cultivated as a vegetable, is yellowish-gray, often a foot long and two inches in diameter. Its flesh is white and contains a considerable proportion of milky juice. The flavor of the root is said to resemble that of an oyster, but many culinary experts insist that it resembles far more the flavor of a globe artichoke.

The Spanish oyster plant, or Spanish thistle, *Scolymus hispanicus,* is a larger plant, with prickly leaves and a root that is lighter in color. Its flavor is not so highly developed as the oyster plant. The black oyster plant, *Scorzonera hispanica,* is the smallest of the three, with broader leaves and a yellow flower. The skin of its root is black and it is similar in flavor to the oyster plant.

Oyster plant is a winter vegetable, although the young leaves of the plant make a delicious spring salad.

Availability and Purchasing Guide—Available from June to March in specialty food stores or vegetable stores catering to people of Spanish, Italian, and Greek extraction.

Select from well-shaped roots of medium size. Avoid large coarse roots or flabby shriveled ones.

Storage—Remove tops, if intact. Rinse, then place in plastic bag or wrap in aluminum foil and refrigerate.

Refrigerator shelf or vegetable compartment: 1 to 4 weeks

Nutritive Food Values—Contains some calcium, phosphorus, iron, and vitamin C.
$3\frac{1}{2}$ ounces, cooked = 77 calories

Basic Preparation—Oyster plant must be scraped before cooking. As each root is scraped, it should be plunged at once into water mixed with a little fresh lemon juice or vinegar to prevent discoloration; the proportions are about 3 tablespoons lemon juice or vinegar to 1 quart water. The roots are then cut into 2- to 3-inch pieces and kept in the acidulated water until cooking time. Boil until just tender, drain, and finish in very hot butter; or fry like French-fried potatoes or fritters; or serve in a well-seasoned white sauce.

OYSTER-PLANT FRITTERS

Scrape and cook oyster plant. Mash as you would mash potatoes. Season with butter, salt and pepper, and if desired add a touch of ground nutmeg. Shape into small round flat cakes, about $1\frac{1}{2}$ inches in diameter. Dip cakes into all-purpose flour. Quickly cook in hot butter until golden-brown, turning once. Serve with meats in place of potatoes, rice, or noodles.

P

PAELLA—A Spanish rice dish that has gained international fame. It is named for the two-handled iron frying pan in which the rice is cooked and served. *Paella* is a casserole which must always be based on rice, but in Spain its other ingredients vary according to the food available locally: *Paellas* in inland Spain generally contain meat, chicken, sausage, and vegetables; whereas the coastal regions specialize in seafood and chicken combinations. Outside of Spain it is the varieties featuring at least some seafood which have come to be most generally associated with *paella*.

It makes an excellent buffet dish and only a salad and dessert are needed with it for a complete meal.

PAELLA A LA VALENCIANA

1 lobster
½ cup olive oil
2 garlic cloves, minced
1 frying chicken (2 to 3 pounds), cut into small pieces
1 chorizo or Spanish sausage, sliced, or hot Italian sausage
3 green peppers, sliced
3 pimientos (fresh or canned), sliced
¼ cup finely diced salt pork
4 medium-size onions, sliced
6 medium-size tomatoes, peeled and cut into wedges
3 cups raw rice
2 teaspoons saffron threads
Chicken bouillon or fish stock
15 shrimps, cooked and shelled
15 mussels or clams, well scrubbed
2 cups green peas or sliced green beans
2 medium artichokes, sliced, or 1 package (9 ounces) artichoke hearts
Pepper (optional)

Cook lobster until red. Remove meat, but only crack the claws and reserve them. In large skillet or kettle heat olive oil and garlic. Sauté lobster meat over medium heat for 2 or 3 minutes. Remove and reserve. Add chicken and cook until brown on all sides. Return lobster meat to skillet and add *chorizo* slices, green peppers, pimientos, pork, onions, and tomatoes. Cook about 5 minutes, stirring constantly. Add rice and saffron soaked in little chicken bouillon and cook for another 5 minutes. Add bouillon to cover, plus 1 inch. Cook, covered, over medium heat for 10 minutes, stirring occasionally. Add shrimps, mussels, peas, and artichokes (Remove tough outer leaves and chokes from fresh artichokes.) Season with pepper. Cover and cook for 10 minutes more, or until rice is tender, stirring frequently. If necessary, add more bouillon, a little at a time; the dish should be dry and the liquid all absorbed. Before serving arrange ingredients so that some of the shrimps will show; place lobster claws on top. Decorate with additional pimiento strips, if desired. Serve hot. Makes 8 to 10 servings.

PALM—A very large family, *Palmaceae*, of highly ornamental tropical and sub-tropical trees and shrubs. They are generally characterized by unbranched stems which vary in size from three feet to a height of more than 100 feet. They have a terminal crown of large leaves, feathery in some varieties, fan-shape in others. Many of the palms are extremely valuable for the food products obtained from them. Chief among these are the betel palm, whose nutlike kernel and leaves yield a potent drink; the cabbage palm, whose tender central leaves are eaten as greens, and whose terminal frond (hearts of palm) is cooked, or pickled; the coconut palm; the date palm; the sago palm; the oil palm from which palm oil and palm nuts come; and the sugar palm from whose sap arrack is distilled.

PANBROIL—This is a dry-heat method of cooking meats, poultry, or fish which can often substitute satisfactorily for broiling. Tender cuts of meat one inch or less thick, frying-chicken parts, and thin pieces of fish such as fillets are particularly suitable. To panbroil, use a heavy skillet and preheat it, but do not add fat or water. Put food into the skillet and do not cover. Cook over medium heat, turning food occasionally. Drain from pan any fat that accumulates and continue cooking until meat is brown on both sides. Season to taste and serve immediately.

PANCAKE by Helen Evans Brown—Pancakes, or griddle cakes, are the oldest form of bread. The first ones were made of pounded grain, mixed with water, and spread upon a hot rock to dry. The ancient Hebrews cooked their unleavened bread on a griddle and in China, the egg roll, really a pancake, has been made for untold oriental ages.

Today, every country has its own version of the pancake. They may serve as appetizers, as the Russian *blini* do; entrées, as do Italian *cannelloni*; desserts, as do French *crêpes Suzette*, but always they are welcome. All the world loves pancakes.

Nutritive Food Values—The nutrients in pancakes vary with the ingredients but they are primarily a source of carbohydrates.

Homemade pancake, 4-inch (1 ounce) = 62 calories

Plain or buttermilk mix, 4-inch (1 ounce) pancake made with milk = 55 calories

Plain or buttermilk mix, 4-inch (1 ounce) pancake made with milk and egg = 61 calories

Buckwheat or other flour mix, 4-inch (1 ounce) pancake made with milk and egg = 54 calories

Basic Preparation—Mix ingredients together lightly and quickly. Mix batter until dry ingredients are just blended and do not try to beat out all the lumps. Overbeating produces tough pancakes. Some pancake batters need to stand before batter can be cooked. Since flours are very variable, add more liquid if the batter is too thick and more flour if the batter is too thin. If you are in doubt, test the batter before using all of it. If you are using a pancake mix, follow directions on the label to prepare the batter.

The griddle you use should heat evenly. Test by dropping some water onto it. If the water sizzles and bounces, the griddle is ready.

If you are using a seasoned griddle, one of the Teflon-coated griddles, or if the batter has shortening or fat in it, it is not necessary to grease the griddle. However if yours is a griddle on which the batter sticks, brush the entire surface with a small amount of fat or shortening before making the pancakes.

When the entire surface of the pancake is covered with unbroken bubbles, turn the pancake only once. The second side takes only half the amount of time needed to cook the first side. Try to serve the pancakes at once. To keep them warm for a short period of time, place them, covered with a towel, in a preheated slow oven (200°F.).

Holiday Breakfast of Pancakes and Sausages

AMERICAN PANCAKES

Sourdough Starter

Boil some peeled potatoes, say 4, in plenty of water to cover. Do what you will with the spuds, but save the water. Mix 2 cups of it, lukewarm, with 2 cups all-purpose flour, 1 tablespoon sugar, and 1 teaspoon salt. Put in a crock and let stand in a warm spot, loosely covered, for 3 or 4 days, or until it's working merrily and has attained a peculiar and, to me, delightful sour odor. "She'll let you know when she's up," one old-timer told me, and you'll see what he means. To hasten this process, you may add a cake of yeast at the beginning, but if you have the time, let it take its natural course. When "ripe," it may be stored in the refrigerator or freezer, or used. Makes about 3½ cups.

SOURDOUGH PANCAKES

Take 2 cups of starter from the crock; add 1 cup each flour and water. Cover bowl and allow to stand in a warm place overnight. Next morning, stir in 1 teaspoon to 1 tablespoon sugar, ½ teaspoon baking soda, salt to taste (about ½ teaspoon), and 1 well-beaten egg. If too thick, add more water; if too thin, more flour. Stir in 2 tablespoons melted butter; allow to stand for a few minutes, then bake on both sides. Makes 6 servings.

NOTE: To have more starter for use at a future time, replace the 2 cups removed with an equal amount of flour and enough water to give the starter its original consistency. Then, after it begins to work again, store it in the refrigerator or freezer until you wish to use it.

BUTTERMILK PANCAKES

Combine 2 cups all-purpose flour, ½ teaspoon salt, 1½ teaspoons baking soda, 1 teaspoon sugar, 2 cups buttermilk, 2 tablespoons melted butter or margarine, and 2 beaten egg yolks. Beat 2 egg whites and fold in. Bake on a hot griddle, making pancakes any size from that of silver dollars to dinner plates. Makes 4 to 6 servings.

SOUR-CREAM PANCAKES

Combine ¾ cup all-purpose flour, ½ teaspoon salt, 1 teaspoon sugar, 1 cup dairy sour cream, ¼ teaspoon baking soda, 1 cup cottage cheese, and 4 well-beaten eggs. Cook slowly on a hot griddle or in skillet until brown on both sides. Makes 4 servings.

YEAST PANCAKES

Scald 1¼ cups milk and cool to lukewarm. Sprinkle 1 package active dry yeast or crumble 1 cake compressed yeast into ¼ cup lukewarm water. Use very warm water (105°F. to 115°F.) for dry yeast; use lukewarm water (80°F. to 90°F.) for compressed. Let stand for a few minutes, then stir until dissolved. Add dissolved yeast to milk, 1 teaspoon salt, 1 teaspoon sugar, 2 tablespoons melted butter or margarine, 2 cups all-purpose flour, and 1 well-beaten egg. Beat for 2 minutes and set aside in a warm place to rise. When doubled in bulk, stir again and cook. Makes 4 servings.

VERMONT GRIDDLE CAKES

Combine 2 cups all-purpose flour, 4 teaspoons baking powder, 2 tablespoons sugar, 1 teaspoon salt, 1 cup milk, ¼ cup melted butter or margarine, and, at the last, 2 well-beaten eggs. Make large cakes and spread while hot with soft butter and grated maple sugar. Stack 6 high and cut like a pie. Another New England trick is to add maple syrup to the batter, replacing the sugar and part of the milk. Makes 4 servings.

FLANNEL CAKES

They are made like the New England griddle cakes, except that the baking powder is increased to 5 teaspoons and the egg yolks and whites are beaten separately, the latter being folded in at the last. You may need a little additional milk, too. Makes 4 servings.

BUCKWHEAT CAKES

Combine 2 cups buckwheat flour with 1 cup all-purpose flour, 3 tablespoons sugar, and 2 teaspoons salt. Sprinkle 1 package active dry yeast or crumble 1 cake compressed yeast into 1 cup warm water. Use very warm water (105°F. to 115°F.) for dry yeast; use lukewarm water (80°F. to 90°F.) for compressed. Let stand for a few minutes, then stir until dissolved. Add 2 cups warm milk and ¼ cup melted butter, margarine, or sausage drippings. Stir into the dry mixture and beat smooth. Allow to rise overnight in a warm place. Next morning stir in ½ teaspoon baking soda dissolved in 1 tablespoon water; mix; cook on a griddle until a heavenly brown. Omit the soda if you wish; the pancakes will then have a pleasantly sour flavor. Serve with butter and syrup. Makes 4 to 6 servings.

PANCAKES FROM OTHER LANDS

MEXICAN CHEESE AND CHILI PANCAKES

Make pancakes from a mix. For each cup of mix add 3 well-beaten egg yolks; then at the end fold in 3 egg whites beaten stiff. Have ready some domino-shape pieces of Jack cheese, or sharp Cheddar. Wrap each one in a strip of canned peeled green chili, each strip about a third of a chili. Drop spoonfuls of the batter onto a hot griddle. When almost done on the bottom, put a piece of the chili-wrapped cheese on one half and fold over the other, like a turnover. Put in preheated moderate oven (350°F.) for 5 to 10 minutes, until cheese is melted.

ENGLISH HAM AND HERB PANCAKES

These herb griddle cakes are made with any batter to which chopped chives, parsley, and thyme have been added in discreet quantities. They are cooked, then spread with cooked ham or crumbled crisp bacon, and rolled.

Mexican Cheese and Chili Pancakes

CRÊPES
[Basic French Pancakes]

The versatile French crêpe is a tender, rich little cake which is useful for many other dishes. When made without sugar, crêpes may be filled with meat, vegetables, fish, or cheese, rolled or folded, and served, usually sauced, for the main dish or as an accompaniment.

For about 32 crêpes, beat 4 eggs well; then add 1 cup milk, 1 cup all-purpose flour, ½ cup melted butter or margarine, 1 teaspoon salt, and if for dessert, 2 teaspoons sugar. A tablespoon of brandy may also be added to dessert crêpes for extra flavor and delicately crispy edges. Mix well; let stand in the refrigerator for 2 or 3 hours. Stir again; if thicker than a heavy cream, add a little more milk. Heat a 7- or 8-inch skillet. (My pet one, made of heavy aluminum, measures 8 inches at the rim, about 6 at the bottom, with curving sides, an omelet pan.) Brush skillet with melted butter and put in 1 generous tablespoon batter. Working quickly, tip and tilt the pan so that the batter flows evenly over the bottom. Cook quickly. As soon as the pancake browns on one side turn quickly and brown the other. Stack and keep warm until all are made. These freeze, beautifully, I find. Pack them in stacks of 6 or 12 and wrap in foil or freezer paper. Thaw thoroughly before separating lest they tear.

Crêpes

BLINTZES

These popular Jewish pancakes are filling enough to make the main course at lunch, although they are usually served as dessert. Fill Crêpes with a mixture of 2 cups cottage cheese, 2 slightly beaten eggs, 2 tablespoons melted butter or margarine, ¼ teaspoon salt, and 2 tablespoons sugar. Grated lemon rind, ground cinnamon, or raisins can be added. Fold or roll filled Crêpes; then brown in butter. Serve hot with cold dairy sour cream and jam, preferably cherry, apricot, or black currant.

GERMAN PANCAKES

Use 6 eggs, separated; beat yolks, and add ¼ cup each flour, melted butter, and milk; season with ½ teaspoon salt, and fold in stiffly beaten egg whites. Cook batter, ⅛ at a time, in plenty of butter in a large skillet. When the edges curl, turn and brown on the other side. The same pancakes—spread with applesauce, jam, jelly, or other fruit or rum sauce, rolled, and served with sugar and butter—make a superb dessert.

These pancakes can also be cooked until firm on one side, then placed in preheated hot oven (400°F.) for 10 minutes or until puffed and golden. Cut into wedges and serve.

German Apple Pancakes

German Apple Pancakes

Pour batter in skillet. Top with very thinly sliced apples and cook until pancake is golden-brown. Turn and brown on the other side.

ITALIAN CANNELLONI

The Basic French Pancakes are filled with any well-seasoned cooked meat or fish which has been moistened with a little gravy or with egg yolks. Some suggestions: chopped chicken with shreds of Virginia ham or prosciutto; chopped cooked brains with hard-cooked egg, minced parsley, and pignolias. Put a generous spoonful of filling on each pancake, roll, and arrange on a buttered flat baking dish or, if preferred, on a bed of well-seasoned puréed spinach. Pour a mixture of olive oil and melted butter over all, sprinkle with grated cheese, and bake until pancakes are heated and the cheese melted.

Russian Blini

RUSSIAN BLINI

The most famous of all appetizer pancakes are, of course, the Russian Blini. They are made exactly as Buckwheat Cakes except that only 1 teaspoon sugar is used and the batter may have to be thinned with a little water, for the cakes should be small and thin. Use melted butter for the shortening. Give each guest a plate and pass the hot pancakes as well as sour cream, melted butter, caviar, sliced smoked salmon, or any smoked or kippered fish that meets your fancy. The *Blini,* which should be about 3 inches in diameter, are buttered, dabbed with sour cream, and topped with fish. They are usually folded before eating.

Chinese Egg Rolls

HUNGARIAN PALACSINTA

Make Basic French Crêpes, and spread with a mixture of dairy sour cream and chopped cooked ham, and stacked 6 or 7 high; cut into wedges for serving. Another filling that may be used is a combination of creamed lobster and mushrooms, not too thin, with both lobster and mushrooms cut fine.

CHINESE EGG ROLLS

These deliciously filled rolls are sometimes made of noodle paste, but those made of a thin egg batter are far better. Beat 2 eggs slightly; add 1 cup all-purpose flour, 2 tablespoons cornstarch, 2 cups water, and ½ teaspoon salt. The batter should be very thin; if not, add more water. Make in a small frying pan like Crêpes, being sure to tilt the pan quickly so that the batter will spread transparently thin. Use little or no butter in pan. Cook on one side only. For filling, mix ¾ cup chopped cooked shrimp, ½ cup finely diced celery; ⅓ cup each minced cooked pork, minced water chestnuts, and minced bamboo shoots. Season with 2 teaspoons wine, 1 tablespoon soy sauce, and 2 tablespoons minced green onion. Mix with a raw egg, and form into finger-shape rolls; lay them on the cooked sides of the pancakes. Roll up, tucking in edges to seal in the filling. A little uncooked batter can be used to help seal. Chill; just before serving, brown in 2 inches of fat. Although usually served as one of the dishes at a Chinese meal, they also make a tantalizing appetizer when cut into 3 or 4 pieces and served on toothpicks.

MORE PANCAKES

FLY-OFF-THE-PLATE PANCAKES

1 cup all-purpose flour
¼ teaspoon salt
1 tablespoon sugar
3 teaspoons baking powder
1 egg
1 cup milk
2½ tablespoons dairy sour cream
2 tablespoons melted butter, at room temperature

Sift dry ingredients into a mixing bowl. In another bowl beat egg, milk and sour cream. Pour into dry ingredients, beating with a slotted spoon or wire whisk to keep from lumping. Add butter and beat until smooth. Cook a cake and if batter is too thick, add a bit more milk. The cakes puff up while cooking, so do not have the mixture too stiff. Keep adding milk, a tablespoon at a time until batter reaches the proper consistency. Drop cakes by tablespoonfuls onto hot, lightly greased griddle. Use 2 tablespoons of batter if you prefer large cakes. Let one side brown until golden. If cakes get too brown, lower heat. Turn and brown on other side. As soon as cakes are brown on both sides, they should be ready to serve. Makes 10 to 12 pancakes. For a breakfast pancake, serve with honey, syrup, jam, jelly or preserves. For a main dish, top with chicken à la king, Newburg, creamed ham or dried beef and egg slices in sherried cream sauce, or whatever you prefer.

Frozen Pancakes

Cook pancakes as directed and as soon as they have cooled to room temperature, wrap each in foil. Place side by side on a flat cookie sheet and freeze. When frozen they can be placed in freezing bags or stored in any container you wish. Do not keep frozen over 2 weeks. To reheat, unwrap each pancake. Put on cold ungreased griddle. Let one side heat, turn on other side and let that get hot also. Brush each side with melted butter and let sizzle on the griddle before bringing to the table. The outside of the pancakes will have a delicious crunchy coating, the inside will be as light as when they were first made and cooked. No extra butter need be served.

Refrigerating Batter

Leftover batter can be refrigerated and will remain fresh several days. Keep in a covered container. It thickens as it stands. Therefore for each cup of batter it may be necessary to add a tablespoon or two more milk in which ½ teaspoon extra baking powder has been dissolved, just before cooking pancakes.

Blueberry or Red-Raspberry Pancakes

Sprinkle a few blueberries or red raspberries over the surface of each Fly-off-the-Plate Pancake as soon as the batter has been placed on the griddle. Cook as in the basic recipe. Serve with Blueberry or Raspberry Syrup made by cooking a pint of berries with ½ cup sugar, ½ cup water and a slice of lemon (if berries are very ripe) until a syrup is formed, about 10 minutes. This is a Maine specialty.

NEW ENGLAND BUCKWHEAT CAKES

2 cups buckwheat flour
¾ teaspoon salt
½ teaspoon baking powder
½ teaspoon baking soda
1 package active dry yeast, or 1 cake compressed yeast
2 cups warm water, or more if needed
1 tablespoon maple sugar or syrup
Milk
Lard or vegetable shortening

The evening before serving these cakes put buckwheat flour, salt, and ¼ teaspoon each baking powder and soda in large bowl. Add yeast mixed with 2 cups water (105° to 115° for dry yeast and 80°F. to 90°F. for compressed). Add sugar and mix well until smooth. Cover and leave at room temperature overnight. Next morning, add remaining ¼ teaspoon each baking powder and soda mixed with 1 or 2 tablespoons milk. Beat to mix. If batter is too thick, add more milk, but add only 1 tablespoon at a time. To cook cakes use a large iron skillet. We prefer a 12-inch one. Heat and add 1 to 1½ tablespoons lard. Heat until fat smokes. Drop batter by tablespoonfuls into the fat, leaving about 2 inches between each as cakes spread while cooking. They require a little more fat than the lighter pancakes, added while they cook. When one side is golden brown, turn and brown on other side. These take a little longer to cook than other pancakes. Serve piping hot. Maple syrup is the favorite topping in New England. Sage-seasoned pork sausage and strong black coffee complete the meal when buckwheat cakes are featured. Makes about 2 dozen.

DOUBLE-APPLE PANCAKES

2 tablespoons sugar
¼ teaspoon ground cinnamon (optional)
2 medium apples, cored and thinly sliced crosswise
1 egg, beaten
½ cup milk
⅔ cup applesauce
1 cup pancake mix
3 tablespoons butter or margarine, melted
Honey or syrup

Combine and mix well sugar and cinnamon. Sprinkle on apple slices and set aside. Combine egg, milk and applesauce and beat well. Pour over pancake mix and beat until smooth. Blend in butter. Bake pancakes in lightly greased heated skillet, using ¼ cup batter for each pancake. Immediately press 2 apple slices down into each pancake. Bake until golden, then turn and bake other side. Serve with honey. Makes 10 pancakes.

FOOLPROOF ALL-PURPOSE THIN PANCAKES (Basic Recipe)

Use this easy recipe to make some of the interesting variations suggested under crêpes (Basic French Pancakes).

- ½ cup all-purpose flour
- ½ teaspoon baking powder
- ¼ teaspoon salt
- 1 egg
- ¾ cup milk
- 2 tablespoons butter, melted

Sift flour, baking powder and salt. Beat egg until light and very slowly add slightly warmed milk and melted butter at room temperature. Gradually add liquids to dry ingredients and beat until smooth and full of bubbles. An electric mixer or beater is fine for this, or use a French wire whisk. Grease a 6-inch skillet with just enough butter or cooking oil to cover the bottom; ¼ to ½ teaspoon should be sufficient for each pancake. Pour 2 tablespoonfuls of batter all at once into skillet, tilting the pan until it spreads and completely covers the bottom. This takes practice, for it must be done quickly. When pancake is brown on one side, turn and brown on the other. Serve plain or fill with creamed meat, fish or vegetables for lunch or supper or use as dessert pancakes. Makes 1 dozen.

Pancakes Russian Style

For an elegant first course, spread each cooked thin pancake with caviar. Sprinkle with a few drops of lemon juice, then add a little finely minced onion and a thin layer of riced hard-cooked egg. Roll up and top with dairy sour cream. Serve 2 to each person.

POORBOY'S PANCAKES

- 1 cup all-purpose flour
- 1 teaspoon salt
- 2 eggs
- 1 cup milk
- ½ cup diced cooked meat
- ½ cup each cooked vegetables, diced
- 4 tablespoons butter or margarine
- 1 cup leftover or canned gravy (optional)

Mix flour and salt in bowl; make a well, break eggs into well, add milk and beat all together with rotary beater until smooth and free of lumps. Add meat and vegetables. Melt 1 tablespoon butter in 9-inch skillet. Pour in enough batter to cover bottom. When pancake is golden brown, flip over and cook other side. Repeat with remaining butter and pancake batter, making 3 more cakes. Keep warm in oven until ready to serve. While preparing pancakes, heat gravy in saucepan. Serve 1 cake per person, adding gravy, if desired.

CLAM PANCAKES

- 2 cans (7½ ounces each) minced clams
- 1 cup each pancake mix and cornmeal
- 1 teaspoon onion salt
- ½ teaspoon salt
- 1 cup milk
- 1 egg, beaten
- 2 tablespoons butter or margarine, melted

Drain clams, reserving liquid. Combine pancake mix, cornmeal and seasonings. Add ½ cup clam liquid, clams and remaining ingredients. Mix well and drop by tablespoonfuls on hot greased griddle or into skillet and cook until browned on both sides and done. Good with catsup. Makes eighteen 4-inch pancakes, or 6 servings.

DESSERT PANCAKES

CONTINENTAL LEMON PANCAKES

As each Crêpe or Dessert Pancake is taken from the pan, dust heavily with sifted confectioners' sugar and squeeze a little lemon juice over it. Roll up and sprinkle again with sugar. Serve at once. Sometimes these pancakes are topped with fresh raspberries or wild strawberries, sweetened to taste, plain or fortified with kirsch.

BLINCHIKI

Here's an unusual dessert which originated in Old Russia. Mix 1 egg, ⅛ teaspoon salt and 1 to 2 tablespoons sugar (to taste) plus 1 teaspoon cinnamon with 1 cup cottage cheese. Spread a tablespoon over each of 12 Dessert Pancakes or Crêpes just before serving; roll and top with 1 cup dairy sour cream sweetened with 2 tablespoons sifted confectioners' sugar and ½ teaspoon cinnamon or more to taste.

JELLY PANCAKES

Spread hot Crêpes or Dessert Pancakes with your favorite jelly: raspberry, currant, blackberry, or grape. Roll up and dust heavily with confectioners' sugar. Serve very hot, 2 to each person.

French Pancake Pie

Make the Crêpes ahead if desired, and when ready to serve, top each one with 1 tablespoon brown sugar, raspberry or strawberry jam, maple sugar, cranberry jelly or Nut Filling. Stack into buttered round shallow piepan or ovenproof dish and place in preheated hot oven (400°F.) until "pie" is heated through, about 5 minutes. Cut in wedges at the table and serve.

Nut Filling For Pancakes

To 1 cup ground filberts, toasted blanched almonds, or pecans, add 2 tablespoons sifted confectioners' sugar or more to taste, and enough vanilla-flavored whipped cream to make a paste stiff enough to spread. Allow about 1 tablespoon of this for each pancake. Fills 12 pancakes.

CRÊPES DREI HUSAREN

- 2 tablespoons butter
- 2 tablespoons all-purpose flour
- ½ cup milk
- 2 tablespoons sugar
- 4 eggs, separated
- 1 teaspoon vanilla extract
- Melted butter
- ⅛ teaspoon salt
- Raspberry Purée
- Vienna Whipped Cream

Melt butter in skillet or saucepan. Stir in flour. Then slowly pour in milk and cook, stirring constantly, until smooth and the consistency of medium white sauce. Remove from heat. With a wire whisk beat in sugar and egg yolks; add vanilla. (If desired, this can be made a few hours ahead, but do not refrigerate. Cover and leave at room temperature. Crêpes are best if made and baked at the last moment, however.) You will need 4 shallow pottery baking dishes 6 inches in circumference and 1 inch deep, or substitute foil piepans. Brush melted butter over the dishes to be used. When you are ready to cook, fold in half the whites beaten stiff with salt. Then quickly fold in other half. Divide batter among the pans and place in preheated hot oven (400°F.). As soon as tops are lightly browned and crêpes no longer shake, they are done; 5 to 10 minutes cooks them. Loosen edges with a dull knife and turn upside down on a dessert plate. Pour a generous amount of Raspberry Purée over them. Surround with stars or dabs made of Vienna Whipped Cream. Makes 4 servings.

Raspberry Purée

Wash and drain 1 pint ripe red raspberries. Place in the blender with ½ cup sugar and whirl until thoroughly blended. Strain through a fine-meshed wire strainer. Refrigerate until ready to serve. If you do not have a blender, press berries with a wooden spoon through a fine-meshed strainer.

Vienna Whipped Cream

Beat 1 cup chilled, heavy cream, being careful not to get it too stiff. Reduce speed, and add 3 tablespoons sifted confectioners' sugar and 1 teaspoon vanilla.

CRÊPES SAINT-DENIS

Use vanilla pudding for filling these rolled pancakes. Flavor with rum to taste and chill. Spread 1 tablespoon of this mixture over each crêpe just before serving. Sprinkle 1 teaspoon of ground, toasted blanched almonds over the filling and roll. Reheat all filled pancakes in ¼ cup butter; turn with a fork to warm evenly. A very light sprinkling of sugar goes over the crêpes followed by ¼ cup dark rum. Heat rum, but do not boil. Flame the crêpes and serve at once. You can use any liquor you wish instead of rum: brandy, applejack, bourbon whiskey, etc., for the filling as well as flaming. If you are fond of spices, a dusting of cinnamon, nutmeg or a combination can be sprinkled over filling before rolling pancakes.

SAUCES AND SYRUPS

FRENCH CARAMEL OR BURNT-SUGAR SAUCE

Put 1 cup granulated sugar in a heavy skillet, iron preferred. Put over high heat. With a wooden spoon stir and stir, scraping the sugar from the bottom of the pan until it forms coarse crumbs or lumps. When it begins to melt, lower heat and continue stirring, scraping particles from bottom and sides of the pan until clear and caramel-brown and resembling maple syrup. Add ½ cup water at once. The mixture will lump once more, but no matter. Continue stirring and cooking over low heat until it once more reaches the consistency of maple syrup. Remove from heat. Do not cook too thick for it thickens as it stands. Makes ⅞ cup.

PANCAKE ORANGE SYRUP

This is especially noteworthy on blueberry pancakes, equally delicious on dessert crêpes.

- Grated rind of 1 orange
- ½ cup orange juice
- 1 cup sugar
- Dash of salt
- Sections from 1 orange

Mix grated rind, orange juice, sugar and salt and let boil in large saucepan until the consistency of maple syrup, 4 or 5 minutes. Add orange sections free of seeds and membrane. Makes 1 cup.

PANFRY—A method of cooking or frying in very little fat in an uncovered skillet or pan on top of the stove. It is a quick-cooking method used for the same types of food as in panbroiling but can also be used for lean meats and vegetables and fish, all of which require the addition of just a little fat to prevent sticking and achieve the desired browning. While there are general similarities between panfrying and sautéing, panfrying can be used for thicker pieces which require slightly longer cooking.

Use a heavy skillet to panfry. Add a small amount of fat to the skillet and allow it to melt over medium heat. Add food and cook over medium heat, turning occasionally until brown on both sides. Food can be seasoned before or after cooking. Do not cover and do not add any liquid. When cooked to desired doneness, drain on absorbent paper and serve at once.

PAPAW or PAWPAW—A North American fruit of the custard apple family, *Asimina triloba,* which grows naturally in rich moist soil from Lake Ontario south to the Gulf of Mexico. It is the only member of this family hardy in the northern United States. Because of the similarity in names it is often confused with the papaya, which is also called a pawpaw.

The pawpaw tree grows to a height of twenty to thirty feet, has large, long, glossy leaves and a purplish flower. The fruit varies from two to six inches in length and is shaped like a short fat banana, dark-brown to blackish in color, with a soft creamy yellow flesh in which many seeds are embedded. It is sweet, rich, custardlike, and slightly aromatic. Not available commercially, the fruit should be picked after the first frost and stored in a cool dry place until soft. They are peeled like a banana and eaten raw.

Nutritive Food Values
3½ ounces = 85 calories

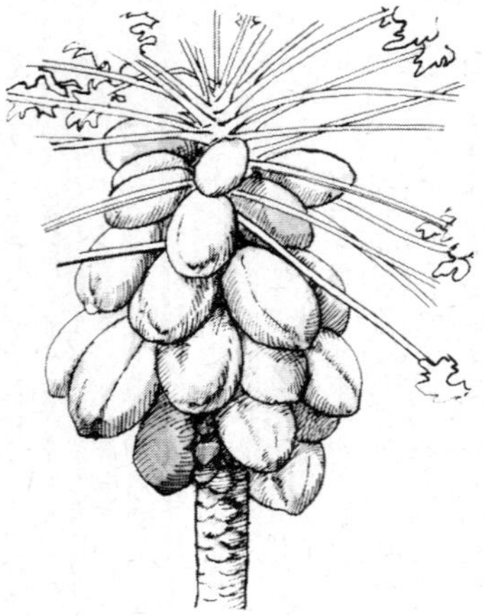

PAPAYA or PAWPAW—A small tropical tree, or more accurately, a very large herbaceous plant *(Carica papaya)* with large, fleshy fruits which grow on stalks from the trunk, just below the leaves. The fruit, which resembles a melon, has a rind and a juicy flesh that is yellow-orange in color; one fruit can weigh up to twenty pounds. Papaya has a delicious, sweet-tart musky taste. It makes an excellent breakfast fruit and appears as a standard part of tropical breakfasts. Papayas are also used for salads, pies, and sherbets. The fruit contains an enzyme called papain which acts as a digestive ferment. Papain is the chief ingredient in meat tenderizers. It is also important in medicine.

The papaya is a true American native; the only point that is in question is whether it came from the West Indies or Mexico. The name is a corruption of the Carib word *ababai.* After Columbus discovered the New World, the plant spread quickly to other tropical countries. By 1600 it had reached the Philippines, India, and very likely Africa, too. Apart from the excellence of the fruit, the papaya tree grows very quickly, maturing in eighteen months from the time the seed is planted.

Papayas are of great importance in tropical Asia, Africa, and Hawaii, both as a staple food and commercially. In the United States, they are grown almost entirely in southern Florida and Texas since the trees are very sensitive to frost.

Availability—Papayas are chiefly available where grown, in Florida and Texas. The fruit does not ship well and cannot be sent great distances. Some papaya juice is being marketed and is sold canned or mixed with frozen juice blends.

Purchasing Guide—The flavor is best when ripe. Ripe fruit has a yellow-orange skin that yields to slight pressure. It has a fruity odor.

Storage—Let fruit ripen at room temperature. When ripe, fruit should be refrigerated.
Refrigerator shelf: 1 to 2 days

Nutritive Food Values—Good source of vitamin A and an excellent source of vitamin C
Fresh, 3½ ounces, raw = 39 calories
Fresh, 1 cup, cubed (6.4 ounces) = 71 calories
Canned juice, 3½ ounces = 48 calories

Basic Preparation—Cut papaya into wedges or quarters without removing outer skin. Remove most of the seeds. Serve with slices of lemon or lime. Or peel and cut into cubes to use in fruit cups or salads.

PAPILLOTE, EN—A French culinary term meaning "wrapped in paper." At one time parchment was used for the wrapping, but nowadays brown paper or aluminum foil is widely used. Dishes are prepared *en papillote* to hold in the juices of the meat or fish during cooking.

PAPRIKA—The Hungarian name given to a spice or condiment made by grinding the ripe dried pods of red *capsicum* or bell peppers. There are a number of paprikas, and their quality, color, flavor, and pungency depend on the variety of the bell peppers used and the way in which they are processed. Usually, paprika is made from sweet red bell peppers. The stems, stalks, and white membrane are removed before grinding because they are bitter hot, but the seeds are ground along with the pulp.

Hungarian *rose paprika* is made from the choicest *capsicum,* with a rich dark-red color and a sweet distinctive flavor and aroma. Another kind of Hungarian paprika is *King's* or *Koenigspaprika,* which has a much sharper flavor since the entire pepper is used.

Paprika is used as a seasoning and as a garnish on practically all nonsweet dishes. The best known paprika-flavored national dish is Hungarian goulash. Spanish, Mexican, Balkan, and Turkish cookery also use paprika, in varying degrees of sweetness or pungency. However, none of these paprikas achieve the excellence of the Hungarian varieties. This is not surprising, since in Hungarian cooking paprika is an essential element.

Availability—Paprika is available ground, almost always in the mild sweet variety. More pungent varieties are available in stores specializing in foreign food products.

Storage—Keep paprika in a cool dry place. Like chili powder and onion and garlic seasonings, paprika picks up moisture from the air if containers aren't tightly closed. Hot and humid storage conditions are particularly bad for paprika, changing both its color and flavor.

VEAL PAPRIKASH

1½ pounds boned veal shoulder, cut into 1½-inch pieces
2 tablespoons fat
2 medium onions, chopped
½ small garlic clove, minced
1 tablespoon paprika
1 green pepper, sliced
1 tomato, peeled and sliced
1 teaspoon salt
Water
1 tablespoon all-purpose flour
1 cup dairy sour cream
Hot cooked noodles

Brown meat on all sides in hot fat. Add onion and garlic, and cook for 2 or 3 minutes. Add paprika, green pepper, tomato, and salt. Cover and simmer for 1 hour, or until meat is tender. Add ¾ cup water when needed to prevent sticking. Just before serving, blend flour with a little cold water and stir into mixture. Cook for 2 or 3 minutes. Add sour cream and heat gently. Serve with noodles. Makes 4 servings.

PAPRIKA CHICKEN WITH SOUR-CREAM SAUCE

1 medium onion, minced
3 tablespoons shortening
1 frying chicken (3 pounds), cut up
5 tablespoons all-purpose flour
1½ teaspoons salt
1 teaspoon paprika
⅛ teaspoon pepper
¼ cup water
1 cup dairy sour cream
5 ounces broad noodles
1 tablespoon poppy seeds

Cook onion in 1 tablespoon shortening until soft. Remove from skillet. Wash chicken and dry on paper towels. Mix ¼ cup flour with ½ teaspoon salt. Dredge chicken with mixture. Brown chicken in remaining 2 tablespoons shortening. Sprinkle with onion, remaining 1 teaspoon salt, paprika, and pepper; add water. Cover and simmer for 30 minutes, or until chicken is tender. Remove chicken to a hot platter. Stir remaining 1 tablespoon flour into skillet juices. Add sour cream; heat to boiling point, stirring constantly. Pour sauce over chicken. Serve with hot cooked noodles sprinkled with poppy seeds. Makes 4 servings.

PAPRIKA CHEESE SAUCE

3 tablespoons butter, margarine, or bacon fat
2 tablespoons all-purpose flour
1½ cups milk
¾ teaspoon salt
⅛ teaspoon pepper
1 cup shredded sharp American cheese
1 teaspoon paprika

Melt butter in a saucepan; blend in flour. Remove from heat and stir in milk. Return to heat. Cook, stirring constantly, for 5 to 8 minutes, until mixture begins to thicken. Add salt, pepper, cheese, and paprika. Makes 6 servings.

PARAFFIN—A flammable waxy substance produced in distilling wood, shale, coal, etc., and occurring also in the earth as a constituent of petroleum or as a solid deposit. Paraffin is sold in solid form in food stores, particularly during the fall months, and is used for coating the tops of jars of jams and jellies to keep out air, thus preventing spoilage. Since it has an extremely low smoking point, it should be melted over hot water and poured over the jam or jelly to the depth of ⅛ inch. Although it is not edible, paraffin is a pure wax.

PARBOIL—To parboil food is to plunge it into boiling water and cook it for a short period of time. Parboiling is used for such vegetables as potatoes or green peppers to cook them partially, or to shorten cooking time. Parboiling is also used to prepare vegetables for freezing; the process shrinks the vegetables for more compact storage and retards action of the enzymes in the vegetable.

PARCH—To dry thoroughly under dry heat. Most parched foods are dried in the sun to the point where they contain very little internal moisture.

All parched foods require long cooking. Parched corn, a specialty of the American Indian, is the best example; corn on-the-cob was dried in the sun to preserve it for winter use.

PARE—To peel thinly with a sharp knife. A short-bladed paring knife is generally used for this process. Potatoes, apples, pears, and turnips are examples of foods which are pared.

PARFAIT—The word for this ice-cream dessert is the French word meaning "perfect," an opinion shared by many.

Originally, a parfait meant only a coffee cream, but in modern French usage a parfait is an ice made of a single flavor in a plain mold.

An American parfait consists of ice cream served with whipped cream or fruit or other sauces, arranged in a tall narrow glass called a parfait glass. The ice cream is layered into the glass with the cream or fruit or sauce. The parfait is often topped with a generous spoonful of sweetened whipped cream and garnished with a maraschino cherry.

PARFAITS

In parfait glasses or small jelly, cheese, shrimp-cocktail, or juice glasses, alternate layers of ice cream and jam, syrup, baby or junior fruit, or marshmallow cream. The sky is the limit on combinations; just remember eye appeal as well as flavors. Here are a few suggestions:

Strawberry ice cream and strawberry jam.

Chocolate ice cream and marshmallow cream.

Vanilla ice cream and red raspberry jam.

Vanilla ice cream and sundae sauce.

Cherry ice cream and almond-flavored whipped cream.

Vanilla ice cream with apricot and apple, or pear and pineapple baby or junior fruit.

FRENCH KIRSCH PARFAIT

1 cup sugar
2¼ cups water
1 envelope unflavored gelatin
⅓ cup fresh lemon juice
½ cup kirsch
2 egg whites
⅛ teaspoon salt

Put sugar and 2 cups water in saucepan. Bring to boil and boil for 10 minutes. Soften gelatin in remaining water, and stir into first mixture. Add lemon juice and kirsch. Pour into refrigerator trays, and freeze until firm. Beat egg whites with salt until stiff, but not dry. Beat frozen mixture until light and fluffy. Fold in egg whites. Pour into 5-cup mold and freeze until firm. Turn mold upside down on serving plate and wrap in a cloth wrung out of hot water. Shake until mold drops onto plate. Makes 6 servings.

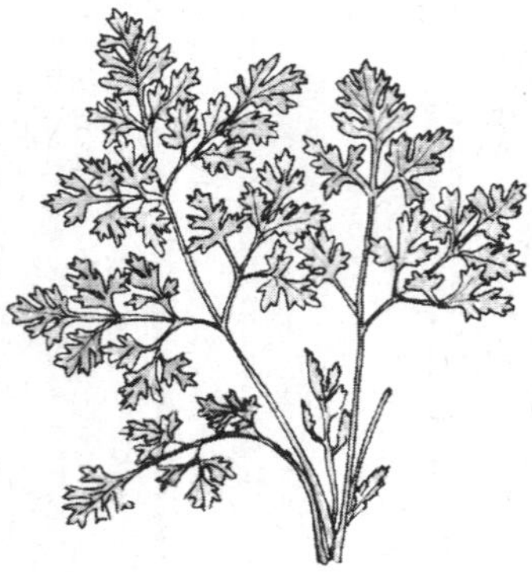

PARSLEY [*Petroselinum crispum*]—A hardy biennial herb plant, native to southern Europe and widely used for flavoring and as a garnish. The parsley family, or *Umbelliferae,* includes many herbs and spices such as anise, dill, angelica, chervil, caraway, coriander, cumin, fennel, lovage, sweet cicely, and the common vegetables celery and carrots.

Parsley is a small green plant of which there are more than thirty varieties. These are distinguished by the shape of their foliage: curled, moss-curled, double-curled, or fern-leaved, for example; and plain or common parsley, often called Neapolitan or Italian parsley, which has comparatively coarse foliage. Hamburg parsley is a subspecies, *P. crispum, var. latifolium,* grown for its fleshy carrotlike root and prepared like any root vegetable.

Bunches of parsley leaves are used whole as a garnish or in a *bouquet garni.* Chopped, either fresh or dried, parsley is used to flavor soups, meat dishes, fish stuffings, cream or cheese sauces, eggs, breads, flavored butter, marinades, and most vegetables and salads.

The word parsley is from the ancient Greek *petroselinon,* "celery growing among rocks," because it often grew there. Although not known for certain, some modern botanists believe Sardinia to have been its birthplace. At any rate, parsley did originate somewhere in the Mediterranean region, and was a widely used plant in the ancient world, often for other than culinary reasons.

The ancient Egyptians, for instance, sprinkled parsley on the graves of their dead. This association with the dead continued into Greek and Roman times, when the bodies of loved ones were strewn with parsley. This linking of parsley and death is also found in an old English proverbial expression "to be in need of parsley" which meant to be at death's door.

Another use of parsley in olden days was to ward off intoxication. No Greek or Roman would dare attempt a long banquet without a parsley wreath to protect him from too much wine. This tradition continued until the 16th century, when an English herbalist, William Turner, suggested that parsley seed taken before a drinking bout "helpeth men that have weyke (weak) braynes to bear drinke better."

Whatever the ancient history of parsley, it was one of the most popular of medieval herbs for gravies, sauces, and relishes. It could even make a quick soup, suggests a Parisian husband to his young bride in the late 14th century. He recommends: "Take parsley and fry it in butter, then pour boiling water on to it and boil it and add salt and serve your soups." Parsley was important in omelets and pickles and in fact in almost every medieval dish that called for herbs.

Since colonial days Americans have grown and used parsley widely. It was such a part of the home garden that Southerners considered it unlucky to transplant it when moving to a new house. Today, we rely on it for flavor and as an attractive garnish, and modern nutritionists support its use by recognizing its important nutritional value.

Availability and Purchasing Guide—All year round; it is grown in many home gardens and is also grown commercially. It is sold fresh in bunches. Look for clean, fresh, bright green leaves. Fresh parsley is also sold mixed with soup greens. Dried parsley flakes are available alone or in dried soup and other mixes.

Storage—Wash, shake water from leaves, and store in a tightly closed container in the refrigerator.

Refrigerator shelf: 3 to 8 days

Refrigerator frozen-food compartment: 2 to 3 months

Freezer: 1 year

Nutritive Food Values—When eaten in quantity it is a good source of vitamins A and C.

1 tablespoon chopped = 2 calories
10 small sprigs = 5 calories

Basic Preparation

To Chop—Hold the stems of several sprigs together. Pinch the parsley leaves together tightly and cut across with a sharp knife or scissors until stems are reached. Discard stems.

To Dry—Cut parsley clusters from heavy stems. Plunge parsley leaves into boiling water for 30 seconds. Drain. Spread the leaves on a wire screen or on a piece of heavy-duty foil that has been punched with a fork over the entire surface. Put sheet into a preheated slow oven (300°F.) until leaves are crisp and dry. Leave the door of the oven partially open. Store in an airtight container.

To Fry—Wash sprigs of parsley and dry well. Fry sprigs in deep hot fat (375°F. on a frying thermometer) for a few seconds, or until they rise to the surface. Drain on absorbent paper and sprinkle with salt. Serve as a garnish.

To Freeze—Choose crisp young parsley. Wash in several changes of water. Trim tough stems. Put parsley into freezer containers allowing ½-inch headspace. Pack parsley in small portions, enough for one preparation. Frozen parsley can only be used for cooking.

CARROT AND PARSLEY SOUP

2 leeks, sliced
4 carrots, sliced
2 cups chicken bouillon
⅓ cup chopped parsley
Salt and pepper

Combine leeks, carrots, and bouillon in a saucepan. Bring to boil, lower heat, and simmer until vegetables are tender. Put parsley into a blender. Add some of the vegetables and bouillon. Whirl until well blended. Pour mixture into a saucepan. Whirl remaining soup and pour into saucepan. Add salt and pepper to taste. If soup is too thick, add more bouillon. Serve with croutons. Makes 4 servings.

PARSLEY SALAD

3 tomatoes, peeled and diced
1 cucumber, peeled and diced
3 scallions, sliced
1 bunch of parsley, washed, stems removed, and chopped (use Italian parsley if possible)
¼ cup fresh lemon juice
½ cup olive oil
Salt and pepper
¼ cup chopped pitted black olives

Mix tomatoes with cucumber, scallions, and parsley. Chill until ready to serve. Beat lemon juice with olive oil. Add salt and pepper to taste. Pour dressing over salad and toss lightly. Serve sprinkled with chopped olives. Makes 4 servings.

PARSLEY-CHEESE TOASTS

1 loaf unsliced white, rye, or whole-wheat bread
½ cup softened butter or margarine
1 tablespoon parsley flakes
⅛ teaspoon garlic powder
13 thin slices of American cheese (about)

Cut bread into ¾-inch slices to within ¼ inch of the bottom of loaf. Leave a solid crust to hold the slices intact. Blend together butter, parsley flakes, and garlic powder. Spread on both sides of each slice of bread and insert a thin slice of cheese between each two. Spread top crust and sides with remaining butter. Put on a buttered cookie sheet. Bake in preheated moderate oven (350°F.) for 15 minutes, or until cheese has melted and bread is brown and crusty. Makes 6 to 8 servings.

PARSLEY EGG AND HAM ROLL

2 tablespoons butter or margarine
6 large eggs, beaten
⅓ cup milk
1 tablespoon parsley flakes
¼ teaspoon salt
⅛ teaspoon pepper
12 large slices of baked or boiled ham

Melt 1 tablespoon butter in 9- or 10-inch skillet. Combine eggs, milk, parsley flakes, salt, and pepper. Pour into buttered skillet. Stir and cook over low heat until eggs are set. Spread on large slices of boiled or baked ham. Roll up as for a jelly roll. Heat ham rolls in remaining butter only until ham is hot. Serve for breakfast, brunch, or supper. Makes 6 servings.

FRIED PARSLEY

Wash parsley. Dry extremely well on paper towel. Make sure not a drop of water remains on parsley or it will make the fat spatter. Drop parsley by clusters into fat or oil heated to 375°F. on frying thermometer. Fry only until parsley comes to the surface and has become crisp. This takes 10 to 15 seconds. Do not overfry or color will change. Drain on absorbent paper. Serve immediately.

PARSLEY SAUCE

¾ cup olive or cooking oil
3 tablespoons plus 1 teaspoon vinegar
Salt and pepper to taste
2 tablespoons finely chopped onion
¼ teaspoon finely minced garlic
¼ cup freshly chopped parsley
¼ teaspoon dried oregano

Combine oil, vinegar, and salt and pepper in a small saucepan. Blend well. Heat thoroughly, but do not boil. Remove sauce from heat. Cool almost to lukewarm and add remaining ingredients. Serve immediately with fish. Makes about 1¼ cups.

ITALIAN PARSLEY SAUCE

2 cups finely chopped fresh parsley
3 garlic cloves, minced
1 small can (2 ounces) anchovies, chopped, and oil
¼ cup finely chopped sweet basil
Black pepper to taste
2 tablespoons wine vinegar
3 tablespoons olive oil
¼ cup pimientos, chopped fine
3 tablespoons drained capers, chopped

Mix all thoroughly; allow to marinate at least 3 hours. The sauce will keep in refrigerator at least 2 weeks. Serve as edible garnish with fish, steak, boiled meats, cold meats, or even as a spread for sandwiches or snack crackers. Makes about 1⅓ cups.

SALSA VERDE

Combine ½ cup each of salad oil and cider vinegar. Add 1 cup chopped parsley and 3 tablespoons drained capers. Season with salt and pepper to taste. Beat well and serve with cold meats and fish. Makes 1⅔ cups.

PARSLEY CHIVE BUTTER

Add ¼ cup each finely chopped parsley and chives and 1 teaspoon brandy to ¾ cup soft butter. Chill and then roll mixture into small balls. Serve on steak or lamb chops. Makes 12 servings.

PARSLEY CHEESE BALLS

Blend 8 ounces cream cheese with ¼ teaspoon salt and ½ teaspoon paprika. Roll mixture into small balls using hands or butter paddles. Roll cheese balls in finely minced parsley. Chill, and serve on watercress as a salad. Makes 4 servings.

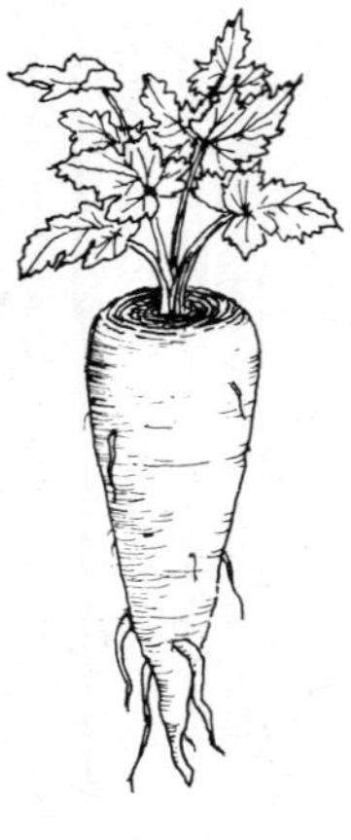

PARSNIP—The edible underground root of a biennial plant, *Pastinaca sativa,* of the carrot family. The parsnip is harder to harvest than some of the other large root vegetables because its root is entirely underneath the ground. The sweet flavor of the parsnip develops only after the first frost, as cold weather changes the starch to sugar. The roots can easily stay in the ground all winter. Parsnips were considered by the early New England colonists to be poisonous until after they were frozen.

Parsnips can be served in many ways. When properly cooked, they make a welcome change from the usual winter vegetables. They also make a good home-brewed wine, often flavored with ginger, especially popular in England.

Availability—Available fresh all year round, with peak crop during winter and spring months.

Also sold mixed with other greens in soup greens.

Purchasing Guide—Look for well-shaped firm roots of small to medium size. Woody cores are likely to be found in the very large roots. Soft shriveled roots are usually pithy or fibrous.

Storage—Refrigerate parsnips.

Refrigerator shelf or vegetable compartment, raw: 1 to 4 weeks

Refrigerator shelf, cooked: 1 to 2 days

Refrigerator frozen-food compartment, prepared for freezing: 2 to 3 weeks

Freezer, prepared for freezing: 1 year

Nutritive Food Values—Contain some iron and vitamin C.

1 cup, cooked = 100 calories

Basic Preparation—Scrub, scrape, or pare. Leave whole or cut into lengthwise strips, slices, or cubes.

To Cook—Cook in ½ to 1 inch of boiling salted water until tender, whole parsnips for 25 to 30 minutes, slices or cubes for 10 to 15 minutes. A little sugar added to cooking water improves the flavor. Drain; add melted butter or margarine.

To Bake—Bake in covered casserole in preheated moderate oven (350°F.) for 30 to 40 minutes. Mash, and serve spiced with a dash of grated orange rind.

To Freeze—Use young tender parsnips. Cut off tops, wash, and pare. Cut into cubes or slices. Blanch in boiling water: cubes for 1 minute; slices for 2 minutes; chill in ice water for 5 minutes. Pack into containers, allowing ½-inch headspace. Seal.

PARSNIP STEW

3 cups diced parsnips
1½ cups sliced raw potatoes
Water
½ cup diced salt pork
4 cups warm milk
2 tablespoons all-purpose flour
Salt and pepper

Cook parsnips and potatoes in water to cover until tender. Brown salt pork and add with its fat and milk to undrained vegetable mixture. Bring to boil and thicken with flour mixed to a paste with small amount of cold water. Add salt and pepper to taste. Serve with toasted crackers. Makes 6 servings.

HONEY-ORANGE PARSNIPS

3 medium parsnips (about 1 pound)
Salt
2 tablespoons butter or margarine
1 tablespoon honey
1 teaspoon grated orange rind
2 tablespoons orange juice

Peel parsnips and cut in ¼-inch diagonal slices. Cook in small amount of lightly salted boiling water until tender. Drain, add remaining ingredients and simmer a few minutes. Makes 4 servings.

SAUTÉED PARSNIPS

Peel parsnips and cook in small amount of lightly salted boiling water until tender. Drain and cool, then slice lengthwise about ¼ inch thick. Sauté in butter until golden brown on both sides. Season to taste with freshly ground black pepper.

PARTIES—Brunch is so easy that a hostess can start her entertaining career with it. The menu is a real buy-ahead one—everything but the fresh mushrooms can be bought ahead. Last-minute preparations are minimal if you do some cooking in advance. Our decorating ideas are simple—flowerpot containers, trimmed with painted or pasted posies and ribbons; a plastic bag holds ice in the drink carafe flower pot. The invitations are made of colored papers.

COME TO BRUNCH!
[Serves 8]

Champagne, or Collins Mix
with Orange Juice
on the Rocks
Grilled Honey-Ham Steak
Eggs, Mushrooms and Peas
au Gratin
Seeded Breadsticks
Glazed Pear Cake Dessert
Coffee

GRILLED HONEY-HAM STEAK

Buy half a ready-cooked ham (butt end) and ask butcher to cut off a steak 2 inches thick (reserve remaining ham for later use). Remove excess fat and score edges. Heat on grill about 8 inches from coals, basting frequently with mixture of ¼ cup honey and 4 teaspoons dry mustard, 30 minutes. Cut in thin diagonal slices. Makes 8 servings.

Easy Brunch for Eight

EGGS, MUSHROOMS AND PEAS AU GRATIN

½ pound fresh mushrooms, sliced
4 tablespoons butter or margarine
1 dozen eggs, hard-cooked and cut in fourths lengthwise
1 package (10 ounces) frozen peas, cooked
1 can (6 ounces) water chestnuts, drained and sliced
1 can (10½ ounces) condensed cream of chicken soup
1 cup dairy sour cream
¼ cup milk
1 teaspoon instant minced onion
¼ cup sherry
3 tablespoons chopped pimiento
Salt and pepper
1 cup soft bread crumbs

Sauté mushrooms in 2 tablespoons butter. Arrange with next 3 ingredients in greased 2½-quart baking dish about 2 inches deep. Mix soup and next 3 ingredients and heat gently. Remove from heat and stir in sherry and pimiento. Season to taste. Pour over ingredients in baking dish. Mix bread crumbs with remaining 2 tablespoons butter, melted, and sprinkle on top. (You can make the dish to this point the day before and refrigerate.) Bake in preheated moderate oven (375°F.) 20 minutes, or until hot and bubbly. Makes 8 servings.

SEEDED BREADSTICKS

Slice 8 frankfurter buns, separating tops and bottoms. Slice bottoms in half lengthwise and tops in thirds lengthwise. Dip sticks in melted butter and sprinkle with sesame or poppy seed. Bake on sheet in 350°F. oven 10 to 12 minutes.
NOTE: Can be made ahead and frozen in foil.

GLAZED PEAR CAKE DESSERT

2 cans (29-ounces each) pear halves
1¾ cups buttermilk biscuit mix
⅔ cup granulated sugar
1 egg
⅓ cup milk
2½ tablespoons butter or margarine
1¼ teaspoons vanilla extract
12 maraschino cherries (see Note)
Slivered blanched almonds
¼ cup peach preserves
1 tablespoon brandy
Brown sugar

Drain pears, reserving ⅓ cup syrup. Set pears aside; put syrup in large bowl of electric mixer with next 6 ingredients. Beat at medium speed 4 minutes, scraping bowl occasionally. Pour into greased and floured 8-inch square baking dish and bake in preheated moderate oven (350°F.) 20 minutes. Remove from oven and arrange 12 pear halves, cherry flowers and almonds on top. Brush with peach preserves, heated with brandy. Sprinkle with brown sugar. Bake 5 to 10 minutes in oven. Serve hot. Makes 8 servings.
NOTE: Make cherry flowers by cutting them with scissors almost to the stem end and spread gently.

SIT-DOWN DINNER
[Serves 4]

Carrot-Juice Cocktail with Green-Onion Muddler
Appetizers—Watercress, Green Pepper, Black Olives and Cheddar Cheese
Baked Stuffed-Cabbage Rolls
Parsleyed Fordhook Limas
Baked Tomatoes and Mushrooms
Toasted Crisp Rye Wafers with Caraway Butter
Apricot-Potato-Almond Torte
Herb Tea

A sit-down dinner does not have to be the classic soup, roast, vegetables, salad and dessert that many of us are so used to. It can be an off-beat menu, like the one here that keeps up with the times—a vegetarian meal that gives you and your friends a delicious taste of one of the big trends in eating today—natural foods.

Our decorating theme reflects the menu with a countrified checked cloth and napkins (you make these from inexpensive permanent-press fabric) and a centerpiece that is a basket filled with vegetables, planted with "fruit" and "vegetable" bubble-bath packets on sticks for favors (they can be real seed packets, of course). The invitation repeats our spring-like garden idea with its cut-out vegetable pasted on a card that carries the message; the card, in turn, is mounted on cardboard covered in fabric to match the tablecloth.

The menu involves fresh vegetables, but they can be picked up a couple of days before the dinner, and the rest of the ingredients a week or more ahead. Most of the cooking will be done just before dinner is served, but a timer should keep that schedule easily under control. Plan to serve the first course in the living room and to use a warming tray or some such device if you want to keep the main dish warm on the table. The cake and its plates and the teacups, of course, can be set out before the guests arrive.

CARROT-JUICE COCKTAIL

Chill pure canned carrot juice. Add seasoned salt and pepper and lemon juice to taste. Serve with a green onion in each glass as a muddler.

APPETIZERS

Arrange on individual trays or plates a few watercress sprigs, thinly sliced green-pepper rings, a few pitted black

olives and 3 x ½-inch Cheddar-cheese sticks. If you wish, the vegetables and cheese can be prepared earlier in the day of the party and refrigerated.

BAKED STUFFED-CABBAGE ROLLS

1 head cabbage (about 2½ to 3 pounds)
Salt
1 cup finely chopped walnuts
1 cup finely chopped celery
2 cups cooked brown rice
2 tablespoons instant minced onion
1 egg
1 cup instant vegetable broth
½ teaspoon celery salt
Dash of white pepper
1 can (10¾ ounces) condensed tomato soup
½ teaspoon dried oregano
2 tablespoons butter or margarine
Parsleyed Fordhook Limas
Baked Tomatoes and Mushrooms

Trim cabbage, cut around center core and drop cabbage into large pot of boiling salted water. Remove 8 large whole leaves as they wilt. Drain on absorbent paper and peel off some of the coarse center core. Divide remaining cabbage in quarters and slice lengthwise in ½ inch wide strips; set aside. Combine next 5 ingredients with ½ cup vegetable broth; add celery salt and white pepper and mix well. Divide mixture evenly onto center of cabbage leaves, fold up sides and shape in roll. Put sliced cabbage in botton of greased shallow 4-quart casserole or oven-proof serving platter, Arrange cabbage rolls, folded side down, on top, Combine soup, remaining broth and oregano, mix well and pour over cabbage rolls. Dot with butter and bake in preheated moderate oven (375°F.) 50 minutes. Arrange limas, tomato halves and mushrooms around rolls. Rice and wilted cabbage can be cooked the day before. Makes 4 servings.

Sit Down Dinner

Parsleyed Fordhook Limas

Cook 1 package (10 ounces) frozen Fordhook lima beans as directed on label. Drain and season with salt, pepper and butter. Add chopped parsley to taste.

Baked Tomatoes and Mushrooms

Arrange tomato halves, cut side up, in small baking pan with ½ pound whole mushrooms. Dot with butter and sprinkle tomatoes with grated Parmesan cheese. Sprinkle with paprika, salt and pepper and bake with cabbage rolls 20 minutes before rolls should be done. Tomatoes and mushrooms can be prepared early in the day. Add cheese and seasonings just before you put dish on oven.

TOASTED CRISP RYE WAFERS WITH CARAWAY BUTTER

Spread rye wafers on baking sheet. Toast in preheated hot oven (400°F.) 7 to 8 minutes; cool. Serve with creamed butter, seasoned with crushed caraway seed to taste; it can be made a day ahead.

APRICOT-POTATO-ALMOND TORTE

- 5 tablespoons margarine
- ¾ cup sugar
- 2 eggs, separated
- 1 teaspoon grated lemon rind
- ¾ cup ground blanched almonds
- 1½ medium potatoes, cooked and finely shredded (about 1 cup)
- 1 can (1 pound) apricot halves, drained
- ⅓ cup apricot preserves
- Chopped nuts

Butter well a round 8-inch layer-cake pan. Line bottom with waxed paper cut in circle to fit pan; butter paper. Cream margarine, sugar, egg yolks and lemon rind until light and fluffy. Add almonds and potato and mix well. Beat egg whites until stiff and fold into cake mixture. Pour into prepared pan. Bake in preheated moderate oven (350°F.) 45 to 50 minutes, or until done. Cool on rack about 5 minutes. Turn out on serving plate, remove waxed paper and cool completely. (Can be done to this point the day before.) Garnish with apricot halves, rounded side up. Heat apricot preserves gently, stirring, until slightly thinned. Spoon on apricots and sprinkle with nuts. Makes 6 servings.

Notes on last-minute countdown: You can assemble the appetizer trays when the guests arrive, putting the carrot juice on each tray. . . . To leave yourself ten minutes or so at serving time to arrange vegetables in casserole, heat wafers, light candles, etc., put the casserole in the oven an hour before you plan to eat. Thirty minutes ahead, put in the tomato-mushroom pan and start the lima beans.

LIGHT LUNCHEON I

Frosted Stacked Sandwiches
Jellied Cucumber and Chinese-Cabbage Salad
Marinated Shrimps
Cherry Tomatoes
Onion Curls
Fresh Strawberries (with confectioners' sugar and liqueur)
Tea, Lemon Wedges

FROSTED STACKED SANDWICHES

- Fillings
- 8 slices each whole-wheat and white bread
- Whipped cream cheese
- Few drops onion juice
- Light cream
- Watercress

Divide and spread fillings among 4 stacks of bread, allowing 2 whole-wheat and 2 white slices to each stack and alternating types. Mix cream cheese with onion juice and add enough cream to make mixture of spreading consistency. Frost filled stacks and cut in half. Put on serving plates and garnish with watercress. Sandwiches can be spread the day before serving. Wrap air-tight and refrigerate. Frost and garnish shortly before serving. Makes 8 servings.

TUNA FILLING

- 1 can (7 ounces) solid-pack white tuna, well drained and finely flaked
- ½ cup minced celery
- 1 tablespoon minced green onion
- ½ cup mayonnaise
- 1 tablespoon minced sweet gherkin
- Salt to taste
- ⅛ teaspoon black pepper

Mix all ingredients together.

HAM FILLING

- 1 can (12 ounces) chopped ham
- ½ cup minced sweet gherkins
- ½ cup mayonnaise
- 1 teaspoon lemon juice

Force ham through coarse blade of food chopper, then mix well with remaining ingredients.

EGG ALMOND FILLING

- 4 hard-cooked eggs
- ½ teaspoon onion salt
- ½ teaspoon dry mustard
- ⅓ cup mayonnaise
- 2 tablespoons minced blanched almonds

Force eggs through ricer or coarse sieve, then mix with remaining ingredients.

JELLIED CUCUMBER AND CHINESE-CABBAGE SALAD

- 2 envelopes unflavored gelatin
- 1½ cups each unsweetened pineapple and grapefruit juices
- 1 to 2 tablespoons sugar
- ½ teaspoon salt
- ⅛ teaspoon white pepper
- 1 medium cucumber
- 1 can (2 ounces) chopped pimientos, drained
- 2 tablespoons minced green onion
- 3 cups thinly shredded Chinese cabbage

Soften gelatin in 1 cup pineapple juice. Dissolve over low heat, then mix with remaining juices. Add sugar and seasonings. Cover bottoms of six 8-ounce molds to depth of ⅛ inch and chill until firm. Partially peel cucumber and cut off 6 thin slices. Cut remaining cucumber in half lengthwise and scoop out seeds. Dice cucumber fine and

Light Luncheon I

set aside. Arrange a few pimiento pieces and a cucumber slice on set gelatin in each mold. Add a small amount of gelatin to bind and chill again until firm. Chill remaining gelatin mixture until slightly thickened. Mix remaining pimiento, cucumber, onion and cabbage with slightly thickened gelatin and spoon into molds. Chill until firm, then unmold. Makes 6 servings.

MARINATED SHRIMPS

Cook large shrimps in well-seasoned broth until pink. Drain, peel and devein. Split lengthwise, using a sharp thin-bladed knife. Marinate in French dressing seasoned with chopped fresh dill or any favorite herb. Cover and chill a few hours.

ONION CURLS

Cut green onions crosswise in 1½ to 2 inch pieces (use both white and green part). With sharp scissors or knife, fringe ends ⅛ inch thick toward center, leaving a ½ inch piece in center intact. Drop into ice water and chill until ends curl.

FRESH STRAWBERRIES

Arrange whole fresh strawberries on individual trays or plates and serve with small bowls or saucers of confectioners' sugar and Cointreau, Grand Mariner, kirsch, white wine or orange juice.

LIGHT LUNCHEON II

Curried Chicken Salad with
Broiled Topping
Raw Relishes
Chutney Rolls
Coconut Ice Cream Balls with
Crushed Strawberries
Minted Iced Tea

CURRIED CHICKEN SALAD WITH BROILED TOPPING

3 cups cooked chicken cut in ½-inch dice
2½ cups thinly sliced celery
⅓ cup French dressing
2 teaspoons curry powder
¾ cup mayonnaise
½ cup dairy sour cream
Salt and white pepper
⅓ cup toasted slivered almonds
2 cups finely crushed potato chips
1 cup coarse shredded sharp Cheddar cheese

Combine first 3 ingredients in mixing bowl and marinate in refrigerator at least 1 hour. Blend well curry powder, mayonnaise and sour cream; combine with chicken mixture. Season to taste with salt and white pepper. Cover loosely and chill (this can be done the day before serving). Fold in almonds and put salad in greased shallow 2½-quart broiler-proof baking dish or in 6 individual ramekins. Mix potato chips and cheese and cover top of salad completely with mixture. Put under preheated broiler, 3 minutes, watching carefully, or until cheese is melted and top is browned and crisp (salad remains cold). Makes 6 servings.

CHUTNEY ROLLS

Combine and mix well 6 tablespoons soft butter or margarine and ¼ cup minced chutney. Split 8 small dinner rolls and spread with mixture. Put on baking sheet and bake in preheated hot oven (400°F.) until hot and bubbly. Makes 16.

COCONUT ICE CREAM BALLS WITH CRUSHED STRAWBERRIES

Line a small baking sheet with waxed paper. Shape any flavor ice cream in balls, using an ice cream scoop. Roll quickly in flaked coconut and put in single layer on baking sheet. Freeze until firm. Meanwhile slice fresh strawberries, sweeten lightly with confectioners' sugar and sprinkle with lemon juice to taste. Let stand a few minutes, then crush with fork. Serve on ice cream balls.

PARTRIDGE—A game bird of the Old World. The two principal species are the Gray, frequenting moors and open country and especially favoring cultivated land, and the Red-legged, or French, partridge. The Hungarian and Bohemain partridges, considered particularly suitable for propagation in the United States are varieties of the Gray species, hardier and somewhat larger than the formerly better-known English variety.

In different parts of the United States, the title of partridge is given to various American birds. Although in strict parlance it is not applicable to any birds indigenous to the western hemisphere, good general usage now applies the name American partridge to the native Ruffed Grouse. In the south it is more generally applied to the Bobwhite.

The delicious plump little partridge has been hunted since the Middle Ages; one of the famous English Christmas carols "Twelve Days of Christmas" stresses the partridge in a pear tree, showing how highly both were thought of.

Availability and Purchasing Guide—The average partridge weighs twelve to fourteen ounces, and one partridge makes one serving. Frozen fresh partridges are available in specialty food stores, as are canned whole and canned smoked partridges.

Caloric Value
3½ ounces, raw = 168 calories

Basic Preparation—After killing, a young bird should be hung in a cool airy place for no longer than 4 days; an older one may be hung for 1 week, depending on one's taste for a high flavor. Young birds should be roasted or broiled, older birds braised or stewed and preferably tenderized by marinating before cooking. Depending on their age and plumpness, partridges may be larded before cooking, that is, wrapped in salt pork or bacon slices or coated with lard. This gives needed additional fat to their lean meat in order to keep it juicy.

To Cook—A simple way to serve young partridges is to roast them. Season the birds with salt and pepper and roast them in preheated moderate oven (325°F.) for 1 to 1½ hours, or until partridge is tender. Serve immediately.

To Freeze—Eviscerate partridges carefully to prevent tainting of meat from undigested food in the intestines. Since a partridge is generally roasted whole, it is frozen whole. Tie the legs and wings closely to the body. Do not stuff the birds until they are ready to be cooked. Wrap birds in moisture-proof wrapping, excluding all air, and seal tightly. Label. Freeze until firm. Storage life in a freezer is 1 year.

PARTRIDGES IN MARINADE

4 partridges, dressed and quartered
¼ cup cooking oil
Salt and pepper to taste
1 cup white wine
1 cup cider vinegar
2 tablespoons each chopped fresh thyme and parsley
2 teaspoons each chopped fresh basil and marjoram
2 garlic cloves, chopped

Brown partridges on all sides in hot oil. Sprinkle with salt and pepper. Add remaining ingredients. Bring to boil, lower heat, and simmer until partridges are tender. Serve hot or cold. Makes 4 servings.

PARTRIDGES WITH CABBAGE AND JUNIPER BERRIES

1 medium-size green cabbage
Bacon fat
6 partridges, dressed and trussed
½ pound sliced bacon
6 carrots, sliced
6 smoked sausages
Salt and pepper to taste
6 juniper berries
2 garlic cloves, minced
2 teaspoons sugar
½ teaspoon ground nutmeg
1 teaspoon grated lemon rind
Bouillon

Separate cabbage into leaves and parboil for 5 to 6 minutes. Drain cabbage and cut into shreds, removing all stalks. Put half of cabbage in a roasting pan with cover. Heat bacon fat and brown partridges on all sides. Put partridges on top of cabbage. Add bacon, carrots, and sausages and sprinkle with salt and pepper. Add remaining ingredients except bouillon. Cover with remaining cabbage. Add enough bouillon to come halfway up the cabbage, and cover. Bake in preheated slow oven (200°F.) about 4 hours. Makes 6 servings.

PASSION FRUIT—The edible fruit of the passiflora or passion flower, a vine with solitary spectacular flowers which is a native of tropical Brazil. The passion flower is so named because it supposedly symbolized the nails, wounds, and crown of thorns of Christ. The fruit is also known as granadilla. It has a sweet-acid flavor, and it is used as a table fruit, as well as for making sherbets, candy, and in very refreshing beverages.

The purple passion fruit, about three inches in length, with many seeds, is found wild in North and South America and Australia. It requires a tropical, sub-tropical,

or warm temperate climate. In Australia, it is a crop of great economic importance. In the United States it is cultivated in Florida and other southern states; but only in California is it cultivated commercially.

Other species of passion fruit are the giant granadilla, which has greenish-yellow fruit that reach ten inches in length, and the sweet granadilla.

Availability—A highly perishable fruit, it is found only in specialty fruit markets in the fall. Some canned passion-fruit nectar is available in specialty food stores.

Caloric Value
Raw, 3½ ounces, pulp and seeds = 90 calories

PASSION-FRUIT CHIFFON PIE

Crust:

2 cups finely rolled graham-cracker crumbs
½ cup sugar
½ cup melted butter or margarine

Filling:

1 envelope unflavored gelatin
Cold water
3 egg yolks, well beaten
Juice of 1 lemon
1 cup puréed passion fruit
3 egg whites
6 tablespoons sugar
Whipped cream, sweetened and flavored with vanilla extract

Mix crumbs with sugar and butter. Press mixture firmly against bottom and sides of 8-inch pie pan. Chill until ready to fill. Sprinkle gelatin into ¼ cup cold water. Let stand for 5 minutes. Beat egg yolks with ⅓ cup water and lemon juice. Cook over low heat, stirring constantly, until smooth and thickened. Stir in gelatin and passion fruit. Chill mixture until it begins to thicken. Beat egg whites until stiff. Gradually beat in sugar, 1 tablespoon at a time, until stiff and glossy. Fold egg whites into fruit mixture. Pour mixture into crumb crust and chill until firm. Top with sweetened whipped cream. Makes 6 to 8 servings.

PASTA COOKBOOK

PASTA—The Italian word for "paste," which in culinary usage describes an alimentary paste made from semolina and water. Semolina is the purified middlings of hard wheat, the best being durum, or macaroni wheat, grown in this country in the western north-central states, chiefly Minnesota. Durum wheat is heavy with gluten, the principal protein component of wheat and other grains.

In the manufacture of pasta, the semolina is moistened with boiling water, then worked to produce a smooth tough dough. This dough is placed in a cylinder and forced through a perforated plate called a "trafila"; then it is dried. The form of the trafila determines the nature of the pasta product. When the trafila has small holes, each with a steel pin in it, macaroni and similar hollow tubular pastas are produced. A bent steel pin turns out elbow macaroni. With smaller holes and no steel pins, the result is spaghetti. For the flat ribbonlike pastas, the trafila is perforated with slits. The short-size pastas and the small fancy shapes are sliced off by rotary knives as the pasta emerges from the trafila. Shells are made by forcing the pasta through a die.

In Italy, the country with which pasta and pasta dishes is most closely associated, there are more than 100 varieties, some large to be stuffed, like lasagna, others small decorative shapes: stars, hearts, animals, and letters, for example. The Italian names for these varieties are wonderfully descriptive. Among them can be found *amorini,* little cupids, *capelletti d'angelo,* angels' hair, *cappelli di prete,* priests' hats, *cappelli pagliaccio,* clowns' hats, *conchigliette,* little shells, *ditalini,* little thimbles, *farfalloni,* big butterflies, *fusilli,* spindles, *lancette,* little spears, *linguine,* little tongues, *lingue di passero,* sparrows' tongues, *lumache, lumachine,* and *lumacone* or snails, little snails, and big snails, *mostaccioli,* little mugs, *occhi di lupo,* wolf's eyes, *ondulati,* wavy ones, *ricciolina,* little curls, *rigatoni,* little fluted ones, *stelline,* little stars, *stivaletti,* little boots, *vermicelli,* little worms, and *ziti,* bridegrooms.

There are also colored pastas. Spinach and beet juice are used to produce green and red pastas, eggs to make bright yellow pastas.

Availablity and Purchasing Guide—Pasta is available packaged in a wide variety of sizes and shapes. In Italian food stores it is occasionally available in bulk, and also packaged in a more complete selection of types. Some pastas, particularly macaroni and spaghetti, are available canned and frozen in combination with other foods.

Look for pasta enriched with thiamin, riboflavin, niacin and iron. Green (spinach) noodles and whole-wheat pastas are also available in some stores.

Select the shapes you prefer for the individual recipe. Macaroni and spaghetti come in about 150 shapes; noodles, which contain eggs, come in fine, medium or wide width. Shapes can be interchanged so long as cooked volume is about the same (macaroni and spaghetti double in volume; noodles stay the same). For 4 servings, cook 8 ounces (2 cups) macaroni or spaghetti, or 4 cups noodles.

Storage—Store in a cool dry place.
Kitchen shelf: 3 to 6 months
Refrigerator shelf, cooked and covered: 4 to 5 days
Refrigerator frozen-food compartment, prepared for freezing: 3 to 4 weeks
Freezer, prepared for freezing: 1 year

Nutritive Food Values—Enriched pastas contain some protein, thiamine, riboflavin, and niacin, and appreciable amount of calcium, phosphorus, and potassium.
Spaghetti, cooked tender, 1 cup = 155 calories
Noodles, cooked, 1 cup = 200 calories
Macaroni, cooked firm, 1 cup = 190 calories
Macaroni, cooked tender, 1 cup = 155 calories

Basic Preparation—Pasta should be cooked *al dente:* to the toothsome stage when it is tender yet still resilient to the bite. To cook pasta properly, it is absolutely essential to have a very big pot with rapidly boiling salted water. Unless the pasta cooks in sufficient water, it cannot expand properly and shed its excess starch. Spaghetti, one of the most popular kinds of pasta, also presents the problem of strands sticking together. The addition of a little olive oil to the boiling water helps keep them apart, but this is not necessary when the pasta is stirred properly.

Another equally important step is to have the pasta reach the table hot, and piping hot at that, the hotter the better. The pasta must be cooked in violently boiling water, drained quickly, poured immediately onto a hot serving dish, served with a sauce that is hot, and preferably on really hot dinner plates. If these rules are observed, making good pasta dishes should present no problem.

To Cook One Pound of Pasta

1. Use kettle large enough to hold 6 quarts of water (½ pound of pasta should be cooked in 3 quarts of water). Add 2 tablespoons salt to 6 quarts water (1 tablespoon salt to 3 quarts water).
2. Bring water to a full, rolling boil. Gradually add pasta, stirring with a long-handle, two-prong kitchen fork. The water should keep on boiling hard.
3. As the pasta begins to soften, fold it over and over in the water so that it won't stick together. Keep on stirring it frequently during the whole cooking process. Occasionally lift out a strand and taste for doneness. Different pastas have different cooking times. Thus tasting is essential to get the pasta right for one's own taste.

   Pasta that is to be cooked further in a casserole should not be more than three-quarters done, or the end results will be mushy.
4. When the pasta is done, drain it immediately into a large strainer or colander. Return to pot and add seasonings. Stir to coat all strands. Serve immediately on heated platter and heated plates. For salads, drain pasta in a colander and rinse twice with cold water. Drain well.

CHOWDER

MACARONI FISH-VEGETABLE CHOWDER

1 cup thinly sliced celery
1 small onion, thinly sliced
¼ cup butter or margarine
1 pound frozen cod fillets, partially thawed and cut in cubes
2½ teaspoons salt
¼ teaspoon pepper
¼ teaspoon dried thyme
¼ teaspoon dried marjoram
1 small garlic clove, crushed
1 bay leaf
1 can (1 pound) cut green beans
1 can (1 pound) sliced carrots
8 ounces elbow macaroni
2 cups milk

Cook celery and onion in butter in kettle or Dutch oven 2 minutes, or until crisp-tender. Add fish and seasonings. Drain beans and carrots and add enough water to liquids to make 1½ quarts. Add to fish mixture, bring to boil and simmer, covered, 15 minutes. Bring to boil and gradually add macaroni. Boil 10 minutes, or until macaroni is tender. Add beans, carrots and milk; heat. Makes about 2 quarts, or 6 servings.

MAIN AND SIDE DISHES

LUXURY LASAGNA

1 large onion, chopped
2 garlic cloves, crushed
⅓ cup olive oil
½ pound chicken livers, chopped
¼ pound prosciutto, chopped
2 cups chopped cooked chicken
2 cans (1 pound each) herbed tomato sauce
2 cans (6 ounces each) tomato paste
1 cup chicken broth
1 cup dry white wine
1 teaspoon salt
½ teaspoon each pepper, dried basil and oregano
1 pound curly lasagna (about 19 pieces)
1 pound ricotta
2 cups grated Parmesan cheese
½ pound mozzarella cheese, sliced

Sauté onion and garlic in oil in skillet until crisp-tender. Add chicken livers and sauté until browned. Add remaining ingredients, except last 4. Bring to boil, cover and simmer, stirring occasionally, 30 minutes. Meanwhile, cook and drain lasagna. Rinse with cold water to make separation easier while working and drain again. Pour a little sauce into greased 16 x 9½ x 2½-inch baking dish (or 2 smaller dishes). Top with a layer of lasagna. Spread with a third of ricotta and sprinkle with a third of Parmesan cheese. Top with more sauce. Repeat layers twice. Arrange mozzarella slices on top and bake in preheated moderate oven (350°F.) 30 minutes, or until bubbly. Makes 8 to 12 servings.

CLAM CASSEROLE

8 ounces noodles
1 can (8 ounces) minced clams
1 can (4 ounces) mushroom stems and pieces
1 can (10½ ounces) condensed cream of mushroom soup
1 green pepper, chopped
1 medium onion, chopped
1 cup shredded Cheddar cheese
½ cup herb-flavored stuffing mix, crushed
2 tablespoons butter or margarine, melted
Paprika

Cook noodles 5 minutes, then drain. Drain clams and mushrooms, reserving liquid. Mix reserved liquid with soup. Mix together all ingredients, except last 3. Pour into greased 2-quart casserole. Mix stuffing and butter and sprinkle on top, then sprinkle with paprika. Cover and bake in preheated 350°F. oven 20 minutes. Uncover and bake 10 minutes longer. Makes 6 servings.

NOODLE-ONION PIE

3 ounces (1½ cups) medium noodles
2 cups thinly sliced onion
2 tablespoons butter or margarine
Cheese Pie Shell
2 eggs, slightly beaten
1 cup milk, scalded
1 teaspoon salt
¼ teaspoon pepper
1 cup grated Cheddar cheese

Cook and drain noodles. Sauté onion in butter in skillet until tender but not brown. Remove from heat, add noodles and toss lightly. Put in unbaked Cheese Pie Shell. Combine eggs and milk, salt, pepper and cheese. Pour over noodles and bake in preheated slow oven (325°F.) 30 to 35 minutes, or until knife inserted in center comes out clean. Cool slightly before cutting. Makes 6 servings.

Cheese Pie Shell

In bowl, combine 1 cup grated Cheddar cheese, ¾ cup all-purpose flour, ½ teaspoon salt, ¼ teaspoon dry mustard and ¼ cup melted butter or margarine. Mix with pastry blender or fork until smooth. Knead about 1 minute to soften, then, without rolling, press firmly on bottom and sides of 9-inch piepan and flute edge.

MACARONI, TUNA AND BEAN POT

3 tablespoons butter or margarine
3 tablespoons all-purpose flour
2 cups milk
1 teaspoon each salt and dried basil
¼ teaspoon pepper
8 ounces elbow macaroni, cooked
1 jar (4 ounces) pimiento, diced
1 package (9 ounces) frozen cut green beans
1 cup diced American cheese
1 can (7 ounces) tuna
¼ cup parsley

Melt butter in saucepan and stir in flour. Remove from heat and gradually stir in milk. Cook over low heat until slightly thickened, stirring constantly. Stir in salt, basil and pepper, then macaroni, pimiento and beans. Simmer for 3 or 4 minutes. Stir in cheese and cook until cheese melts. Add tuna, drained and broken in chunks, and parsley. Heat through and serve. Makes 6 servings.

FUSILLI [SPIRAL MACARONI] WITH VEGETABLE SAUCE

1 medium eggplant
½ cup olive oil
2 medium zucchini, cut in ½-inch slices
2 medium onions, thinly sliced
2 medium green peppers, thinly sliced
2 garlic cloves, minced
5 firm medium tomatoes, peeled and sliced
2 teaspoons salt
½ teaspoon each coarsely ground pepper, dried basil and oregano
1 tablespoon capers
¼ cup chopped parsley
1 pound fusilli
Grated Parmesan cheese (optional)

Peel eggplant and cut in 3-inch strips ½ inch thick. Sauté quickly on both sides in ¼ cup oil in kettle or Dutch oven. Remove and add remaining ¼ cup oil to kettle. Add zucchini, sauté quickly and remove. Add next 3 ingredients to oil remaining in kettle and sauté 2 to 3 minutes. Arrange tomato slices on top, cover and cook 5 minutes. Gently stir in eggplant, zucchini and remaining ingredients, except fusilli and cheese. Cover and cook slowly 25 minutes. Cook fusilli, drain and put in serving dish. Pour sauce over top, and serve with cheese, if desired. Makes 6 to 8 servings.

SALADS

MACARONI-TUNA-VEGETABLE SALAD

8 ounces elbow macaroni, cooked
⅓ cup salad oil
1 tablespoon cider vinegar
½ teaspoon dried oregano
¼ teaspoon dried basil
1 green pepper, cut in thin strips
1 can (13 ounces) tuna
1 can (14 ounces) artichoke hearts
Salt and pepper
Red radish roses
Celery hearts
1 can (3¼ ounces) pitted ripe olives
2 tomatoes, cut in wedges

Cook macaroni in 3 quarts rapidly boiling salted water, stirring occasionally, until tender. Drain in colander. Rinse with cold water, drain again. Return macaroni to pot. Add next 7 ingredients and salt and pepper to taste; toss to mix. Cover and chill for several hours. To serve, toss salad lightly; arrange on serving platter. Garnish with chilled radish roses, celery hearts, olives and tomatoes. Makes 6 servings.

MEDLEY MACARONI SALAD

8 ounces macaroni
¼ cup bottled French dressing
1 cup dairy sour cream
Salt and pepper to taste
½ pound bacon, cooked crisp and crumbled
1 cup diced cooked chicken
2 hard-cooked eggs, chopped
¼ cup chopped pimientos
1 large tomato, diced
2 tablespoons lemon juice
1 small avocado, peeled and sliced
Crisp chicory

Cook macaroni, drain, rinse with cold water and cool. Combine dressing with sour cream, mixing well. Add macaroni and mix. Add remaining ingredients, except last 3, and toss lightly. Place in salad bowl. Sprinkle lemon juice on avocado. Garnish salad with avocado and chicory. Makes 6 to 8 servings.

acaroni-Tuna-Vegetable Salad

PASTA CASSEROLES

by SHIRLEY SARVIS

MUSHROOM-HAM CASSEROLE WITH PEA PURÉE

4 ounces broad egg noodles
Pea Purée
1½ pounds lean smoked ham or leftover roast ham, cut into 2-inch slivers
1 tablespoon each butter or dry sherry
½ pound mushrooms, thickly sliced
2 egg yolks
Tarragon Sour Cream
1 cup fine soft bread crumbs (about)
3 tablespoons butter, melted (about)
2 tablespoons grated Romano cheese
½ cup slivered almonds

Cook noodles according to package directions; rinse and drain well. Toss noodles with Pea Purée and arrange on bottom of a buttered shallow 2-quart baking dish. Season with salt if necessary. In a skillet, brown ham slivers slowly in their own fat about 5 minutes. Add butter, sherry and mushrooms; cover and cook just until mushrooms are tender. Spread ham and mushrooms over noodles. Beat egg yolks and mix with Tarragon Sour Cream; pour evenly over ham and mushrooms. Toss bread crumbs with melted butter and sprinkle over top. Sprinkle with Romano, then with almonds. Bake in preheated hot oven (400°F.) 20 to 25 minutes. Makes 6 servings.

Pea Purée

Combine in a saucepan 2 packages (10 ounces each) frozen peas, ½ cup each chopped onion and water, 1 teaspoon chicken stock concentrate and ½ teaspoon dried oregano. Bring to a boil; then cover and simmer until peas are very tender, about 25 minutes. Cool slightly; then whirl in blender or press through food mill to purée.

Tarragon Sour Cream

Mix ¾ cup dairy sour cream, 2 teaspoons minced shallots or white part of green onions, 1 teaspoon dried tarragon and ½ teaspoon celery salt; let stand 30 minutes.

BROILED ORIENTAL-STEW CASSEROLE

2 cups wheel macaroni, or 3 cups broad egg noodles broken into 2-inch pieces
2 tablespoons peanut oil
6 green onions with part of green tops, cut diagonally into 1-inch lengths
1 large green pepper, cut into strips about ¼ x 1-inch
3 stalks celery, cut diagonally into ¼-inch crescents
½ pound small mushrooms (about), cut in half
1½ cups fresh (or 7-ounce package frozen, thawed) Chinese snow peas or 1 cup fresh (or thawed frozen), green peas
1 cup (6 ounces) slivered boiled or baked ham (about)
Rich Bouillon or heat together 3 cans (10½ ounces each) beef bouillon, 1 cup water and ⅔ cup dry white wine)
12 large oysters, drained and dried
3 tablespoons butter (about), melted
½ cup fine dry bread crumbs (about)
½ teaspoon dried thyme (about)
Lime twists
Thin tomato wedges

Cook macaroni according to package directions; drain. Heat oil in a large skillet; add onions, green pepper, celery, mushrooms and snow peas. Sauté over medium-high heat about 2 minutes, tossing lightly; reduce heat to low, cover and cook 3 to 4 minutes more, or until vegetables are crisp and barley tender. Toss vegetables with macaroni and ham. Turn into greased 3-quart casserole or 6 individual ovenproof casseroles. Pour in enough of hot bouillon just to cover vegetable mixture. Dip oysters into melted butter, then into bread crumbs mixed with thyme; place on surface of casserole. Broil about 3 inches from heat 5 minutes, or until crumbs brown and oyster edges curl. Garnish with lime twists and tomato wedges. Serve in individual casseroles or soup bowls. Makes 6 servings.

Rich Bouillon

Combine in a saucepan 3 cans (10½ ounces each) beef bouillon, 1 cup water, ⅔ cup dry white wine, 6 celery tops, 1 grated carrot, 3 tablespoons chopped onion, 8 parsley sprigs, 4 teaspoons catsup, 1 strip lemon peel about ½ x 2 inches, halved, 1 garlic clove and ¼ teaspoon dried thyme. Bring to a boil, then cover and simmer 45 minutes. Strain. Makes about 4½ cups.

CARAWAY CHICKEN-CURRY CASSEROLE

2 small-to-medium sweet onions, very thinly sliced
Caraway Butter Sauce
Fruited Seasoning Sauce
1 frying chicken (2½ to 3 pounds), cut into serving pieces
Salt and pepper
4 ounces (about ¾ cup) moist dried apricots
Toasted-Sesame Pasta
Thin lemon and lime wedges

Break onions into rings in bottom of greased shallow 2½ to 3-quart casserole. Add 2 tablespoons Butter Sauce and toss to coat onions well. Spoon on about one third Fruited Seasoning Sauce. Dry chicken pieces well and season with salt and pepper. Dip into Butter Sauce and place in a single layer over onions. Bake, uncovered, in preheated moderate oven (375°F.) 15 minutes. Reduce oven heat to slow (325°F.) and bake 45 minutes more, or until tender. Tuck in apricots among chicken pieces. Spoon remaining Seasoning Sauce over chicken and fruit. Bake 15 minutes more. Put Sesame Pasta in center of casserole and spoon curry juices over chicken and noodles. Put in oven a few minutes to heat through. Garnish with lemon and lime wedges. Makes 4 servings.

Caraway Butter Sauce

Melt 6 tablespoons butter over medium heat; add 2 teaspoons caraway seed and 2 to 3 teaspoons curry powder. Cook, stirring, about 1 minute. Stir in ½ teaspoon ground cardamom, ¼ teaspon chili powder, 1 garlic clove, minched or crushed, and 3 tablespoons dry vermouth. Cook and stir over very low heat about 2 minutes.

Fruited Seasoning Sauce

Mix ¼ cup each dry vermouth and plum jam, 1 tablespoon each catsup and chicken stock concentrate, ¾ teaspoon grated fresh ginger or ½ teaspoon ground ginger, and 1 bay leaf, finely crumbled.

Toasted-Sesame Pasta

Cook 4 ounces green (or white) noodles according to package directions; drain well. In a small pan, melt 2 tablespoons butter; add 2 tablespoons sesame seed and cook over low heat, stirring, until brown. Remove from heat and stir in 1 teaspoon lemon juice. Toss pasta with butter.

WALNUTTED SHRIMP CASSEROLE

1½ cups (4 ounces) small seashell macaroni
1 pound cooked small shelled shrimp
1 large green pepper, cut into ¾-inch slivers
2 large stalks celery, very thinly sliced
Herb Sour Cream
2 cups finely chopped walnuts
3 tablespoons butter, melted
2 hard-cooked eggs, finely sieved
¼ cup minced parsley (about)

Cook macaroni according to package directions; rinse and drain well and blot dry with paper toweling. Combine shells with shrimp, green pepper, celery and half of Herb Sour Cream; toss gently to mix, then turn into buttered shallow baking and serving 2-quart casserole. Toss walnuts with butter and sprinkle evenly over top. Bake in preheated moderate oven (350°F.) 25 minutes, or until heated through. Put sieved eggs in the center of casserole. Sprinkle parsley over eggs. Pass remaining Herb Sour Cream as a sauce. Makes 6 generous servings.

Herb Sour Cream

Mix together thoroughly: 2 cups dairy sour cream; ⅔ cup mayonnaise; ¼ cup lemon juice; 8 green onions with part of green tops, thinly sliced; 2 teaspoons each crumbled dillweed and dry mustard; 1 teaspoon dried tarragon; and ½ teaspoon each salt, celery salt, and pepper.

LAYERED TAGLIARINI AND SPINACH CASSEROLE

4 ounces tagliarini (or spaghetti), broken into 1½-inch pieces
Ricotta Custard
¾ cup shredded Monterey Jack or domestic Muenster cheese
Basil Spinach
Lemon-Nutmeg Meatballs
½ cup grated Parmesan cheese
Tomato-Mushroom Sauce

Cook tagliarini according to package directions; rinse in cold water; drain well. Combine tagliarini and Ricotta Custard; spread on bottom of buttered shallow 2-quart casserole. Sprinkle with Jack cheese. Spoon Basil Spinach on cheese and gently spread with fork to make an even layer. Nest meatballs into spinach. Sprinkle with Parmesan. Cover and bake in moderate oven (350°F.) 15 minutes; remove cover and bake 15 to 20 minutes more, or until custard is set. Serve with Tomato-Mushroom Sauce. Makes 6 generous servings.

Ricotta Custard

Beat 2 eggs slightly and mix with 1 cup (½ pound) ricotta cheese, ½ cup milk, ½ teaspoon salt and ¼ teaspoon ground nutmeg.

Lemon-Nutmeg Meatballs

Mix together thoroughly: 1 pound ground round, ¾ cup fine fresh bread crumbs, 2 tablespoons each catsup and dry red wine, 2 teaspoons olive oil, ½ teaspoon salt, ¾ teaspoon celery salt, ½ teaspoon grated lemon rind, ¼ teaspoon ground nutmeg and ¼ teaspoon garlic powder. Beat 2 eggs with ¼ cup milk and mix in thoroughly (mixture will be moist). Form into 1 to 1¼-inch balls. Brown over low heat in a small amount of oil. Add 1 tablespoon each dry red wine and water, cover pan, and simmer for 15 minutes.

Tomato-Mushroom Sauce

Place in a large kettle 1 teaspoon olive oil, ½ pound ground round, and ½ pound mild Italian link sausages cut from casings and crumbled. Cook over medium-low heat, stirring, until meat loses pinkness and some fat accumulates. Add 1 large onion, finely chopped, and continue cooking until onion is tender. Add 1 can (1 pound) stewed tomatoes; 2 cans (6 ounces each) tomato paste; ½ cup dry red wine; 3 cups stock or water; 2 cloves garlic, minced or mashed; 2 strips lemon peel, each about ½ by 2 inches; 1 bay leaf, crushed; 1 teaspoon each salt, dried rosemary and dried sweet basil; ½ teaspoon sugar; ½ pound thinly sliced fresh mushrooms; 2 teaspoons Angostura bitters (optional); and 1 teaspoon Worcestershire (optional). Cover loosely and simmer 3 hours or more, stirring occasionally.

Basil Spinach

Cook 2 packages (10 ounces each) frozen chopped spinach according to package directions until barely tender. Drain well; stir in ¾ teaspoon celery salt and ½ teaspoon crumbled dried sweet basil.

PASTEURIZE—To heat milk or other liquids to certain temperatures and thus kill harmful bacteria. Pasteurization kills all pathogenic bacteria, making milk that might otherwise be hazardous quite safe for human consumption. The process does not change the food value of milk to any significant degree, and the benefits of pasteurizing to prevent undulant fever and other diseases transmitted by raw milk are obvious. The sale of raw milk is illegal in most of the United States, and most civilized nations of the world have enacted laws requiring that milk be pasteurized before it is sold.

Although pasteurization is most commonly associated with milk, the process was actually discovered for beer and wine. Louis Pasteur (1822-1895), the famous French scientist, experimented for years, starting in 1854, to discover the reasons for the spoilage of beer and wine and developed the process given his name. He published his final and most complete paper on fermentation in 1876. His work saved the wine and beer industries of France, and was later applied to milk.

PASTIES, REGAL FARE by Roland A. Browne—The pasty, a type of meat pie or turnover peculiar to the British Isles, is as much a part of my heritage as the English language. What chowder is to the Down-Easter and haggis to the Scot, pasties are to the Cornish and Devon folk from whom my mother is descended. They occupy a unique place in my personal hierarchy of gustatory delights.

Pasties (the word rhymes with fast rather than with taste) are a dish of great antiquity, as integral with the English tradition as Magna Charta, the longbow, and Robin Hood. In fact, you will find references to "pastes of venysoun" in the Robin Hood ballads, and I am reasonably sure that I have run across mention of pasties in Chaucer and Shakespeare. The Cornish version of the pasty, such as my grandmother and mother made, and which I still construct, probably differs but little from those that nourished Drake's crew of Devonshiremen and so fortified them that they defeated the invincible Armada of Spain, a demonstrable fact unaccountably omitted from practically all history books.

To construct pasties (I use the verb "construct" deliberately, for they have definite architectural elements), you must assemble the necessary building materials: potatoes, onions, turnips, beef, pork, and piecrust dough. The dough should be of a sort that will make a reasonably flaky crust, not excessively rich, and moist enough to handle easily. A standard mix of about three parts flour to one of shortening, plus salt and ice water, will be fine.

Take a chunk of pastry and roll it out on a lightly floured dish towel until it makes an oval about the size of a dinner plate and about one eighth of an inch thick. If it's too thin, you'll break it for sure. If you develop any holes, patch them by wetting the broken spot with water and pressing on a moistened piece large enough to make the break watertight.

We have now to make the floor or foundation layer of the pasty. This consists of about half an inch of thinly sliced raw potatoes. This should almost cover one half of the oval of dough, leaving a clear edge of pastry about an inch wide for later use in sealing, and should not intrude on the remaining half, which will later be folded over the top as a cover. Salt the potatoes lightly. Incidentally, Maine potatoes will cook up better than Idahoes in a pasty, and will not be so granular.

Next should come a light garnish of thinly sliced onions as a sort of carpet upon which to establish a solid stratum of lean beef. For this you can use round steak cut into half-inch cubes or you can cut up a sirloin tip roast. I suppose you could use a cheaper cut of beef, but I've never had the heart to try. A respectable pasty has a lot of beef in it, a double handful or more. When this is in place, apply salt and pepper judiciously and add the next layer, which consists of enough thin slices of raw turnips (either white or yellow) to cover the layer of beef. Slice them, as well as the potatoes, as thinly as

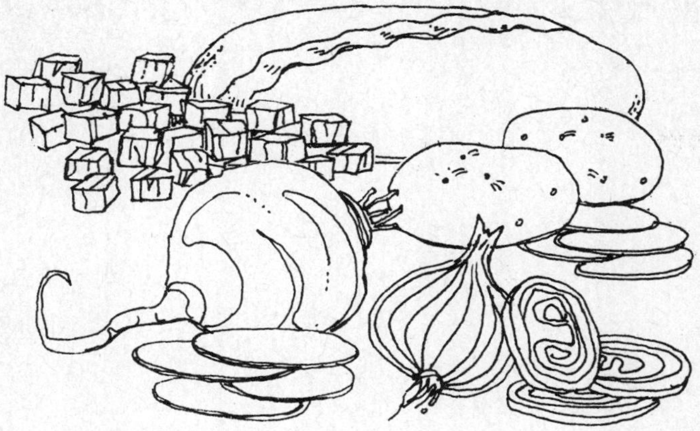

possible and put on a couple of layers, like shingles. Now should come a layer of fresh pork, reasonably lean and cubed like the beef. You can either use slices from a fresh ham or cut up a butt pork roast. Use about half as much pork as you did beef, and only a little of it can be fat. More salt and pepper are now in order. Finish off your edifice with a good layer of sliced onions. Dot the pile here and there with a slice of butter and, by way of good luck, sprinkle it lightly with marjoram or thyme.

Now, moisten the outer inch of pastry all around with a finger dipped into warm water. Wait a minute and repeat the operation. A pasty has to stick together at the seams, or it is of no account. Using the cloth to help you, ease the uncovered half of the pastry over the top of the pile and match its edges with the bottom half. You may have to roll it out a little larger. Press all around the outside with the edge of your thumb, making the indentations overlap one another to produce a tight seal. Moisten the top of the resulting seam and turn it back on itself far enough to repeat the sealing operation.

Now comes the tricky part. Gently tilt the side of the cloth next to the seam so as to rotate partly the whole pasty and bring the seam part way up over the top, instead of flat on the side.

Prick half a dozen vent holes in the crust with a kitchen fork to let steam out but keep all the juices within. Transfer the pasty gingerly to a large baking dish (I like a cookie sheet), and start making another pasty. You should allow one pasty per adult, half a pasty per child, or else make a junior-size model for the youngsters.

When your pasties are all on the pan ready to bake, slide them into a preheated moderate oven (350°F.) for the first half hour to set the crust; after which you should lower the heat to slow (300°F.), so that the pasties can bake slowly. I like to allow from 2 to 2½ hours of baking, half near the bottom and half near the top of the oven.

A pasty properly cooked is neither dry nor runny inside. Instead, the filling is uniformly moist and succulent. The flavor of the onion, delicately titillated with thyme, is carried down by the melted butter into the pork, and the pork juice impregnates and ennobles the turnips, which in turn lend a strange, poetic bouquet (half sweet, half bitter, like the memory of an old love) to the hearty, jovial whang of the beef, and the essences of all these separate ingredients finally infiltrate the potatoes, where they are combined and entrapped for the delectation of honest folk.

There is a definite ritual to the eating of pasties. I can still see the family assembled at the long dining table, my older brothers for once promptly and unbidden in their seats; my mother flushed but triumphant, with a little flour on one cheek; myself, not more than five, enveloped to the chin in a damask napkin and suitably elevated on two volumes of the *Encyclopaedia Britannica;* and my father, his gentle, scholarly countenance alight, poising a carving knife over a Blue Willow platter of gargantuan pasties, from which a scented steam arose and misted his glasses. Or were they tears of delight?

No matter. As each pasty was cut into two, my father placed one half on the recipient's plate and with a pencil wrote the person's initials on the crust of the other half for later reference. My father was a methodical man who liked to avoid family arguments.

Served smoking hot, eating them involved considerable blowing on each bite, unless you adhered to the school of thought (to which I belong) that believed in tipping up your half of pasty and pouring within a quantity of rich, thick cream to cool it. There are purists who regard this as heresy, but I suspect most of them are Scots and Welshmen.

The reason for initialing the other half of each pasty became apparent as the motion of jaws slowed down and a desultory conversation began to flicker up around the heretofore silent board. Half a pasty at one time is enough for anybody; the other half, properly identified, was set aside to be eaten later when cold, along with a tall glass of milk.

I have eaten pasties off and on since I got my first teeth and to this day I can't decide whether they taste better hot or cold.

PASTILLE—The French name for a confection which we call a "drop." Pastilles are made from sugar, water, and flavoring, and sometimes they contain medicinal ingredients, as in cough drops.

Pastilles are an old form of candy. Often they were chewed to sweeten the breath. They were made from dissolved sugar and water poured hot, drop by drop, onto a cold marble slab.

PASTRAMI—A preserved meat of eastern European origin, made from plate, brisket, or round of beef dry-cured with salt and saltpeter. The beef is then rinsed and rubbed with a paste of garlic powder, ground cuminseed, red pepper, cinnamon, cloves, and allspice, smoked and cooked. In the larger cities packaged pastrami, in slices or bigger pieces, is available in food stores. Sliced pastrami is available in delicatessens.

PASTRY COOKBOOK

PASTRY—The word has two culinary meanings. First it refers to a dough made of flour, shortening, salt, and water or other liquid. Pastry doughs, shorter and flakier than bread doughs, are used for pies, tarts, small sweet foods served as desserts, and nonsweet foods served as appetizers and snacks. Commercial mixes for standard pastry dough are available.

In its second meaning, the word pastry describes a baked food. It may be one which is made with a pastry dough; or one which has the characteristic tenderness and flakiness of food made with a pastry dough, such as Danish pastry; or one which is served as pastries are, cream puffs, for example.

PASTRY DOUGHS

TWO-CRUST PIES

1. Prepare proper amount of Standard Pastry for pan size to be used. (See Chart) Divide pastry about in halves. Round up on lightly floured board or other surface.
2. Cover a rolling pin with stockinet and rub flour into it. Flatten one pastry half with hand, and roll out not quite ⅛ inch thick. Roll lightly, being careful not to add extra flour as it makes pastry tough. Keep rounding the edge of pastry. If pastry breaks, pinch broken edges together immediately. Roll pastry about 1 inch larger all around the inverted pie pan, keeping it circular as you roll.
3. Fold in half and carefully transfer to pie pan. Unfold pastry and ease loosely into pan, being careful not to stretch it. (Stretching causes pastry to shrink during baking.) Or roll pastry carefully around rolling pin and unroll in pan.
4. Prepare desired filling and put in pastry-lined pan. Trim overhanging edges with scissors.
5. Roll second half of pastry for top crust, making it large enough to extend 1 inch beyond edge of pie pan. Measure by holding pie pan over rolled round of pastry.
6. Fold pastry in quarters. Make several slits near center to allow steam to escape or top crust will puff up. Moisten edge of bottom crust with water. Put folded pastry evenly on filling and unfold. Trim with scissors ½ inch from edge of pan.
7. Fold edge of top crust under edge of lower crust on rim. Seal well by pressing with fingertips. Build up a high standing rim. Make a fluted edge by firmly placing the right index finger on the inside of the rim, left thumb and index finger on outside of pastry at that point. Pinch. Repeat all around edge. Pinch each point firmly to sharpen.
8. Bake as directed in individual recipe.

LATTICE PIES

1. Prepare proper amount of Standard Pastry for pan size to be used. (See Chart, following.) Complete Steps 1 through 3 for Two-Crust Pies. Trim, leaving 1 inch overhanging edge. Fill with desired filling.
2. Roll remaining pastry and cut into ½-inch strips. (Use a pastry wheel to scallop edges.)
3. Moisten edge of bottom pastry with water. Lay half of pastry strips across filling 1 inch apart. Weave first cross strip through center. Add another cross strip, first folding back every other strip going the other way. Continue weaving until lattice is complete. Fold lower pastry over strips and press firmly around edge to seal.
4. Bake as directed in individual recipe.

UNBAKED PIE SHELLS

Prepare amount of Standard Pastry for pan to be used. (See Chart, following.) Complete Steps 2 and 3 for Two-Crust Pies. Trim, ½ inch from edge of pan. Fold pastry under, even with pan. Build up a high standing rim. Make a fluted edge by firmly placing the right index finger on outside of pastry at that point. Pinch. Repeat all around edge. Pinch each point firmly to sharpen. Fill and bake as directed in individual recipe.

BAKED PIE SHELLS

Follow directions for making Unbaked Pie Shells, above. With fork, prick shell close and deep on bottom and sides. Bake in preheated very hot oven (450°F.) for 12 to 15 minutes, or until golden-brown. Fill and complete pie as directed in individual recipe.

UNBAKED PIE TOP
[For meat pies or deep-dish pies]

Prepare proper amount of Standard Pastry for pan size to be used. (See Chart, following.) Roll pastry about 1 inch larger around than baking pan or casserole. Make several slits in crust for steam to escape during baking. Put crust on filling, fold edge over, and flute just inside edge of pan. Bake as directed in individual recipe.

BAKED TART SHELLS

Prepare Standard Pastry. (See Chart, following.) Divide pastry into 6 or more pieces, depending on size of tart pans. Roll each piece into a round and fit into individual pans. Trim edges. Prick with fork to prevent puffing during baking. Put pans on baking sheet and bake in preheated very hot oven (450°F.) about 10 minutes. Cool, and remove from pans.

NOTE: If tart pans are not available, fit pastry rounds over backs of muffin cups or custard cups, making pleats so pastry will fit closely. Prick with fork and bake as directed.

CHART OF INGREDIENTS FOR STANDARD PASTRY

CRUST SIZE	SIFTED ALL-PURPOSE FLOUR*	SALT	LARD OR HYDROGENATED SHORTENING	COLD WATER
8- or 9-inch shell or 8- or 9-inch round or square top for deep-dish or meat pie	1 cup	½ teaspoon	⅓ cup plus 1 tablespoon	2 tablespoons
8- or 9-inch 2-crust pie or 8-, 9-, 10-, or 11-inch lattice pie or 10- or 11-inch shell or 13- x 9-inch top for deep-dish or meat pie or six to eight 4½- x 1¼-inch tart shells or eight to ten 3½- x 1-inch tart shells	2 cups	1 teaspoon	⅔ cup plus 2 tablespoons	¼ cup
10- or 11-inch 2-crust pie	3 cups	1½ teaspoons	1 cup plus 3 tablespoons	6 tablespoons

**When using instant-type flour, follow recipe of individual manufacturer*

TO MAKE PASTRY: Mix flour and salt; cut in lard. Mix in water.

BOILING-WATER PASTRY

For one 2-crust, 8-inch or 9-inch pie or two shells:

⅔ cup hydrogenated shortening or lard
⅓ cup boiling water
2 cups sifted all-purpose flour
1 teaspoon salt

Put shortening in bowl and gradually add water, creaming with fork until well mixed. Add flour and salt, mixing thoroughly with fork. Follow directions for Two-Crust Pies for rolling, cutting, etc.

OIL PASTRY

For one 2-crust, 8-inch or 9-inch pie or two shells:

2 cups sifted all-purpose flour
1 teaspoon salt
½ cup vegetable oil
3 tablespoons cold water

Mix flour and salt. Add oil and mix with fork or pastry blender until well blended and mixture resembles fine crumbs. Sprinkle with water, and mix in with fork. Gather pastry together so that it cleans bowl. If too dry to form a ball, work in 1 to 2 tablespoons more oil. Press firmly into a ball. Divide dough almost in half. Using larger half for the bottom crust, put pastry between two long strips of wax paper crossed in the center, forming a 12-inch square. Wipe table with damp cloth to keep paper from slipping. Roll pastry in a circle to edges of square. Peel off top paper and put pastry in pan, paper-side up. Peel off paper and fit pastry loosely into pan. Follow Steps 4 through 8 under Two-Crust Pies for filling, etc.

For one 1-crust unbaked shell:

Prepare Oil Pastry, using the following proportions: 1½ cups sifted all-purpose flour, ½ teaspoon salt, ⅓ cup vegetable oil, and 2 tablespoons cold water. Roll and fit into pan as in Oil Pastry recipe. Trim pastry ½ inch from edge of pan. Fold pastry under, even with pan. Follow directions for Unbaked Pie Shells, for fluting edge. Fill and bake as directed in individual recipe.

For one 1-crust baked shell:

Prepare Oil Pastry, using the following proportions: 1½ cups sifted all-purpose flour, ½ teaspoon salt, ⅓ cup vegetable oil, and 2 tablespoons cold water. Roll and fit into pan as in Oil Pastry recipe. Trim pastry ½ inch from edge of pan. Fold pastry under, even with pan. Follow directions for Unbaked Pie Shells, for fluting edge. With fork, prick shell close and deep on bottom and sides. Bake in preheated very hot oven (450°F.) for 12 to 15 minutes or until golden-brown.

SPECIAL PASTRY FOR MEAT PIES

For one 8-inch round or square baking dish:

2 cups sifted all-purpose flour
1 teaspoon salt
⅔ cup lard
1 egg, separated
3 tablespoons water

Mix flour and salt. Cut in lard until pieces are the size of peas. Mix egg yolk and water and stir into first mixture. With hands, press together into a firm ball. Smooth edges and roll on lightly floured board ¼ to ½ inch thick. Cut to fit top of hot meat mixture in baking dish. Fold over once and cut several slits to allow for escape of steam. Put on top of meat mixture and open to fit top of dish. Brush with slightly beaten egg white. Bake in preheated hot oven (425°F.) for 10 minutes. Reduce heat to moderate (350°F.) and bake for 20 to 25 minutes longer.

CREAM-CHEESE PASTRY

Especially good for open fruit pies such as cherry, peach, blueberry, or boysenberry, or for citrus-flavored chiffon pies.

For one 2-crust 8- or 9-inch pie, or two 8- or 9-inch shells:

2 cups sifted all-purpose flour
½ teaspoon salt
⅔ cup butter, margarine, or hydrogenated shortening
12 ounces cream cheese

Mix flour and salt. Cut in butter and cream cheese. With hands, press together into a firm ball. Smooth edges. If pastry seems very soft, chill for 30 minutes, or until firm enough to roll.

NONSWEET FRENCH PASTRY
[Pâte Brisée]

For one 2-crust 8- or 9-inch pie, 24 tarts, or 36 turnovers:

2 cups plus 2 tablespoons sifted all-purpose flour
¾ teaspoon salt
1 cup soft butter
2 egg yolks
¼ cup light cream
2 tablespoons dry white wine

Sift flour and salt into bowl. Cut in butter. Add combined egg yolks, cream, and wine; mix with fork until blended and smooth. Knead lightly in bowl until bubbles begin to appear on the surface of dough. Cover and chill for 1 hour. Roll to ⅛-inch thickness on floured board. Fold twice lengthwise, then twice crosswise. Chill for 15 minutes. Roll and fold twice more. Store, wrapped in moisture-proof paper, in refrigerator.

SWEET FRENCH PASTRY
[Pâte Brisée Sucrée]

For one 9-inch tart, flan, or 2-crust pie, two 9-inch shells, or 12 medium-size individual pies or tarts:

½ cup sugar
¼ teaspoon salt
¾ cup butter, at room temperature
2 egg yolks
¼ teaspoon vanilla extract
2 cups all-purpose flour
Grated rind of 1 lemon

Put all ingredients in bowl and blend with fingers, kneading until mixture holds together. Press firmly into a ball, smoothing edges. If pastry seems very soft, chill 30 minutes, or until firm enough to roll.

PUFF PASTE

Puff paste can be used for a great variety of pastries. Among them are cream horns, which are cone shapes baked on forms and filled with whipped cream; napoleons; patty shells, both large and small; squares or circles filled with marmalade or jam, folded, sealed, and baked; fancy shapes cut out and baked for individual deep-dish pies; heart shapes baked, with a spoonful of jam put in the center of each and a fluted edge of whipped cream added; or in strips to be put together with jam or marmalade to make sandwiches.

1 pound (2 cups) unsalted butter
4 cups all-purpose flour
1 teaspoon salt
1 tablespoon fresh lemon juice
1¼ cups cold water (about)

Shape butter into a brick about 3 x 5 x ¾ inches. Roll butter in ¼ cup flour, coating all sides. Wrap in wax paper and chill. Put remaining 3¾ cups flour in a large bowl. Make a well in the center. Add salt and lemon juice. Gradually begin to add water, only enough to make a rather firm, slightly sticky dough.

Knead dough thoroughly on floured board for 20 minutes. Pound it on the table at intervals to achieve the right consistency. It should be very elastic and smooth. Form it into a ball; place on well-floured cloth. With a rolling pin, form the ball of dough into the shape of a four-leaf clover. Roll ends out, leaving the center thick. Well-rolled, the dough will have a thick cushion in the center and four thinner "petals." Put brick of butter in the center of the four-leaf clover. Fold "petals" over dough by stretching them over butter and sealing all the edges so that the butter is completely enclosed. Wrap in waxed paper and chill for 20 minutes.

On a well-floured cloth, gently roll out the block of dough as evenly as possible into a rectangle slightly less than ⅓ inch thick, and about 3 times as long as it is wide. Do not roll over ends lengthwise, but when dough is long enough, roll it lightly across the width, flattening ends to same thickness as the rest of the dough. Fold down into thirds, making three layers, and chill for 20 minutes. Turn folded side toward you, roll out dough, and fold again into thirds. (Rolling, folding, and turning is called a "turn.") It is necessary to make a total of 6 turns, after which the dough is ready for use. The dough should be chilled about 20 minutes between each turn. Wrap in moisture-proof paper and refrigerate until ready to use. Dough will keep 2 weeks.

NONSWEET BAKED APPETIZER PASTRIES

CURRIED SHRIMP DIAMONDS

⅔ cup soft butter or margarine
1½ cups sifted all-purpose flour
½ teaspoon salt
1 teaspoon instant minced onion
1 teaspoon water
1 teaspoon Worcestershire
1 cup finely chopped cooked shrimps
1 teaspoon curry powder
1 egg yolk
1 tablespoon milk

Cut butter into flour and salt. Soak onion for a few minutes in combined water and Worcestershire. Add with shrimps and curry powder to flour mixture, sitrring with fork until blended. Roll out on floured board ½ inch thick and cut into 1½-inch diamonds. Put on greased cookie sheet and brush with egg yolk beaten slightly with milk. Bake in preheated moderate oven (375°F.) about 30 minutes. Serve hot or cold. Makes about 2 dozen.

APPETIZER CREAM PUFFS

Use recipe for Cream Puffs. Level off 1 teaspoon dough onto greased cookie sheet. Then, using this amount as a guide for size, drop remaining dough onto cookie sheet. Bake in preheated hot oven (400°F.) about 20 minutes. Fill with crabmeat, tuna, chicken, or lobster salad; pimiento, Cheddar, or other cheese spread. Makes about 10 dozen.

ANCHOVY PUFFS

Roll Nonsweet French Pastry ⅛ inch thick. Cut into 1½-inch rounds. Put half on greased cookie sheet; put an anchovy in center of each. Top with remaining rounds. Prick tops; crimp edges with fork. Brush with egg yolk beaten with 1 tablespoon milk. Bake in preheated very hot oven (450°F.) for 10 minutes. Makes 2 to 3 dozen.

Shrimp Puffs

Cut rounds of pastry as for Anchovy Puffs. Substitute canned shrimps for the anchovies. Put ½ teaspoon sandwich spread (mayonnaise-pickle type) or tartare sauce on shrimps. Proceed as directed.

CHEESE HEARTS

¼ cup soft butter or margarine
1 cup buttermilk biscuit mix
¼ teaspoon each salt and chili powder
1 cup grated sharp Cheddar cheese
Water
Paprika

Cut butter into biscuit mix; add salt and chili powder. Add cheese and just enough water to hold mixture together. Force through cookie press onto greased cookie sheets (Y-shape disk forms hearts). Sprinkle with paprika. Bake in preheated hot oven (425°F.) for 10 minutes. Makes about 36.

SWISS PETIT PUFFS

½ recipe Cream Puffs
2 cups shredded Swiss cheese
½ cup butter or margarine, softened
3 tablespoons heavy cream
Dash of hot pepper sauce

Drop cream-puff mixture by half-teaspoonfuls onto ungreased cookie sheets. Bake in preheated hot oven (425°F.) about 20 minutes. Cool. Beat remaining ingredients together until blended. Use as filling for puffs. Makes about 5 dozen.

SWEET BAKED PASTRIES

HUNGARIAN CHEESE PASTRIES

½ cup plus 1 tablespoon soft butter or margarine
1⅔ cups sifted all-purpose flour
⅛ teaspoon salt
1 egg yolk, beaten
1½ tablespoons heavy cream (about)
Cheese Filling
Confectioners' sugar
Black-currant or other jelly

To make pastry cut butter into flour and salt. Add egg yolk, mixing with fork. Add just enough cream to hold mixture together. Chill overnight. Roll about one third of dough to form an 8-inch square a little more than ⅛ inch thick. Put in pan 8 x 8 x 2 inches. Take slightly more than half of remaining dough and roll and cut in strips about 1 inch wide. Fit around sides of pan. Pour in Cheese Filling and spread evenly. Roll out remaining dough and cut into ¾-inch strips. Put on top of filling, lattice-fashion. Bake in preheated moderate oven (350°F.) about 40 minutes. Cool on rack. Just before serving, sift confectioners' sugar over top. Cut into 2-inch squares and garnish each with jelly. Makes 16.

Cheese Filling

Press 1 pound dry cottage cheese through fine sieve. Add ¼ cup sugar, grated rind of ½ lemon, 2 egg yolks, and 2 tablespoons melted butter. Beat 4 egg whites stiff with ¼ teaspoon salt. Fold into cheese mixture.

RICH BANBURY TARTS

¼ cup each dry currants, seedless raisins, and chopped candied pineapple
½ cup chopped pitted dates
⅓ cup chopped nuts
1 cup firmly packed light brown sugar
2 eggs, slightly beaten
2 tablespoons all-purpose flour
¼ teaspoon salt
Grated rind and juice of 1 lemon
Nonsweet French Pastry
1 egg yolk
1 tablespoon milk

Mix well all ingredients except last 3. Roll Nonsweet French Pastry ⅛ inch thick and cut into 4-inch squares. Put about 1 tablespoon of filling mixture in the center of each square and fold the corners to meet in center. Put on greased cookie sheet and brush with egg yolk beaten with milk. Bake in preheated very hot oven (450°F.) for 12 to 15 minutes. Makes about 2 dozen.

DANISH PASTRIES

- ¾ cup milk, scalded
- Sugar
- 1½ teaspoons salt
- 1¾ cups butter or margarine
- ½ cup water*
- 2 packages active dry yeast, or 2 cakes compressed yeast
- 1 whole egg
- 1 egg, separated
- 1½ teaspoons grated lemon rind
- 3½ cups all-purpose flour
- 2 tablespoons cornstarch
- Jelly
- 1 tablespoon water

Pour milk over ½ cup sugar, salt, and ¼ cup butter. Mix well and cool to lukewarm. Put water in large bowl. *Use very warm water (105°F. to 115°F.) for dry yeast; use lukewarm (80°F. to 90°F.) for compressed. Sprinkle dry yeast or crumble cakes into water. Stir until dissolved. Add lukewarm milk mixture. Beat whole egg and 1 egg yolk; reserve remaining white. Add yolk mixture and lemon rind to yeast mixture. Add 1 cup flour and mix well. Mix cornstarch and remaining 2½ cups flour. Stir into batter until just mixed. Refrigerate. Spread remaining 1½ cups butter on wax paper to form rectangle 10 x 12 inches. Chill for 1 hour. Roll chilled dough into a rectangle 12 x 16 inches. Put butter slab on three quarters of dough. Fold uncovered quarter over middle section. Fold over remaining section to enclose butter. Give dough a quarter turn; roll to a rectangle 12 x 16 inches; fold as above. Turn, roll, and fold once more; chill for 1 hour. Repeat procedure of two rollings, foldings, turnings, and chilling two more times. Then refrigerate overnight. Shape half of dough at a time, refrigerating remainder. Roll half of dough to a rectangle 12 x 9 inches. Cut into 3-inch squares. Put ½ teaspoon jelly in the center of each square. Fold to form triangles, then seal edges. Put 2 inches apart on greased baking sheets. Chill for 1 hour. Mix reserved egg white with water. Brush on pastries and sprinkle lightly with sugar. Bake in preheated moderate oven (375°F.) for 15 to 20 minutes. Makes about 2 dozen.
NOTE: It is important to work the dough as little as possible when shaping the pastries. Handle quickly to keep dough cold.

CREAM PUFFS

- 1 cup water
- ½ cup butter
- ¼ teaspoon salt
- 1 cup sifted all-purpose flour
- 4 eggs, beaten
- Vanilla Cream Filling
- Confectioners' sugar

In saucepan heat water, butter, and salt to full rolling boil. Reduce heat and quickly stir in flour, mixing vigorously with wooden spoon until mixture leaves the sides of the pan in a ball. Remove from heat and add eggs in 6 additions, beating after each addition until mixture is very smooth. (An electric mixer at a low speed makes this procedure easier.) Drop dough from metal mixing spoon onto greased cookie sheets, forming mounds 3 inches apart. Bake in preheated hot oven (400°F.) for 40 to 45 minutes. Remove at once to racks and cool away from drafts. Split; fill with Vanilla Cream Filling. Sprinkle with confectioners' sugar, or frost as desired. Store in refrigerator. Makes 12 large or 16 medium puffs.
NOTE: Freeze puffs without filling. To recrisp, put in oven for a few minutes.

PETITS PUFFS

Use Cream Puff recipe above. Level off 1¼ teaspoons dough onto greased cookie sheet. Then, using this amount as a guide for size, drop remaining dough onto cookie sheet. Bake in preheated hot oven (400°F.) about 20 minutes. Fill and frost. Makes 8 dozen.

ÉCLAIRS

Use recipe for Cream Puffs, forcing mixture through pastry tube, or shaping with spatula into 16 fingers, 4 inches long and 1 inch wide. Bake as for Cream Puffs. Fill with Vanilla Cream Filling (below) and spread with thin chocolate frosting. Makes 16.

VANILLA CREAM FILLING

- 3 cups milk
- ¾ cup sugar
- 6 tablespoons cornstarch
- ½ teaspoon salt
- 3 eggs, beaten
- 1 tablespoon butter
- 2 teaspoons vanilla extract

Scald milk in top part of double boiler over boiling water. Mix sugar, cornstarch, and salt. Stir in milk. Cook, stirring constantly, until thick. Cover; cook for 10 minutes longer. Add small amount of mixture to eggs; return to double boiler; cook for 5 minutes, stirring constantly. Add butter. Put in bowl and sprinkle small amount of sugar over top to prevent skin from forming. Chill; add vanilla.

Chocolate Cream Filling

Use recipe for Vanilla Cream Filling. Melt 3 ounces (3 squares) unsweetened chocolate in milk and beat until smooth. Proceed as directed.

Fluffy Cream Filling

Use either Vanilla or Chocolate Cream Filling recipes, reducing milk to 2½ cups. Just before using, fold ½ cup heavy cream, whipped, into chilled mixture.

ORANGE-PLUM TWISTS

¼ cup soft butter
2 cups buttermilk biscuit mix
2 tablespoons granulated sugar
1 teaspoon grated orange rind
1 egg
⅓ cup heavy cream
½ cup damson-plum preserves
Confectioners' sugar

Cut butter into biscuit mix. Stir in granulated sugar and rind. Beat egg and cream until blended; with fork, stir into first mixture. Put on floured board and knead a few times. Roll out to form a rectangle 15 x 3 inches. Spread with preserves; fold twice lengthwise to form a rectangle 1 x 15 inches. Cut crosswise into 1-inch strips. Twist each strip twice to form a spiral. Put on foil-covered cookie sheet and bake in preheated very hot oven (450°F.) for 10 to 12 minutes. Sift confectioners' sugar over tops while twists are warm. Serve warm or cold. Makes 15. Can be frozen.

CHERRY-COCONUT PASTRIES

1 box (10 or 11 ounces) pastry mix
2 tablespoons granulated sugar
3 eggs, beaten
1 cup firmly packed brown sugar
½ teaspoon baking powder
2 tablespoons all-purpose flour
1½ teaspoons vanilla extract
½ cup flaked coconut
½ cup chopped nuts
½ cup chopped maraschino cherries

Prepare pastry as directed on the label, adding granulated sugar. Press into bottom and on sides of pan, 9 x 9 x 2 inches. Bake in preheated hot oven (425°F.) for 10 minutes. Mix remaining ingredients; pour into pastry. Bake in preheated moderate oven (325°F.) for 35 minutes. Cool; cut into bars 3 x 1½ inches. Makes 18.

RASPBERRY MAIDS OF HONOUR

⅓ cup butter or margarine
1 box (10 or 11 ounces) pastry mix
Raspberry jam
½ box (2-layer size) white-cake mix or 1 box (1-layer size)
Confectioner's-Sugar Frosting
Candied violets, angelica, colored candies

Cut butter into pastry mix. Add just enough of the liquid indicated on pastry-mix label to hold dough together. Chill if necessary. Roll out ⅛ inch thick, and cut into 24 rounds with 3½-inch cutter. Fit into 2½-inch muffin-pan sections. Put about 1 teaspoon jam into each. Prepare cake mix, and put a spoonful of cake batter on jam. Bake in preheated moderate oven (350°F.) for 20 to 25 minutes. Cool in pans and remove to racks. Spread tops with Confectioners'-Sugar Frosting. Decorate. Makes 2 dozen.

Confectioners' Sugar Frosting

Mix 1 cup sifted confectioners' sugar with enough milk or water to make of spreading consistency. Tint with food coloring and flavor with almond or vanilla extract.

LEMON TARTS

2 eggs, beaten
¾ cup sugar
⅛ teaspoon salt
Grated rind of ½ orange
Juice of 1 large lemon
2 tablespoons butter
½ recipe Sweet French Pastry (use 6 tablespoons butter)

Mix all ingredients except Sweet French Pastry in top part of small double boiler. Cook over boiling water, stirring constantly, until thickened. Cool. Line tiny scalloped tart pans or muffin-pan sections with pastry. Bake in preheated very hot oven (450°F.) about 12 minutes. Cool and remove from pans. Shortly before serving, fill shells. Makes 24 tiny tarts.

STRAWBERRY ICE CREAM TARTS

1 pint strawberries
Juice of 1 lemon
⅔ cup sweetened condensed milk
⅛ teaspoon salt
1 cup heavy cream
Graham-Cracker Tart Shells
Fresh mint

Wash and hull berries; reserve 4 and crush remainder; add lemon juice, milk, and salt. Fold in cream beaten to consistency of soft custard; blend well. Pour into refrigerator tray. Freeze for 30 minutes; then stir. Continue freezing. Fill Graham-Cracker Tart Shells with strawberry ice cream. Garnish each with 2 strawberry quarters and mint sprigs. Makes 8 servings.

Graham-Cracker Tart Shells

1¼ cups fine graham-cracker crumbs
¼ cup sugar
⅓ cup soft butter or margarine

Mix crumbs, sugar, and butter thoroughly. Using back of spoon, press firmly onto sides and bottoms of 8 greased 4-inch tart pans. Bake in preheated moderate oven (350°F.) about 10 minutes. Cool. Remove from pans.

LANCASTER SQUARES

Standard Pastry (1-cup flour recipe)
½ cup firmly packed brown sugar
2 tablespoons soft butter or margarine
⅓ cup chopped nuts

Roll pastry out on lightly floured board to form a 9-inch square. Lift pastry onto a baking sheet. Cream sugar and butter together. Spread on pastry and sprinkle with nuts. Cut into 1½-inch squares. Bake in preheated hot oven (425°F.) for 12 to 15 minutes. Makes about 3 dozen.

PÂTÉ—A meat or fish paste or a pie or patty with a filling such as meat or fish paste. Or occasionally the word is used to describe a fruit or vegetable mixture. Originally pâté referred only to the pie form since the word means "pie" in French. The most famous is the *pâté de foie gras,* or goose-liver pâté. Other noted examples are the chicken and ham pâtés from Rouen, France; those of truffled game and poultry from Périqueux, Angoulême, and Nérac; woodcock from Montreuil; duck from Amiens; game from Pithiviers, Chartres, and Nogent-le-Rotrou; and fish from Abbeville.

HOW TO COOK SUPERBLY: PÂTÉS

by HELEN EVANS BROWN

Pâté, to most of us, means *pâté de foie gras,* a sinfully expensive concoction made of livers from specially fat-

Pâté in Aspic   Pâté en Croute

tened geese, and usually studded with truffles. But in France, a pâté is made of less exalted livers and of other meats, and is often known as a *pâté maison* or as a *terrine.* Originally the difference between a pâté and a *terrine* was that the former was enclosed in pastry, the latter made in a covered dish called a *terrine,* from which it is usually served. In today's restaurants you can only be sure which you are ordering if it is listed as *pâté en croûte.* At home, however, you can be sure of delighting your family and guests if you make your own, and that is not as difficult as you may have thought. It will take time, but it's wonderful fun, and it's almost as easy to produce several as one.

A pâté or *terrine* is really a glorified meat loaf because its foundation is nothing more than well-seasoned ground meat. This forcemeat, or *farce* as it's known in French culinary circles, is usually layered with diced meat or with strips *(batons)* of meat, or mixed with other ingredients so that, when sliced, the pâté will have a mosaic look. *Terrines* are sometimes coated with aspic, and sometimes even treated both ways. There is no particularly difficult technique involved in any of them.

EQUIPMENT

For a *terrine* you will need the ordinary kitchen equipment such as measuring spoons and cups, a sharp knife, a meat grinder, and loaf pans or straight-sided casseroles, with or without covers. Or, if you want to be very fancy, a French *terrine* especially made for the purpose is nice. They are usually white, with straight sides and domed covers. They may be oval, round or rectangular. (The latter, I think, is best as the slices will be uniform.) If you are making a *pâté en croûte,* you will also need a special *croûte* mold that can be opened, or else a springform mold or straight-sided pan with a removable bottom although, if you are extremely careful, a glass loaf pan can be used.

BASIC FORCEMEAT
Spice Mixture

Mix ½ teaspoon each ground ginger, nutmeg, and cloves, and 1 tablespoon white pepper.

Forcemeat

- 1 cup minced onions
- ½ cup sherry
- 1 pound ground fresh pork fat
- 1 pound ground lean pork
- 1 pound ground veal
- Spice Mixture (see above)
- 3 eggs
- 1 tablespoon salt
- 3 garlic cloves (or more or less to taste), puréed or very finely minced

Cook minced onions in sherry until liquid has evaporated and onions are soft. Watch carefully so they do not burn. (Madeira, port, or ¼ cup brandy may be used instead.) Add finely ground meats, 1 teaspoon Spice Mixture and other ingredients, and mix well. (If you want to taste for seasoning, cook a small piece, either in the oven or in a dry skillet.) Other ground meat, up to 1 pound, may be added also. Duck is good, as is any game, particularly birds or rabbits. Ham or liver is also widely used. You now have about 6 cups forcemeat which can be used with or without garnishes.

Garnishes—The usual garnishes or decorations are *batons* or dice of various ingredients. *Batons* are strips of meat such as veal, smoked tongue, ham, or pork fat. They should be cut ¼ to ⅜ inch in width and thickness and 2 to 4 inches long. The same meats, cut into ¼- to ½-inch dice may also be used, as may whole chicken or duck livers. You can use from 1 to 1½ pounds *batons* or dice for the above amount of forcemeat. Sliced or diced truffles and whole blanched pistachio nuts, anywhere from 1 tablespoon to 1 cup, are nice additions, too. These garnishes should be marinated in a mixture of ¼ cup brandy or sherry, 1 teaspoon salt, and ½ teaspoon Spice Mixture. Drain and mix liquid with forcemeat.

Pan Lining—The *terrines* or pans used for pâtés are lined with thin slices of fresh pork fat before the mixture is added. You may be able to get this from your butcher. Ask him to give you unsalted fat back. Have it sliced about ¼ inch thick, then put it between pieces of paper and pound it thinner. If you can't get the fresh fat, slice salt pork ⅛ inch thick, and soak it in cold water for several hours. Or use sliced bacon, 1 pound for the above amount of forcemeat.

Assembling and Baking—First measure the *terrines,* pans, or casseroles you intend to use. The above ingredients will make 8 to 9 cups, or 2 bread-size loaves. Use 1 large *terrine,* or several smaller *terrines* if you prefer. Line them with the sliced fat, allowing the slices to hang over the top. Press about one third of the forcemeat mixture you have allotted for the *terrine* evenly over bottom. For instance, if your *terrine* is a 3-cup one and you are using ½ pound (1 cup) garnishing, you'll need 2 cups forcemeat. The fat lining doesn't have to be figured in. Arrange half your *batons* or diced meats or whole livers along the top of the forcemeat layer in a symmetrical manner, alternating colors; have *batons* parallel. If truffles or pistachios are used, arrange between the meats or in a separate layer. Add another third of the forcemeat, pressing evenly as before, then the remaining garnishes. Top with the last of the forcemeat, and fold the fat over the top, covering it completely. Put a whole bay leaf and sprig of thyme or a good big pinch of dried thyme on top. Cover with a double layer of foil and with lids, if available. Put the filled *terrines* in a larger pan and pour in enough boiling water to come halfway up the outside. Bake in preheated moderate oven (375°F.) for 1½ to 2 hours, depending upon the size; a 5-cup loaf pan takes about 1½ hours. The pâté is done when the fat runs clear when it is pierced with a sharp knife. Leave the *terrines* in the outside pan, remove covers but not the foil, and weigh down their contents. This last is important for texture and easy slicing. Use a slightly smaller vessel of the same shape, or cut cardboard to fit, cover with heavy foil, and place on top. Weigh down with canned goods or other heavy objects. Cool thoroughly. Serve either directly from the *terrine,* slicing through the fat, or turn out and slice, fat and all. Serve with toast or on lettuce.

Keeping Pâtés and Terrines—Terrines will keep, refrigerated, at least 2 weeks if they are removed from molds, wiped of any juices that have jellied on the outside, and either wrapped in foil or placed in washed pans. They can be frozen but the texture is not quite as perfect. If aspic is used, add it only a day or two before serving. *Pâté en croûte* will keep for a week or so, and can also be frozen with the same results.

Once you've mastered these basic types of pâtés, you can invent your own and call it, of course, *pâté maison* or *pâté chez nous.* You'll find it really isn't much more difficult than a meat loaf, but so much more exciting.

PÂTÉ IN ASPIC

If you prefer, the pâté can be encased in aspic. When planning this, don't quite fill the *terrine* before baking. Make an aspic with 2 cans (10½ ounces each) condensed beef bouillon, ⅓ cup sherry or Madeira, and 2 envelopes unflavored gelatin softened in ⅓ cup water. Heat until dissolved, then cool until gelatin begins to set. Remove cooked pâté from the pan and scrape off fat. Wash pan, rinse in cold water, and dry. Pour about ½ inch of cooled aspic into pan and allow to set. Place scraped pâté carefully on top, centering it. Pour more aspic on until it covers the top, preferably by ½ inch or more. Allow to set, then turn out on a platter and slice.

PÂTÉ EN CROÛTE

Pâté in a crust is made as above but it is baked in a crust. For the crust Puff Paste, regular pie pastry, or *pâte brisée* may be used, but because the *pâté* contains so much fat the following pastry is preferable. Using your fingertips or a pastry blender, mix ½ cup butter, or butter and shortening combined, into 4 cups all-purpose flour and 1 teaspoon of salt. Gradually add cold water, about ½ cup, until the mixture holds together. Form into a ball, wrap in wax paper, and allow to rest in a cool place for 2 to 8 hours. Roll ⅛ to ¼ inch thick and line *croûte* mold or loaf pan, pressing it firmly to sides first. Cut piece of dough to fit bottom and press in. Be sure corners are completely covered with dough. Make sure there are no holes in the pastry. If *croûte* mold has no bottom, place on a cookie sheet. Allow ¼ inch of pastry to hang over the top. Fill with forcemeat and garnishings as above. Moisten edge of pastry and top with another piece. Press edges firmly together, then cut off excess by passing a rolling pin over the top. If you wish, cut extra pieces into fancy shapes and decorate top. Brush with slightly beaten egg; then make a hole in the top and insert a small funnel or a tube of foil. Bake in preheated moderate oven (375°F.) for 1½ to 2 hours, or until fat in funnel runs clear. Cool. When perfectly cold, aspic may be poured in the hole at the top. As the meat shrinks this will fill up the spaces and look extra pretty when aspic is firm and paté is sliced.

QUICK AND EASY CHICKEN-LIVER TERRINE

½ cup chopped onion
1 tablespoon butter or chicken fat
½ cup sherry
1¼ pounds chicken livers
1 pound sausage meat
1½ teaspoons salt
½ teaspoon Spice Mixture
2 eggs, beaten
½ pound bacon

Cook onion in butter until wilted. Add sherry and cook until almost dry. Remove 3 whole chicken livers and grind remainder finely or whirl in the blender. Mix with other ingredients except bacon. Line sides and bottom of 5-cup ovenproof bread pan with bacon. Pour in half of mixture, arrange whole chicken livers lengthwise in the center; then add rest of mixture. Cover top with remaining bacon and with foil. Bake as directed in Assembling and Baking in preheated moderate oven (375°F.) for 1½ hours.

COUNTRY-STYLE TERRINE

Make Basic Forcemeat; add 2 to 3 cups finely diced meat of your choice: ham, tongue, veal, fat pork, lean pork, or game. Mix well and bake in a 2½-quart terrine for about 2 hours, as above.

MUSHROOM-LIVER PÂTÉ WITH BROCCOLI

½ pound fresh mushrooms, minced
3 tablespoons butter or margarine
12 ounces cream cheese, at room temperature
2 pounds liverwurst
Dash of garlic salt
Garnish: 1 package (3 ounces) cream cheese fresh-broccoli buds and thin slices partially peeled broccoli stems

Sauté mushrooms in butter in skillet until very well browned. Add next 3 ingredients and beat well. Pack into oiled 9 x 5 x 3-inch loaf pan and put in refrigerator until thoroughly chilled. Unmold on serving platter and pipe edges with softened cream cheese forced through pastry tube. Garnish with broccoli buds and slices.
NOTE: Pâté, covered, will keep well several days in refrigerator.

BASIC PORK PÂTÉ

1 pound pork liver
1 cup milk
1 pound pork fat
1½ pounds lean pork
2 eggs, beaten
5 garlic cloves, puréed
¼ cup all-purpose flour
2 teaspoons salt
2 teaspoons dried tarragon
½ teaspoon Spice Mixture
¼ to ½ cup blanched pistachio nuts (optional)
¼ to ½ cup diced cooked ham

Soak liver in milk for 2 hours; drain. Slice half of pork fat for lining a 4- or 5-cup *terrine* or loaf pan. Grind remaining fat with lean pork and liver. Add remaining ingredients and mix well. Put in fat-lined pan and bake as directed in Assembling and Baking in preheated moderate oven (375°F.) for 1½ hours, or until fat is clear.

PATTY—A small, round, flat mass of food: dough, cereal, potato, or other vegetable, ground meat, fish, poultry, or nuts; or a combination of meat and/or other vegetables. In another usage of the word, a dough shell baked to form a container for creamed dishes is referred to as a patty shell.

The word is also used to describe the small flat candies usually made of peppermint-flavored fondant.

BAKED LAMB PATTIES

1 pound ground lamb
1 cup fine fresh-bread crumbs
2 eggs, slightly beaten
¾ teaspoon salt
⅛ teaspoon dried thyme
½ teaspoon dry mustard
1 teaspoon Worcestershire
¼ teaspoon pepper
Tomato sauce

Mix all ingredients except tomato sauce lightly but thoroughly. Shape into 8 patties, and put in shallow dish. Bake in preheated moderate oven (350°F.) about 1 hour. Serve with heated tomato sauce. Makes 4 servings.

FRANKFURTER AND CORNMEAL PATTIES

¾ cup yellow cornmeal
2 teaspoons salt
3 cups boiling water
½ pound frankfurters, cooked and ground or minced very fine
¼ cup fat

Gradually add meal to salted boiling water, stirring constantly. Cook until thick. Remove from heat and add frankfurters, mixing well. Drop by heaping tablespoonfuls on to platter, and let stand until cold. Cook patties slowly in hot fat until browned on both sides. Makes 4 servings.

POTATO PATTIES

Shape 3 cups cold mashed potato into 8 patties. Dredge with flour. Cook slowly in small amount of hot margarine or bacon fat in skillet until browned on both sides. Makes 4 servings.

Squash Patties

Follow recipe for Potato Patties, substituting an equal amount of mashed cooked squash for the potato.

PATTY SHELLS

Prepare one fourth of the recipe for Puff Paste. Roll dough into a rectangle 18 x 6 inches. Cut out 12 rounds with 3-inch cutter. Remove the center from half the rounds with a smaller cutter to make rims and tops. Put both size plain rounds on a cookie sheet covered with two thicknesses of brown paper. Moisten the edges of the large rounds, and set the rings on them. Press gently. Chill for 20 minutes, or longer. Put in preheated very hot oven (500°F.) After 5 minutes, reduce the heat 50° every 5 minutes, and bake until shells are well-risen and browned, about 25 minutes. Turn as necessary to brown evenly. Fill as desired and top with small baked rounds. Good fillings are chicken à la king; creamed mushrooms, lobster, etc.; or newburg mixtures. Makes 6 shells.

PAUCHOUSE, POCHOUSE, or POUCHOUSE—A French name for a bouillabaisse made of fresh-water fish. It is made with five kinds of fish, almost always including eel and pike. The fish is sliced, cooked with a little water and seasoning, or with court bouillon, salt pork which has been cubed and browned, white or red wine, and heavy cream.

PAUPIETTE—A meat or fish roll made from thin slices of meat or fish stuffed with forcemeat, or other dressing, browned and braised. It is more commonly called a "bird" in the United States: veal birds, beef birds, etc.

BEEF PAUPIETTES

4 cube steaks (about 1 pound)
Salt and pepper to taste
Italian herbs
Meat tenderizer
1 small carrot, cut into strips
1 green pepper, cut into strips
1 teaspoon all-purpose flour
½ teaspoon paprika
2 tablespoons fat
1 small onion, chopped
1 cup bouillon
Dash of hot pepper sauce

Sprinkle steaks with salt and pepper, herbs, and tenderizer. Put a few strips of carrot and pepper on each, roll up and tie with string. Dredge with flour mixed with paprika. Brown on all sides in fat. Add remaining ingredients, cover, and simmer for 1½ hours, or until meat is tender. Makes 4 servings.

PAVLOVA—A dessert of Australian origin which is very popular at special teas, birthday buffets, or other celebrations. It consists of a meringue topped with whipped cream and berries, or whipped cream, passion fruit, and banana slices, or whipped cream and sliced kiwi fruit.

STRAWBERRY PAVLOVA

6 egg whites, at room temperature
¼ teaspoon salt
1½ teaspoons cream of tartar
1½ cups granulated sugar
1 teaspoon vanilla extract
1 cup heavy cream, whipped
1 pint strawberries
1 teaspoon kirsch
Confectioners' sugar

Beat egg whites with rotary beater or electric mixer until frothy. Sprinkle salt and cream of tartar over top; beat until stiff but not dry. Gradually beat in granulated sugar,

2 tablespoons at a time. Add vanilla and continue beating until mixture is very stiff. On a 12-inch chop plate, spread about one third of meringue to within 1 inch of edge of plate. Pile remaining meringue about 2½ inches high around meringue base, leaving center unfilled. Bake in preheated very slow oven (250°F.) about 1¼ hours. Turn off heat and leave in oven for 15 minutes longer. Cool. Fill center with whipped cream. Wash and hull berries and put about three fourths of them on top of cream. Press remaining berries through a sieve. Add kirsch and confectioners' sugar to taste. Pour this mixture over berries and cream. Makes 8 servings.

PEA—The seed and plant of a cool-season hardy annual, *Pisum sativum.* Chief among the many varieties are the garden, or green, pea and the field, or stock, pea, *P. sativum var. arvense.* Garden peas are grown for their seed primarily, although one type, the sugar pea, which the French graphically call *mangetout,* has soft thick edible pods. The seeds of garden peas can be classified as smooth-skinned or wrinkled, the former being a hardier type, but the latter being a better quality pea. Field peas, which have a small hard seed, are used chiefly for making yellow split peas and as livestock fodder.

Peas are an old vegetable; they originated in western Asia and the adjacent sections of Europe. The earlier peas were grown for dried seeds, such as we use today in split-pea soup. The Greeks and Romans used peas long before Christian times, but they were not grown in Europe very widely before the middle of the 17th century, when they became most fashionable in gourmet circles. England grew and grows excellent peas, since this vegetable thrives where the summer temperatures are cool and where there is much moisture. Dried, or split, peas, made into the "pease porridge hot, pease porridge cold" of the nursery rhyme, were for centuries a basic staple in the English diet. Peas have been known in America since the earliest days when the colonists brought the dried seeds with them.

Availability—California produces 60 per cent of the fresh green peas used in the United States; March, April, and May are the peak months. There are also shipments from August through November.

Canned green peas and frozen green peas are available, as are frozen peas in butter sauce, frozen peas and onions in cream sauce, and frozen carrots and peas.

Packaged split (dried and de-hulled) peas are available: yellow (made from field peas) and green (made from green peas). Whole dried green peas, with hulls, are available in health food stores for any dried pea recipe, but especially for sprouting.

Purchasing Guide—Fresh green peas should be fresh, tender, and sweet. Look for large, bright-green, well-filled pods with a velvety texture.
1 pound in shell = 1 cup shelled

Storage—Refrigerate fresh peas, unshelled.
Fresh, refrigerator shelf, unshelled: 3 to 5 days
Fresh, cooked; and canned, opened, refrigerator shelf: 4 to 5 days
Fresh, prepared for freezing; and frozen, refrigerator frozen-food compartment: 2 to 3 months
Fresh, prepared for freezing; and frozen, freezer: 1 year
Canned, kitchen shelf: 1 year
Split peas, kitchen shelf: 6 to 8 months

Nutritive Food Values—Peas are a fair source of protein, iron, vitamin A, and also have some niacin and vitamin C.
Fresh, shelled, ½ cup = 58 calories
Fresh, 1 cup, boiled and drained = 115 calories
Fresh, edible-pod, 4 ounces, boiled and drained = 49 calories
Canned (early or June peas), 1 cup, solids and liquid = 165 calories
Canned (early or June peas), ½ cup, drained solids = 76 calories
Canned (early or June peas), dietary pack, 4 ounces, solids and liquid = 55 calories
Canned (early or June peas), dietary pack, 4 ounces, drained solids = 88 calories
Frozen, ½ cup (3 ounces), boiled and drained = 57 calories
Split peas, ½ cup (3-4 ounces), cooked = 112 calories

Basic Preparation—Shell fresh peas just before cooking. Cook, covered, in 1 inch of boiling salted water for 8 to 12 minutes.

To Cook Split Peas—When bought in packages, they have been sorted and washed, and so need only be rinsed. They may or may not need soaking according to directions on the package. Some dried peas are prepared for quick cooking. Consult package for length of cooking time. Loose peas should be sorted and washed thoroughly.

If it is necessary to soak dried peas, cook in the soaking water to save flavor and nutrients. Add salt to soaked peas (1 teaspoon for each cup of dried peas). For special flavor, cook with ham, bacon, or salt pork (less salt will be needed), herbs, chopped onion, carrot, or celery. Cover pot, bring to boil, reduce heat, and cook gently until tender. If peas are to be used in soup, cook until they can be easily mashed. A dash of ground allspice gives an excellent flavor.

To Freeze—Choose sweet tender peas. Shell peas but do not wash. Blanch in boiling water: small peas for 45 seconds; large peas for 60 seconds. Chill in cold water for 3 minutes. Drain. Pack in containers, leaving ½-inch headspace. Seal.

SPLIT-PEA PURÉE

Cover 1¼ cups green split peas with water. Add 1 onion, 1 dried mushroom (optional, but tasty), and 1 teaspoon sugar. Bring to boil, then simmer until tender and thick, about 1½ hours. Put through blender or fine sieve. Bind with 1 tablespoon all-purpose flour mixed to paste with 1 tablespoon water. Season to taste with salt and pepper and simmer a few minutes longer. Serve topped with crisp fried onions, if desired. Makes 4 servings.

YELLOW PEA SOUP WITH SMOKED PORK

1 smoked pork shoulder butt (2 to 3 pounds)
3 quarts water
1 large onion, chopped
1 pound yellow split peas
1 teaspoon dried thyme
1 bay leaf
½ teaspoon coarsely ground black pepper
1 teaspoon salt

Put pork in kettle, and add water and onion. Bring to boil and simmer, covered, for 1½ to 2 hours, or until tender. Remove meat, and skim off most of fat from broth. To broth, add peas and remaining ingredients. Simmer, covered, stirring occasionally, for 1½ to 2 hours, or until soup is almost a purée. Slice meat thin and add to soup. Heat well and serve. Makes 6 servings.

CHUTNEY-GLAZED CHICKEN BREASTS, CURRIED RICE AND PEAS

12 whole chicken breasts
½ cup butter or margarine
Salt and pepper
Water
1 cup chutney
2 tablespoons cornstarch
2 packages (6 ounces each) curried-rice mix
2 packages (10 ounces each) frozen peas, cooked

Allow 1 whole chicken breast per person. Remove all bones, except the main breast bone. Brown chicken in butter and season with salt and pepper. Put in shallow baking dish, skin side up. Add 2½ cups water and chutney to skillet drippings. Bring to boil and pour over chicken. Cover and bake in preheated slow oven (325°F.) 30 minutes. Uncover and bake about 30 minutes longer, basting several times with pan juices. Blend cornstarch with a little cold water; stir into pan juices and bake about 5 minutes longer. Prepare curried rice according to package directions. To serve, put rice in the center of the dish and surround with chicken. Top center with cooked peas. Pour gravy over chicken breasts and serve the rest of the gravy separately. Makes 12 servings.

TUNA, PEAS, AND RICE

1 small onion, minced
¼ cup butter or margarine
3 cups hot cooked peas
3 cups hot cooked rice
1 or 2 cans (7 ounces each) tuna
Salt and pepper to taste
Grated Parmesan cheese

Sauté onion in butter until golden. Toss lightly with remaining ingredients, except cheese. Serve hot, sprinkled with cheese. Makes 6 to 8 servings.

FRENCH PEAS

¼ cup butter or margarine
Large outside lettuce leaves
2 cups shelled fresh peas
Salt and pepper

Put 1 tablespoon butter in a large skillet with a tightly fitting cover. Wash lettuce leaves and allow a little water to cling to them. Arrange several leaves over butter. Add peas and remaining butter, and cover with more lettuce leaves. Cover tightly and cook over high heat until butter is bubbly hot. Lower heat and steam gently until peas are just tender. This takes about 15 minutes. Discard lettuce, and season peas with salt and pepper to taste. Makes 4 servings.

MUSHROOM-PIMIENTO PEAS

Cook 1½ cups shelled fresh peas or 1 package (10 ounces) frozen peas. Add 3 tablespoons butter or margarine, 1 can (4 ounces) drained sliced mushrooms, and 2 chopped canned pimientos; heat. Makes 3 servings.

CURRIED PEAS AND ONIONS

Cook 1½ cups shelled fresh peas or 1 package (10 ounces) frozen peas. Drain off all but about 1 tablespoon liquid. Add 1 can (1 pound) onions, drained, 3 tablespoons butter or margarine, and 1 teaspoon curry powder. Heat, stirring lightly once or twice. Season to taste with salt and pepper. Makes 4 to 6 servings.

PEAS WITH MUSHROOMS AND ONIONS

1½ tablespoons butter
2 tablespoons water
½ cup thinly sliced mushrooms
1½ cups shelled fresh peas or 1 package (10 ounces) frozen peas
1 small onion, thinly sliced
½ teaspoon salt

Melt butter in saucepan. Add remaining ingredients. Cover pan tightly, and cook until peas are tender. Shake pan occasionally. Makes 4 servings.

SAVORY PEAS

½ cup sliced green onions
2 tablespoons butter or margarine
1½ cups (1½ pounds in the pod) shelled fresh peas
½ teaspoon sugar
¼ teaspoon dried savory
¼ teaspoon dried basil
1 tablespoon snipped parsley
½ cup water
1 teaspoon salt
⅛ teaspoon pepper

Sauté green onions in butter for 5 minutes, or until tender. Add peas, sugar, herbs, water, salt, and pepper. Cook, covered, over low heat for 10 minutes, or until peas are tender. Makes 4 servings.

CORN AND PEAS IN CREAM

1 package (10 ounces) frozen whole-kernel corn
1 package (10 ounces) frozen peas
1 cup light cream
1 teaspoon instant minced onion
2 tablespoons butter or margarine
Salt and pepper
1 cup slivered cooked ham

Cook corn and peas separately as directed on labels; drain and combine. Add cream, onion, and 1 tablespoon butter; heat, and season to taste. Sauté ham lightly in 1 tablespoon butter. Pour vegetables into serving dish and top with ham slivers. Makes 6 servings.

HERBED CORN AND PEAS

Combine 3 cups cooked shelled fresh peas and 2 cups cooked whole-kernel corn. Add ½ cup water in which peas were cooked, a few chopped parsley sprigs, and ½ teaspoon dried marjoram or oregano. Heat; season to taste with butter or margarine and salt and pepper. Makes 6 servings.

Peas Crown Chutney-Glazed Chicken Breasts on Curried Rice

Menus

50 Menus to help you plan more varied meals

BREAKFASTS AND BRUNCHES

Peach-Orange Compote
French Omelet
Oatmeal Butter Sticks
Jam
Coffee or Tea

Grilled Pineapple
Broiled Mullet
Crisp Bacon
Bread Crumb Pancakes
Wild Honey
Campfire Coffee

Vegetable Juice Cocktail
Double Apple Pancakes
Maple Honey Sauce
Frizzled Ham
Coffee

Baked Apples Cream
New England Buckwheat Cakes
Canadian Bacon
Pancake Orange Syrup
Coffee or Tea

Cranberry Juice
Puffy Omelet
Grilled Ham Steak
Coffeecake
Beverage

Grape Juice
Crisp Sausage Links
Buttermilk Pancakes
Honey Butter
Coffee

Tomato Juice
Fried Salt Pork with Cream Gravy
Scrambled Eggs
Oat Scones
Coffee or Tea

Carrot Juice with Lemon
Puffy Ham Omelet
Toasted Anadama Bread
Butter
Spiced Peach Jam
Coffee

LUNCHES OR SUPPERS

Raw Vegetables
Mustard-Mayonnaise Dip
Canadian Bacon
Corn Pudding
Oat Crumb Coffeecake
Fresh Applesauce
Tea or Coffee

Apricot-Pineapple Juice
Cheese Omelet
Crisp Bacon
Dumfunnies
Warm Maple Syrup
Coffee

Yellow Pea Soup with Smoked Pork
Fresh Pear and Cucumber Aspic
Buttered Oatmeal Bread
Brownies
Beverage

Mandarin Orange Segments
Harry Hamblet's Golden-Fried Oysters
Southern Onion Bread
Butter
Apple Slump
Coffee

Melon with Berries
Broiled Liver and Crisp Bacon
Indian Meal Raised Bread
Fresh Pineapple Pie
Coffee

Oxtail and Vegetable Soup
Cheese Sticks
Green Salad
Fresh Peach Pie
Beverage

Orange-Chicken Salad
Toasted Crisp Rye Wafers with Caraway Butter
Fresh Pears
Cheese
Beverage

German Pancakes with Spinach
Buttered Turnips
Baked Rhubarb Compote
Beverage

Vegetable Soup Cup
Crackers
French Onion Quiche
Bibb Lettuce with Walnut-Oil Dressing
Prune Refrigerator Cookies
Green Tea

French Onion Soup
Eggs Baked in Tomatoes
Parsley Cheese Toasts
Fresh Strawberries
Beverage

Jellied Tomato Broth
Grated Lemon Rind
Curried Chicken Salad with Broiled Topping
Toasted Buttered Crackers
Coconut Ice Cream Balls with Strawberries
Beverage

Split-Pea Purée
Vegetable-Ham Salad
Chutney Rolls
Grapes Nuts
Beverage

Walnutted Shrimp Casserole
Whole-Wheat Muffins
Orange Marmalade
Frozen Lime Cream
Beverage

Chicken Salad
Hot Rolls Butter
Lemon Tarts
Tea

Macaroni, Fish, Vegetable Chowder
Sea Biscuits
Green Salad
Trifle
Beverage

Carrot Juice Cocktail
Spaghetti with Chili Franks
Romaine Salad
Diced Fresh Fruit in Orange Juice
Beverage

DINNERS

Cream of Mushroom Soup
Chicken and Oyster Sauté
Oat Biscuits
Oranges in Red Wine
Coffee or Tea

Cold Roast Chicken
Banana-Peanut Salad
Hot Cheese Bread Butter
Grape-Nuts Puff Pudding
Coffee or Tea

Marinated Shrimps
Spanish Omelet
Mexican Potato Chips
Ripe Olives
Chocolate-Pecan Pie

Chicken Broth
Mushroom-Ham Casserole
with Pea Purée
Parsleyed Tomato Slices
Coconut Ice
Honeyed Orange Peel
Coffee or Tea

Celery and Carrot Curls
Crusted Mushrooms and
Oysters
Orange-Grape-Grapefruit
Salad
Angel Cake
Coffee or Tea

Meat-Vegetable Bundles
Barbecued Beans
Green Salad with
French Dressing
Ice Cream Sundae
Coffee or Tea

Italian Cannelloni
Tomato-Cucumber Salad
Italian Whole-Wheat Bread
Fruit Cup with Marsala
Italian Cookies
Espresso

Baked Lamb Patties
Tomato Sauce
Spiced Mustard Greens
Orange and Watercress Salad
Hungarian Cheese Pastries
Coffee or Tea

Oyster Bisque
Beef Moussaka
Parsley Salad
Fresh Orange Chiffon Pie
Coffee or Tea

Macaroni, Tuna and Bean Pot
Red and White Cabbage Salad
Strawberry and Almond
Cheesecake
Coffee or Tea

Chutney-Glazed Chicken
Breasts
Curried Rice and Peas
Spinach and Radish Salad
Italian Bread
Orange Soufflé
Espresso

Pâté in Aspic
Creamed Ham over Noodles
Orange and Belgian-Endive
Salad
Molasses Chiffon Pie
Coffee or Tea

Herbed Baked Chicken
Rice
Tomato Aspic on Coleslaw
Hot Buttered Rolls
Cherry-Coconut Pastries
Coffee or Tea

Borscht
Pot-Roasted Veal Shoulder
Steamed New Potatoes
Asparagus Salad
Fresh Fruit and Cheese
Coffee or Tea

Boiled Dinner, New England
Style
English Mustard
Boston Cream Pie
Coffee or Tea

Clam Casserole
Field Greens with Wine Vinegar
and Oil
Italian Bread
Italian Orange-Rum Cake
Coffee or Tea

Wine and Honey Ribs
Baked Okra
Shoestring Potatoes
Fresh-Pear Salad
Fudge Cookies
Coffee or Tea

Hot Clam Juice Cocktail
Pork Chops with Onions
Boiled New Potatoes
Savory Peas
Lettuce Salad with
Cheese Dressing
Minted Pineapple
Coffee or Tea

South American Onion Soup
Paella a la Valenciana
Ginger Peach Mold
Tea

Tomato Soup
Beef and Onion Pie
Basil Spinach
Peach Cobbler
Coffee or Tea

DINNER PARTY MENUS

Hungarian Palacsinta
(with ham)
Broiled Tomatoes
Snow Pudding with Nesselrode
Sauce
Demitasse

Baked Crab in Shells
Onion and Orange Salad
Tiny Biscuits with Sweet Butter
Pineapple Ice with Créme
de Menthe

Orange-Stuffed Veal
Fettucine
Asparagus and Pimiento Salad
with Vinaigrette Dressing
Yellow Cake with Chocolate
Frosting
Liqueurs

Veal Paprikash
Poppy-Seed Noodles
Pecan and Apple Salad
Nutmeg Logs
Espresso

Roast Duck
Orange Rice for Duck
Braised Celery
Buttered Dinner Rolls
Frozen Raspberry Nut Roll
Demitasse

Noodle-Onion Pie
Vegetable Relish
Finnochio Ripe Olives
Italian Bread Sticks
Oranges in Red Wine
Florentines
Espresso

EQUIVALENTS

Table of Equivalents

few grains	= less than 1/8 teaspoon (tsp.)
3 tsp.	= 1 Tablespoon (Tb.)
4 Tb.	= ¼ cup
8 Tb.	= ½ cup
5 Tb. plus 1 tsp.	= ⅓ cup
16 Tb.	= 1 cup
1 cup	= ½ pint (pt.)
2 cups	= 1 pt.
4 cups	= 1 quart (qt.)
4 qts.	= 1 gallon
16 ounces (oz.)	= 1 pound (dry weight)
16 oz.	= 1 pt. (liquid measure)